THE ROSWELL UFO CRASH

THE ROSWELL UFO CRASH

WHAT THEY DON'T WANT YOU TO KNOW

KAL K. KORFF

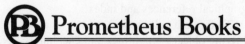

Prometheus Books

59 John Glenn Drive
Amherst, New York 14228-2197

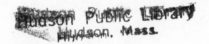
Published 1997 by Prometheus Books

01 00 99 98 97   5 4 3 2 1

Library of Congress Cataloging-in-Publication Data

Korff, Kal K.
   The Roswell UFO crash : what they don't want you to know / Kal K. Korff.
      p.   cm.
   Includes bibliographical references and index.
   ISBN 1–57392–127–0 (cloth : alk. paper)
   1. Unidentified flying objects—Sightings and encounters—New Mexico—Roswell. 2. Conspiracies—United States. I. Title.
TL789.5.N6K67   1997
001.942′09789′43—dc21   97–1555
                                                                CIP

Printed in the United States of America on acid-free paper

This book is dedicated with all my love
to the two most important
women in my life:
my mother and my sister.

In accordance with both
their wishes and mine,
this book is also for those
who desire to know the facts about
the Roswell UFO "crash" of 1947.

Contents

Acknowledgments

I would like to take this opportunity to thank the many individuals and organizations who, in their own unique and various ways, helped make this book possible.

ORGANIZATIONS AND COMPANIES

Apple Computer Inc., Cupertino, California. Bellevue Public Library, Bellevue, Washington. The Bettman Archive, New York, New York. Capitol Color and also the Claris Corporation, both of Santa Clara, California. *Forbes* magazine. *Fort Worth Star-Telegram,* Fort Worth, Texas. Kiviat Productions, Los Angeles, California. KOMO, Seattle, Washington. Louisiana State University Registrar's Office. Microsoft Corporation, MSNBC, and the Redmond Public Library, all of Redmond, Washington. The National Personnel Records Center (Military Personnel Records), St. Louis, Missouri. Neil Media, Menlo Park, California. The *Roswell Daily Record,* Roswell, New Mexico. The *Skeptical Inquirer,* Buffalo, New York. The Truman Library, Independence, Missouri. National Archives and Records Administration, the United States Air Force, the United States Pentagon, the United States Secret Service, and the White House, all of Washington, D.C.

The nonprofit organizations, the Center for UFO Studies (CUFOS), Chicago, Illinois. The Committee for the Scientific Investigation of Claims of the Paranormal (CSICOP), Buffalo, New York. The Mutual UFO Network (MUFON), Seguin, Texas.

RESEARCHERS AND ASSOCIATES

Walt Andrus; Casey Baker; Jeremy, Jesse, Kyra, and Tom Bridgeman; Peter Brookesmith; Jerome Clark; Aimee Cox; Robin Dalmas; Elizabeth Davis; George Early; Carl, Carol, Rick, Valerie, and Ashley Finwall; Stanton T. Friedman; Dr. Richard F. Haines; Lt. Walter Haut; Kent Jeffry; Tom Jennings; Bob Kiviat; Philip J. Klass; Nadya Klass; Kalvin Korff; Kurtis Korff; Gina Kramer; Marylynn Kretchun; Laura Lee; Arthur S. Levine; Capt. Jim McAndrew; Richard Mead; Charles B. Moore; James W. Moseley; Sarah, Pascal, and Jordan Marriott; Mrs. Florence Menzel; William L. Moore; Roy Neil; Joe Nickell; Carl Otsuki; Karl Pflock; Paul Roberts; Rob Rutledge; Ken Schram; Rebecca Shatte; Dan Smith; Debbie Smith; Brad Sparks; Valerie Sparks; Bill Swagerty; Dorothy Toone; Val R. Toone; Mary and Mark Vermillion; Capt. Mark Uriarte; and Dr. Roger Woodward.

SPECIAL ACKNOWLEDGMENTS

I would like to thank Dr. Paul Kurtz, Chairman Emeritus of Prometheus Books, for once again believing in me and my research. I cannot express in words what his faith in me has meant, and what an *honor* it is to have him as my publisher. Dr. Kurtz's confidence in my research is one of many sources of strength I draw from in order to continue my investigations, which sometimes put a great personal toll on me.

To Robert Todd, who is probably the unsung hero in the Roswell investigation and who, through his diligent efforts, first discovered the Project Mogul connection. I hope I have done justice to Mr. Todd by finally bringing out some of the lesser known facts of his research.

To Steven L. Mitchell, Editor-in-Chief of Prometheus Books.

Although this book had an extremely tight deadline because of my late proposal to Prometheus to do the book in the first place, Steven nonetheless patiently helped guide the whole project through to completion, and went to bat for me yet again.

To Michael Boyle, who allowed me to virtually take over portions of the bottom floor of his wonderful house so that I could be isolated to meet the tight deadline for this book. Without Mike's endless willingness to help, I don't think I could have done it.

To William J. Marriott, who also allowed me free reign of his house, refrigerator, and computing equipment in order to help this project out. Bill has been one of my closest friends for nearly ten years and has always encouraged me to be myself.

Finally, to Ms. Karen Johnson, who allowed her personal needs to be set aside for a while so that I could concentrate on this book. I very much appreciate it.

Preface

When I first began studying UFO reports more than twenty-three years ago, I suspected someday I would probably write a book on the phenomenon if and when my analyses ever produced any meaningful results.

Like my previous work, the critically-acclaimed and widely endorsed *Spaceships of the Pleiades: The Billy Meier Story,** this book is also about a very famous UFO case, the legendary 1947 Roswell flying saucer "crash" in New Mexico.

As a UFO researcher, my responsibility as I see it is to study as objectively as possible reports of unidentified flying objects. However, unlike several of my colleagues, I feel that another, equally important responsibility is to the *public*. The public has *a right to know,* whenever it is possible to determine, the truth behind a purported UFO claim or experience.

It is for this reason that I have written this book, to expose what appears to be the final truth about what is easily the most famous UFO case involving the alleged crash and recovery of an alien spacecraft.

Let me state for the record that while I hold no objections to the *possibility* of visitations to Earth by extraterrestrials, clearly, the

---

*(Amherst, N.Y.: Prometheus Books, 1995).

13

burden of proof for such an occurrence rests squarely on the shoulders of those who advocate such a hypothesis. If a claimant's "evidence" fails to withstand the rigors of serious, scientific scrutiny, then one must question the validity of such evidence.

I am confident that the facts presented here, many of which have *never been published before,* are far more than enough to establish with sufficient, indeed probable certainty, the truth about the so-called Roswell incident and the cover-up that surrounds it. Its true nature will shock you.

As 1997 marks the fiftieth anniversary of the alleged UFO crash near Roswell, the worldwide media and especially the American people will once again ponder the question of what really happened in the New Mexico desert in 1947. There is no disputing the fact that the incident as it has been recounted—in several books, on television, and in Hollywood movies—has had a profound impact on our culture.

The world deserves an explanation about the events related to Roswell, and now that a final verdict can more than reasonably be rendered, I can think of no greater gift to give to the public than to share with you what I believe is the final truth.

Although many of you who read this book will find its contents startling, this work contains a truth that *anyone can independently verify* should he or she wish to do so. This fact alone distinguishes this work from others that have been written on Roswell.

I welcome your comments and/or criticisms.

Kal K. Korff
President and CEO, TotalResearch

1

The Roswell UFO Crash: A History, the Claims

"The most important UFO encounter of our century!"[1]

"The presence in New Mexico of very strange substances from the wreckage of the two [UFO] crashes has been testified to by so many people that it is virtually proved."[2]

According to widely held public opinion, the United States government successfully recovered the remains of a crashed UFO along with its extraterrestrial occupants near Roswell, New Mexico, in July 1947. In what is now popularly known as "the Roswell incident," the U.S. military is said to have quickly covered-up the affair, and continues to shroud it in extreme secrecy even today.[3]

If these events surrounding Roswell in the summer of 1947 actually took place, as have been claimed in several books on the subject and by numerous UFO researchers, it would certainly constitute the story of the millennium and be the greatest government-sponsored cover-up of all time. Indeed, should irrefutable evidence ever surface that *any* government on this Earth possessed the physical remains of either an extraterrestrial spacecraft or its occupants, it is an understatement to say that such a revelation would fundamentally transform humanity as we know it.

What does one do with the numerous claims about Roswell that have surfaced over the years? How does one begin to determine the truth about what really happened in 1947 and sort the fact from the fiction?

The Roswell incident, and all that surrounds it, is a complex web of events, not easily understandable nor explainable until examined fully and in painstaking detail. In order to try and determine the truth, let's begin by reviewing the chronological timeline history of Roswell and the alleged events as they are claimed to have occurred according to the various books that have been written on the subject.

In constructing the Roswell "timeline" of events presented in this chapter, I have combined all the divergent claims that exist among the seven major books that have been written about the topic.*

ALLEGED ROSWELL-RELATED TIMELINE OF EVENTS

Tuesday, July 1, 1947

- While watching radar screens at Roswell Army Air Base, White Sands and Alamogordo, New Mexico, military personnel observe a "strange object" whose speed and flight maneuvers indicate that it cannot be from this planet. Subsequent checks of the radar tracking equipment reveal "no malfunction that would account for the [unusual] display."[4]

---

*These are: *The Roswell Incident* by Charles Berlitz and William L. Moore (Berkeley Books, 1990); *UFO Crash at Roswell* by Kevin D. Randle and Donald R. Schmitt (Avon Books, 1991); *The Roswell Report: A Historical Perspective* (The J. Allen Hynek Center for UFO Studies, 1991); *Crash at Corona* by Stanton T. Friedman and Don Berliner (Paragon House, 1992); *The Truth about the UFO Crash at Roswell* by Kevin D. Randle and Donald R. Schmitt (Avon Books, 1994); *Roswell UFO Crash Update—Exposing the Military Cover-Up of the Century* by Kevin D. Randle (Global Communications, 1995); and *Top Secret/MAJIC* by Stanton T. Friedman (Marlowe & Company, 1996).

Wednesday, July 2, 1947

- At approximately 9:50 P.M., Mr. and Mrs. Dan Wilmot of Roswell, New Mexico, observe from their front yard an oval-shaped object that looks like "two inverted saucers faced mouth to mouth." Describing the vehicle as self-luminous, the craft flies over their house heading in a northwest direction, toward Corona, New Mexico. The duration of the Wilmot's UFO sighting is an estimated forty to fifty seconds.[5]

Thursday, July 3, 1947

- Radar installations located at White Sands, New Mexico, continue to track the mysterious object as it "flashes" through the atmosphere. A military radar expert watches the tracking screens for nearly twenty-four hours.[6]

Friday, July 4, 1947

- William M. Woody and his father, working at night on their farm, see a bright light with a "flame-like" tail streaking across the sky. The Woodys observe the object for some twenty to thirty seconds before it disappears below the horizon, some "forty miles north of Roswell."[7]

- Between 11:00 and 11:30 P.M., two Catholic nuns, Mother Superior Mary Bernadette and Sister Capistrano, at Saint Mary's Hospital in Roswell, record in a log book entry seeing "a brilliant light plunge to Earth." The location of the object is north of Roswell and the nuns believe it to be a disabled aircraft.[8]

- During the "worst lightning storm he had ever seen," William W. "Mac" Brazel, who operates the J. B. Foster ranch, hears an "odd sort of explosion, not like ordinary thunder, but different."[9]

- At 11:27 P.M., the radar sites operated by military personnel continue to track the UFO which has befuddled them for three days now. The object seems to "pulsate" repeatedly, then explodes in

a "starburst." The military believes that the object they have been
tracking has suddenly crashed.[10]

- Jim Ragsdale and Trudy Truelove are out camping in the New
  Mexico desert roughly forty miles northwest of of Roswell. Suddenly, a "flaring bright light" from an object "roars" over their
  heads, crashing within seconds into the ground roughly one mile
  from their campsite.

  Ragsdale convinces Truelove to join him in a search for the
  downed mystery object. Driving across the desert in Ragsdale's
  Jeep, the couple arrive at the edge of a cliff. Using only a flashlight with batteries that are running low, the two see a craft stuck
  in the side of a small slope. Observing no activity, they decide to
  return the next day after the sun is up.[11]

Saturday, July 5, 1947

- Mac Brazel is out riding in a pasture on his horse when he comes
  across a large quantity of strange debris scattered over an area
  about a "quarter mile long or so, and several hundred feet wide."
  Brazel "knew this stuff was like nothing he had ever seen
  before."

  The material is highly unusual in nature and consists mostly
  of tin foil type strips, only darker in color. The strange thing
  about the metal is that "you could wrinkle it and lay it back down
  and it immediately resumed its original shape. It was quite pliable, yet you couldn't crease or bend it like ordinary metal. It was
  almost more like a plastic of some sort, except that it was definitely metallic in nature."

  Brazel also finds pieces that are "like balsa wood in weight,
  but a bit darker in color and much harder." The stick-like material is also described as "pliable, but wouldn't break," an attribute
  it seems to share with the strange metallic foil.

  Brazel also discovers some "thread-like material." While it
  looks like silk, it was not. "You could take it in two hands and try
  to snap it, but it wouldn't snap at all."

  Finally, Brazel notices that on some of the debris there are
  mysterious markings, or "figures." Brazel would later describe

them as being comparable to New Mexican Indian petroglyphs (prehistoric cave drawings).[12]

- Dr. W. Curry Holden and a group of archaeologists working nearby accidentally stumble across the impact site where the ship has crashed. One of the members of the group heads toward the nearest phone and calls Chavez County Sheriff George Wilcox.

  Wilcox telephones the Roswell Fire Department who dispatch a fire truck in response to the call. Fireman Dan Dwyer is part of this crew. Officers from the Roswell Police Department escort Dwyer and the rest of the firemen to the crash site.[13]

- Jim Ragsdale and Trudy Truelove arise early and, with the sun now shining, drive immediately to the crash site. For the first time the couple get a clear look at the strange craft. Ragsdale and Truelove notice that there is loose debris scattered everywhere. They collect some of the pieces and put them in their car. Ragsdale later says about the material that "You could take that stuff and wad it up and it would straighten itself out."

  While the debris the couple handles is unusual, a more astounding sight can be seen near the craft itself. According to Ragsdale, there were "bodies or something lying there. They looked like bodies."[14]

- At 5:30 A.M. the United States military, having figured out the location of the downed spacecraft, "move in" with an "elite" team of men to recover the object. Eventually, five alien bodies are found at the crash site.[15]

  Ragsdale and Truelove become frightened when they observe a military convoy approaching. The couple scurry for safety, fleeing via their Jeep into a thicket of brush and some trees for cover. While the soldiers swing into action, Ragsdale and Truelove eventually drive away undetected and return to their campsite.

- By the time the U.S. military arrives, there are already a number of civilians—part of the group of archaeologists—on the scene. The military police, under the command of Maj. Edwin Easley, escort all civilian personnel off of the premises. Easley's MPs take the archaeologists to the base at Roswell Army Air Field for questioning. The group is interrogated, threatened, and eventually sworn to secrecy.[16]

- Dan Dwyer and his fellow firemen from the Roswell Fire Department arrive at the crash site. Members of the Roswell Police Department are already present. The New Mexico state police are also there. Dwyer observes two body bags being loaded into one vehicle, and a live alien being put in another. The creature did not appear to have been injured.

  The U.S. military completely secures and "cleans up" the crash site in a total of six hours, leaving no trace of the remains. The soldiers were very thorough in their task and "used individual vacuums to clean the site."[17]

- Sgt. Melvin E. Brown, who is on guard duty at the impact site, is ordered to climb into the truck carrying the alien bodies. He is further admonished not to look under the tarps that cover them. While no one is noticing, he violates orders and "peeks." Brown sees the bodies "of the alien flight crew," and describes them as "small [in size], with large heads and skin that is yellow or orange."[18]

- On the Plains of San Augustin, just west of Socorro, New Mexico, Gerald Anderson and his family, while out searching for moss agate, stumble upon the wreckage of a flying saucer and its occupants. Within minutes, five archaeology students and their college professor, Dr. Winfried Buskirk, arrive at the scene. A short time later, Grady L. "Barney" Barnett, who was doing some work in the area, drives up in his pick-up truck and is yet another witness to the crashed UFO and its alien crew.

  Barnett is there for only a few minutes before the U.S. military arrives and seals off the area. The officers in charge swear all the witnesses to secrecy through a combination of threats and admonitions that it is their patriotic duty not to tell anyone what they have seen.

  At this second crash site there are four alien bodies discovered: two dead, one badly injured, and the other apparently unharmed. This is the *second* extraterrestrial spacecraft with its crew that crashes in the New Mexico desert.[19]

- At approximately 1:30 P.M. mortician Glenn Dennis of the Ballard Funeral Home in Roswell, receives the first in a series of phone calls from the base mortuary officer at Roswell Army Air

Field. The Ballard Funeral Home had a contract with the base at Roswell to provide mortuary services in 1947.

During the first phone call, Dennis reports that he is asked about "hermetically sealed caskets: What was the smallest one they could get?"

Approximately thirty to forty minutes later, Dennis receives a second telephone call from the Roswell base mortuary officer inquiring about how to best preserve bodies that have been exposed to the elements and what procedures the Ballard Funeral Home uses.[20]

- In the late afternoon or early evening, William "Mac" Brazel picks up a few fragments of the unusual debris that had fallen on the Foster Ranch that he discovered earlier that morning. Brazel drives over to the house of his nearest neighbors, Floyd and Loretta Proctor, and tells them about his find in addition to showing them a piece of the material that he can "neither burn nor cut." Brazel tries, but is unsuccessful, in getting the Proctors to come over to the Foster ranch to view the strange material for themselves. The Proctors suggest that Brazel notify the authorities about his discovery.[21]

- At approximately 6:00 P.M. or 7:00 P.M., Glenn Dennis takes an injured airman back to the base infirmary at Roswell.* Driving an ambulance, Dennis is waived through the front gate at Roswell Army Air Field and pulls into the back of the base hospital and parks in the emergency area. While walking the injured airman into the building, Dennis passes a series of ambulances, one of which is filled with unusual debris. Describing the material as looking "like [the bottom] half of a canoe," Dennis also reports seeing "a row of unrecognizable symbols, several inches high."[22]

Dennis is at the base infirmary for only a short time when he is questioned, intimidated, and threatened by military authorities. One of them is described as a red-haired captain, and the other a black sergeant. Dennis is told by the officer in no uncertain terms, "There was no crash here. You did not see anything. You don't go

---

*The Ballard Funeral Home held a contract for ambulance services in the city.

into town. You don't tell anybody you saw anything. If you do, you'll get into serious trouble."

After telling the captain that he could "go to hell," Dennis claims that he was told "Don't kid yourself, young man. Somebody'll be picking your bones out of the sand."

"Or you'll make good dog food," chimed in the black sergeant.[23]

Glenn Dennis is then literally carried out of the infirmary by two military policemen and escorted all the way back to the Ballard Funeral Home.

Approximately two or three hours later, he receives another phone call threatening him once again if he tells anyone.

- That evening, at Roswell Army Air Field, the bodies of the dead aliens are "sealed into a long crate" which is then taken to a hangar for overnight storage. Military police guards are stationed all around it while spotlights shine on the precious cargo.[24]

    Sgt. Melvin Brown is one of the personnel assigned to the security detail and stands guard outside the hangar where the crate is stored.

Sunday, July 6, 1947

- Mac Brazel arises early and loads some of the small pieces of the unusual wreckage he discovered onto his pick-up truck. Brazel makes the long trek into Roswell, roughly seventy-five miles away.

    Once in Roswell, Brazel first telephones the weather bureau and describes the material he found to them. The bureau recommends that he notify the sheriff instead.

    Following the weather bureau's advice, Brazel walks into the office of Chavez County Sheriff George A. Wilcox and reports to him the news of his unusual find. Brazel shows Wilcox some of the debris and the sheriff decides that he should notify the military authorities at Roswell Army Air Field. In the interim, Wilcox orders two deputy officers to drive out to the location at the Foster ranch where Brazel found some of the wreckage.

- Before Wilcox telephones the Army, Frank Joyce, a reporter and announcer for radio station KGFL in Roswell, calls Sheriff Wilcox to see if there's anything newsworthy to report. Wilcox tells Joyce about Mac Brazel's story and Joyce interviews Brazel on the phone.

- Maj. Jesse Marcel is just sitting down to have lunch at the officer's club at Roswell Army Air Field when he receives a phone call. Sheriff Wilcox is on the line and recounts Brazel's story. Marcel drives to the sheriff's office after finishing his lunch and interviews Brazel and examines some of the debris.

  Marcel decides that the affair is worth reporting so he notifies Col. William H. Blanchard, the commanding officer at Roswell Army Air Field. Marcel arranges to meet Brazel back at the sheriff's office "in an hour or so," and returns to the base at Roswell.

- Blanchard and Marcel meet at the base in person. After discussing the matter, they believe at first that a "downed aircraft of some unusual sort" might be involved.[25] Colonel Blanchard orders Marcel to proceed to the site where Brazel discovered the debris and to take with him a Counter Intelligence Corps (CIC) Agent.

  CIC Agent Capt. Sheridan Cavitt later accompanies both Maj. Jesse Marcel and Mac Brazel back to the Foster ranch.

- After Brazel, Cavitt, and Marcel leave to go to the debris field, the two deputies that had been previously dispatched by Sheriff Wilcox return. They are unable to find the actual pasture where the unusual-looking material had been discovered, but report seeing instead a "burned area." Reporting that the "sand has been turned to glass," the consensus is that "something circular" has landed on the ground.[26]

- Under orders from Maj. Gen. Clements McMullen, then the acting commander of the Strategic Air Command at Andrews Army Air Field in Washington, D.C., Colonel Blanchard is instructed to put some of the debris he receives into a sealed pouch. The courier bag is then flown to Fort Worth Army Air Field in Texas, where it is received by Col. Thomas J. DuBose.

  DuBose, acting on orders, then hands the pouch, with its seal still intact, to Col. Al Clarke, who is the base commander at Fort

Worth. Clarke attaches the pouch via handcuffs to his wrist. General McMullen orders Colonel Clarke to personally accompany the material on a special B-26 flight to Washington, D.C.

• Brazel, Cavitt, and Marcel, all in separate vehicles, arrive at the Foster ranch too late in the day to conduct a thorough investigation. Major Marcel checks some of the debris with a Geiger counter but finds no evidence of radiation. Marcel and Cavitt spend the night at the property.

Monday, July 7, 1947

• Brazel, Cavitt, and Marcel begin their examination of the debris site at the Foster ranch. The wreckage is scattered over an area "three-quarters of a mile long and two to three hundred feet wide." In addition, there is a "gouge" that starts at the north end and is approximately 500 feet long. The presence of the gouge is evidence that something "touched down and skipped along."[27]

Marcel describes the material he observed as being as thin as aluminum foil but extremely strong. Marcel tries to bend, tear, and cut it, but is unable to do so. Later, Marcel reports that even repeated blows with a sixteen-pound sledge hammer fail to dent the material!

Marcel and Cavitt also find several small "beams" of balsawood like material. Like the mysterious metal, they too are very hard and cannot be broken or burned. On some of the beams there appears some "hieroglyphic-type" writing which is undecipherable.

Sheridan Cavitt finds a small black box that has no apparent way of being opened. The box is retrieved and thrown in with the rest of the debris into Cavitt's vehicle to be taken to Roswell Army Air Field.

• Glenn Dennis talks on the telephone to Naomi Maria Selff, a nurse stationed at Roswell Army Air Field with whom he is acquainted. She agrees to meet him for lunch and Dennis drives out to the base. During their luncheon, Selff confirms to Glenn Dennis that there were alien bodies on the base at Roswell. She describes to him their anatomy and appearance and makes several sketches on a small note pad.

Dennis notices that the nurse appears to be on the verge of a "collapse from the emotional trauma" of the event. After their lunch together Dennis drops the nurse off at her barracks.[28]

- Sometime in the afternoon, Captain Cavitt returns to Roswell Army Air Field while Marcel stays behind and loads more debris into his automobile.

- At 4:00 P.M. Lydia Sleppy, a teletype operator for radio station KOAT in Albuquerque, New Mexico, receives a telephone call from Johnny McBoyle, who is a reporter and also a partial owner of an affiliated station, KSWS in Roswell. McBoyle is excited, and claims that he has a "scoop" for Sleppy.

  McBoyle informs Sleppy that a flying saucer crashed and that he's serious. McBoyle then tells Sleppy that he has seen it, and that the Army is going to pick it up. McBoyle also mentions to Sleppy that there's talk of "little men being on board" and asks her to begin immediately typing up his story on the teletype so that they can put it on the ABC wire as soon as possible.[29]

  Sleppy begins typing McBoyle's astonishing story when after only a few sentences her teletype machine suddenly stops working. The Federal Bureau of Investigation (FBI) office in Dallas has intercepted her transmission. She informs McBoyle of this fact and notices that he seems to be arguing with someone on the telephone.

  Within seconds, Sleppy's teletype machine begins transmitting an ominous message *back to her* that reads: "ATTENTION ALBUQUERQUE: DO NOT TRANSMIT. REPEAT DO NOT TRANSMIT THIS MESSAGE. STOP COMMUNICATION IMMEDIATELY."

  Sleppy asks McBoyle for further instructions. McBoyle replies, "Forget about it. You never heard it. Look, you're not supposed to know. Don't talk about it to anyone."[30]

- Lt. Gen. Nathan F. Twining, commander of the Air Materiel Command, suddenly alters his plans and abruptly flies to Alamogordo. Twining's abrupt schedule change is due to the UFO-related events near Roswell.

- Walt Whitmore Sr., owner of radio station KGFL in Roswell, hears about the saucer debris discovery by Brazel through reporter Frank Joyce. Whitmore drives out to the Foster ranch to speak directly with Brazel and convinces him to come into town to do an interview. Brazel agrees, and stays overnight as a guest in Whitmore's house.

   The Army, not knowing Brazel's whereabouts, starts "having a fit" because they cannot locate "the rancher who had found the flying saucer." The Army's objective is to put Brazel "out of circulation" so that he does not talk about his discovery.[31]

Tuesday, July 8, 1947

- At approximately 2:00 A.M., Jesse Marcel stops at home on his way into Roswell Army Air Base. He wakes his wife, Viaud Marcel, and his eleven-year-old son, Jesse Marcel Jr., and shows them some of the unusual material. Major Marcel tells his family that the debris is from a flying saucer.

   The elder Marcel brings in several pieces from his car and spreads it out on the kitchen floor of his home in an attempt to reconstruct the shape of the object.

   In subsequent interviews with UFO researchers, Jesse Marcel Jr. testifies as to the unusual nature of the debris, describing it as a "flying saucer that had apparently been stressed beyond its designed capabilities." He also vividly recalls the strange "I-beams" with "pink and purple" hieroglyphics on them.[32]

- Walt Whitmore Sr. tries to put the wire recording that he made of his interview with Mac Brazel onto the Mutual radio wire for broadcast. However, Whitmore is unable get his call through. In the interim, Whitmore begins announcing locally on radio station KGFL that he has interviewed the rancher who recovered the flying disc.

   Suddenly, Whitmore receives a phone call from a man called "Slowie," who is the Secretary of the Federal Communications Commission (FCC) in Washington, D.C. Slowie informs Whitmore that the story about the recovered flying disc is a matter of national security, and tells him that if he proceeds with the broadcast that his station could lose its FCC operating license!

While Whitmore ponders the threat, a second telephone call comes in from Sen. Dennis Chavez of New Mexico. Chavez admonishes Whitmore that he's not to broadcast his interview and that he had better "obey the FCC directive."[33]

• Colonel Blanchard instructs Lt. Walter Haut to draft a press announcement for release to the media disclosing that his group has recovered the remains of a "flying disc." Haut writes the press release and distributes copies to the various radio stations and newspapers in Roswell who then begin to publicize the story.

Haut's press release announcement reads as follows:

Roswell Army Air Base, Roswell, N.M.

8 July, 1947 A.M.

The many rumors regarding the flying disc became a reality yesterday when the intelligence office of the 509th Bomb Group of the Eighth Air Force, Roswell Army Air Field, was fortunate enough to gain possession of a disc through the cooperation of one of the local ranchers and the sheriff's office of Chaves County [*sic*].

The flying object landed on a ranch near Roswell sometime last week. Not having phone facilities, the rancher stored the disc until such time as he was able to contact the sheriff's office, who in turn notified Maj. Jesse A. Marcel of the 509th Bomb Group Intelligence Office.

Action was immediately taken and the disc was picked up at the rancher's home. It was inspected at the Roswell Army Air Field and subsequently loaned by Major Marcel to higher headquarters.[34]

Haut's startling statement is quickly featured on radio stations and in the print media worldwide. Newspapers such as the *New York Times, San Francisco Chronicle,* and London *Times* all carry the story. Colonel Blanchard's office is besieged with phone calls.

• After the contents of Haut's press release are publicized through the media, Brig. Gen. Roger M. Ramey, the commanding officer of the Eighth Air Force at Carswell Air Force Base in Fort Worth,

Texas, receives a phone call from Lt. Gen. Hoyt S. Vandenburg, the Deputy Chief of the Air Force. Vandenburg tells Ramey that pieces of the announced recovered "saucer" are actually at the base in Roswell.

Ramey telephones Colonel Blanchard and conveys to him both General Vandenburg's and his own "extreme displeasure" over the fact that a press release was issued without proper authority. Ramey then directs Blanchard to have the saucer debris flown directly to his office.[35]

- The newspaper the *Roswell Daily Record* prints a front-page, banner headline story announcing "RAAF Captures Flying Saucer on Ranch in Roswell Region." Mentioned in the story are Major Marcel and Sheriff Wilcox. The article also notes that "Major Marcel and a detail from his department went to the ranch and recovered the disk." The Wilmots' earlier UFO sighting of Wednesday, July 2, 1947, is also cited.[36]

- At 3:00 P.M., under orders from Colonel Blanchard, a B-29 bomber is loaded up with the saucer wreckage. Maj. Jesse Marcel is instructed to accompany the debris in a special flight to Fort Worth and deliver it to Brig. Gen. Roger Ramey. According to Major Marcel, the amount of saucer wreckage loaded aboard the plane is enormous, it fills up half of the B-29 airplane.

- Colonel Blanchard "suddenly and conveniently" goes on leave. Command at Roswell Army Air Field is temporarily turned over to Lt. Col. Payne Jennings.

- James Bond Johnson, a reporter for the *Fort Worth Star-Telegram,* is told by one of his editors to proceed to General Ramey's office. Johnson is instructed to bring his camera because the saucer debris is due to arrive shortly at the base.

- Major Marcel and the B-29 loaded with the flying saucer wreckage land at Fort Worth. Marcel is instructed to bring some of the material up to Ramey's office for examination. The flying saucer remnants are placed on top of some brown paper and spread out on the floor.

- General Ramey allows the press to enter his office and photograph the actual flying saucer wreckage, although they are not allowed to touch it. One of the photographers present is J. Bond Johnson, who takes several pictures. Johnson manages to capture Major Marcel on film holding some of the actual saucer debris that he recovered at the Foster ranch.

- A short time later, the shredded remains of an ordinary weather balloon are brought into Ramey's office and quickly *substituted* for the real saucer wreckage.

  At the official press briefing that follows the "bait and switch" maneuver, General Ramey announces that the whole flying saucer affair has been a mistake, and that the debris recovered by Maj. Jesse Marcel is nothing more than the remains of a weather balloon!

  To prove his point, Ramey brings in Warrant Officer Irving Newton, the base weather officer, who promptly identifies the material as "parts of a balloon" and "a regular Rawin sonde"— an aluminum covered, balsa wood frame attached to balloons and launched for the purposes of weather and radar tracking operations. Officer Newton was certainly qualified to make such a determination, because during his career he had launched "thousands" of such devices.[37]

  Warrant Officer Newton is photographed holding up some of the substituted wreckage that now lays on the floor of General Ramey's office.

- While General Ramey continues to assure the press that "This whole affair has been most unfortunate," and reiterates the mistaken identification explanation, the *real* UFO wreckage is secretly flown to Wright-Patterson Air Force base in Ohio.[38]

- At 6:17 P.M., the FBI's Dallas field office receives official word from Eighth Air Force Headquarters that a "flying disc" has been recovered near Roswell, New Mexico. In a teletype communication to both FBI Director J. Edgar Hoover and the FBI's office in Cincinnati, Ohio, the FBI Dallas office reports the following:

FBI DALLAS 7-8-47 6-17 P.M.

DIRECTOR AND SAC [Strategic Agent in Charge], CINCINNATI

FLYING DISC, INFORMATION CONCERNING MAJOR CURTAIN, HEAD-
QUARTERS EIGHTH AIR FORCE, TELEPHONICALLY ADVISED THIS
OFFICE THAT AN OBJECT PURPORTING TO BE A FLYING DISC WAS
RECOVERED NEAR ROSWELL, NEW MEXICO, THIS DATE. THE DISC IS
HEXAGONAL IN SHAPE AND WAS SUSPENDED FROM A BALLOON BY
CABLE, WHICH BALLOON WAS APPROXIMATELY TWENTY FEET IN
DIAMETER. MAJOR CURTAN FURTHER ADVISED THAT THE OBJECT
FOUND RESEMBLES A HIGH ALTITUDE WEATHER BALLOON WITH A
RADAR REFLECTOR, BUT THAT TELEPHONIC CONVERSATION BETWEEN
THEIR OFFICE AND WRIGHT FIELD HAD NOT BORNE OUT THIS BELIEF.
DISC AND BALLOON BEING TRANSPORTED TO WRIGHT FIELD BY SPE-
CIAL PLANE FOR EXAMIN. INFORMATION PROVIDED THIS OFFICE
BECAUSE OF NATIONAL INTEREST IN CASE AND FACT THAT NATIONAL
BROADCASTING COMPANY, ASSOCIATED PRESS, AND OTHERS
ATTEMPTING TO BREAK STORY OF LOCATION OF DISC TODAY. MAJOR
CURTAN ADVISED WOULD REQUEST WRIGHT FIELD TO ADVISE
CINCINNATI OFFICE RESULTS OF EXAMINATION. NO FURTHER INVES-
TIGATION BEING CONDUCTED.

- Throughout the evening, numerous radio stations and newspapers begin to publicize the story of General Ramey's announcement, that the Roswell "saucer" is simply a misidentified weather balloon.

Wednesday, July 9, 1947

- The *Roswell Daily Record,* in a huge banner headline story spread across the front page, announces "Gen. Ramey Empties Roswell Saucer." Like many papers across the country, the *Roswell Daily Record* carries Ramey's explanation of the "saucer" wreckage. The paper also includes an interview with Mac Brazel, under the headline "Harassed Rancher Who Located 'Saucer' Sorry He Told About It."[39]

- Military personnel conduct a sweep of all radio stations and newspaper offices in Roswell and retrieve all copies of Lt. Walter Haut's press release which had announced the recovery of the flying disc.

- Robert Smith, a member of the First Air Transport Unit, helps load several crates filled with the UFO debris on board a group of C-54 Skymaster cargo planes. Smith sees a piece of the flying saucer metal and describes it as "two or three inches square." Smith further testifies that "You could crumple it up, let it back out; you couldn't crease it. When you crumpled it up, it then laid back out."[40]

   The C-54s that Smith helps load leave for Albuquerque and eventually arrive at Los Alamos. The crates are stenciled with the words "Top Secret" on them because of their contents.

- At Fort Worth Army Air Field, several military officers greet one of the many secret, incoming flights. A bombardier on board the plane recognizes one of the people who is there to meet him "as a mortician with whom he went to school."

   When Jesse Marcel is driven out to the plane, he is ordered to return to Roswell. No debriefing is given, and the flight in fact is a "diversion." The alien bodies have already been flown to Andrews Air Force Base.

- Mac Brazel discusses his situation with reporter Frank Joyce. He tells Joyce that "it will go hard on him" if he doesn't change his story about the discovery of the UFO debris.[41]

- Major Marcel returns to Roswell Army Air Field. He asks CIC Agent Sheridan Cavitt if he can see the reports about the discovery of the UFO wreckage that "have been filed in his absence." Cavitt denies Marcel's request and claims he is under orders from Washington, D.C. Marcel reminds Cavitt that he outranks him. Cavitt remains firm, and tells Marcel that if he has a problem, he is to "take it up" with officials from Washington.[42]

Friday, July 11, 1947

- Glenn Dennis learns that Naomi, the nurse friend who had told him about the alien bodies that had been brought into Roswell Army Air Field, has been abruptly transferred. No one appears to know where she is. All attempts to make contact with the nurse by Dennis are "met with obstruction."[43]

Saturday, July 12, 1947

• Bill Brazel, Mac's son, arrives with his wife, Shirley, at the Foster ranch. They observe that no one is present, not even the military, and find no remnants of any debris.

Tuesday, July 15, 1947

• Mac Brazel, who has been sequestered by the military for several days so he is "out of the way of reporters," finally returns to the Foster ranch. He is bitter about his experience, but has been sworn to secrecy and agrees not to tell anyone about the true nature of the device he discovered.[44]

Late July, 1947

• Mac Brazel complains to Lyman Strickland, a friend of his, about the treatment the military subjected him to while he was in Roswell.

August 1947

• Mac Brazel is riding a horse with one of his ranch hands, Tommy Tyree. The two men spot a piece of the saucer wreckage floating in the water of a sinkhole. Because of the enormous amount of trouble and stress Brazel has previously endured at the hands of military authorities, the piece is never recovered.

September 1947

• Counter Intelligence Corps agent Lewis S. Rickett is assigned to work with Dr. Lincoln LaPaz. LaPaz's task is to try and determine the UFOs' speed and trajectory when it impacted. The two men discover a mysterious burnt circle some five miles from the debris field. Describing it as a "touchdown point," the men note that the sand has been "crystalized," and they also find some of the unusual "foil-like" material. LaPaz, unaware that alien bodies were recovered previously, concludes that the UFO was an "unoccupied probe from another planet."[45]

- Glenn Dennis is informed that Naomi Selff has been killed in an airplane accident while stationed in London, England. Dennis learns this information after a letter he had sent her in the mail was returned marked "deceased."

November 1947

- Arthur Exon, later the commanding officer at Wright-Patterson AFB, flies over the debris field and the impact site. He observes the "gouge" that the craft made.

Summer 1949

- Bill Brazel has managed to accumulate several small pieces of debris from the saucer wreckage at the Foster ranch. These are bits and pieces he discovers "after a good rain" while riding in the pasture where the military had previously collected the material.

  While in a bar in Corona, New Mexico, Brazel casually mentions to some people there that he has in his possession some of the pieces of the saucer wreckage his father discovered. The next day, four military personnel come out to the Foster ranch and politely ask Brazel to give them the material.

  Captain Armstrong, one of the officers who is present, reminds Brazel that his father gave an oath of secrecy regarding the event. Armstrong appeals to Brazel's sense of patriotic duty, and Brazel agrees to hand over all of the material he has found to the military.

July 1969

- As the American astronauts are walking on the moon, Sgt. Melvin E. Brown mentions to his family that he once saw the remains of an extraterrestrial spacecraft and its alien crew.

1978

- Pappy Henderson, a highly decorated World War II pilot who was also stationed at Roswell in 1947, tells his dentist, Dr. John Kromschroeder, that he flew the remains of a crashed saucer to Wright-Patterson Air Force base in Ohio. Henderson also pulls out of his pocket a piece of the strange metal from the UFO at Roswell that he has secretly kept for all of these years.

  Kromschroeder, who has an interest in metals, examines the fragment and says he had "never seen anything like it." He tries to bend the metal but is unable to do so.[46]

1981

- After reading a story in the papers about the 1947 UFO crash at Roswell, Pappy Henderson tells his wife and daughter about his involvement in flying the saucer debris to Wright-Patterson Air Force Base in Ohio.

✳   ✳   ✳

As is readily apparent by now, the myriad purported events that are collectively known as "Roswell" are very complex. What makes this affair seem impressive at first glance, and certainly worthy of objective investigation, are the plethora of names, dates, places, people, and testimonies that have been offered up as evidence.

Did an extraterrestrial spacecraft *really* crash in the New Mexico desert in 1947? Or did *two* such spaceships crash as has been claimed? Are the numerous stories of unusual debris and "alien bodies" actually true? Was there indeed a massive military cover-up instituted by the Air Force, one which persists to this very day?

Finally, were military personnel and ordinary civilians sworn to secrecy, intimidated, and threatened with death if they talked about the crashed flying saucer and its alien crew?

In order to try and determine the truth about what actually did happen near Roswell, New Mexico, in 1947, our quest begins with a systematic examination of all the available evidence offered to date, beginning with the testimonies of those people who claim to have been involved.

NOTES

1. Charles Berlitz and William L. Moore, *The Roswell Incident* (New York: Grosset & Dunlap, 1980), front cover.
2. Stanton T. Friedman and Don Berliner, *Crash at Corona* (New York: Paragon House, 1991), p. 114.
3. Kevin D. Randle and Donald R. Schmitt, *The Truth about the UFO Crash at Roswell* (New York: Avon Books, 1992). See also, Berlitz and Moore, *The Roswell Incident*; Friedman and Berliner, *Crash at Corona;* Kevin Randle, *Roswell UFO Crash Update—Exposing the Military Cover-Up of the Century* (New York: Global Communications, 1995); and Kevin D. Randle and Donald R. Schmitt, *UFO Crash at Roswell* (New York: Avon Books, 1991).
4. Randle and Schmitt, *The Truth about the UFO Crash at Roswell,* p. 195.
5. Berlitz and Moore, *The Roswell Incident,* p. 23.
6. Randle and Schmitt, *The Truth about the UFO Crash at Roswell,* p. 196.
7. Kevin Randle, *Roswell UFO Crash Update,* p. 185.
8. Randle and Schmitt, *The Truth about the UFO Crash at Roswell,* p. 4.
9. Berlitz and Moore, *The Roswell Incident,* p. 85.
10. Ibid., p. 196.
11. Randle and Schmitt, *The Truth about the UFO Crash at Roswell,* pp. 4–5.
12. Berlitz and Moore, *The Roswell Incident,* pp. 86–89.
13. Randle and Schmitt, *The Truth about the UFO Crash at Roswell,* p. 197.
14. Ibid., pp. 8–9.
15. Ibid., p. 197.
16. Ibid., pp. 9, 11, and 272.
17. Ibid., pp. 13 and 21.
18. Ibid., p. 198.
19. Friedman and Berliner, *Crash at Corona,* pp. 91 and 192.
20. Ibid., p. 115. See also, Randle and Schmitt, *The Truth about the UFO Crash at Roswell,* p. 14.
21. Randle and Schmitt, *The Truth about the UFO Crash at Roswell,* p. 199. See also, Berlitz and Moore, *The Roswell Incident,* pp. 92–94.
22. Friedman and Berliner, *Crash at Corona,* pp. 116–17.
23. Randle and Schmitt, *The Truth about the UFO Crash at Roswell,* p. 20.
24. Ibid., p. 200.
25. Berlitz and Moore, *The Roswell Incident,* pp. 70–71.
26. Randle and Schmitt, *The Truth about the UFO Crash at Roswell,* p. 201.
27. Ibid., p. 202.
28. Friedman and Berliner, *Crash at Corona,* pp. 118–19.

29. Berlitz and Moore, *The Roswell Incident,* pp. 15–16.
30. Ibid., p. 16.
31. Ibid., pp. 97–98.
32. Friedman and Berliner, *Crash at Corona,* p. 74.
33. Berlitz and Moore, *The Roswell Incident,* p. 98.
34. *San Francisco Chronicle,* July 9, 1947, p. 1.
35. Berlitz and Moore, *The Roswell Incident,* pp. 30–31.
36. *Roswell Daily Record,* July 8, 1947, p. 1.
37. Berlitz and Moore, *The Roswell Incident,* pp. 36–37.
38. Ibid., p. 75.
39. *Roswell Daily Record,* July 9, 1947, p. 1.
40. Friedman and Berliner, *Crash at Corona,* p. 124.
41. Randle and Schmitt, *The Truth about the UFO Crash at Roswell,* p. 209.
42. Ibid.
43. Friedman and Berliner, *Crash at Corona,* p. 119.
44. Randle and Schmitt, *The Truth about the UFO Crash at Roswell,* p. 211.
45. Ibid., p. 212.
46. Ibid., p. 214.

2

The Original Roswell Eyewitnesses

wit•ness: a person who saw, or can give a firsthand account of, something.

"When someone lies about their background, one has to wonder what else they [*sic*] might be lying about."[1]

Perhaps the most remarkable aspect of the Roswell incident—what distinguishes it from most other UFO cases—is the number of seemingly credible, independent eyewitnesses. The consistency of their accounts is also astounding. The pro-UFO community uses these testimonies to support the argument that the debris recovered was extraterrestrial in origin.

While the sheer *number* of these apparent original eyewitnesses is at first impressive, an objective examination of their statements reveals a curious pattern that is both illuminating and disturbing. Suffice it to say, the truth is not what we've been led to believe.

The "original" Roswell witnesses referred to in this book are those persons whose existence was first publicized through the dogged research efforts of UFOlogists Stanton T. Friedman and William L. Moore.

Friedman is regarded as the "father" of the basic Roswell story as the world knows it today because it was he who initially uncovered many of the eyewitness leads which "broke open" the case.

Bill Moore is co-author, with Bermuda Triangle myth huckster Charles Berlitz,* of the original bestselling book *The Roswell Incident,* which put the case on the map for the first time in 1980.

In order to try and understand the true nature of just exactly what reportedly "crashed" near Roswell in 1947, let us critically examine the statements of the original witnesses as they were first presented in Moore and Berlitz's book.† But first, a lesson in simple math is in order.

ORIGINAL ROSWELL "WITNESS" NUMBERS GAMES

In the pro-UFO community, much fanfare has been made over the years about the "dozens" or even "hundreds" of eyewitnesses to the alleged UFO crash near Roswell.

If the near-holy reverence for the number of alleged witnesses surrounding the Roswell affair were limited to just the UFO buffs who have conducted no direct research of their own, this situation might be understandable. However, this is not the case; the Roswell *authors* play the numbers game as well.

In the pro-UFO book, *The Truth about the UFO Crash at Roswell,* Kevin Randle and Donald Schmitt note the fact that Bill Moore interviewed "more than seventy witnesses who had some knowledge of the [Roswell UFO crash] event."[2] Indeed, both Friedman and Moore, around the time of the initial publication of

---

*For an objective book which thoroughly *disproves* the "mystery" of the so-called Bermuda Triangle, see David Lawrence Kusche's excellent work, *The Bermuda Triangle Mystery—Solved* (Amherst, N.Y.: Prometheus Books, 1986).

†Although *The Roswell Incident* was coauthored by Berlitz and Moore, it was actually Stanton Friedman and William L. Moore who did "95% of the research for the book." Berlitz conducted no interviews with any of the Roswell witnesses, and according to an interview I had with Stanton Friedman in May 1980, was used by Moore as a writing partner because he could secure a large monetary advance from the publisher. On page 45 of *Crash at Corona,* Friedman writes that he received "limited credit in the book and some royalties" in exchange for his help and efforts with the project.

The Roswell Incident in 1980, boasted that they had interviewed more than "ninety witnesses."[3]

While these double-digit figures are certainly accurate, the presentation of such a seemingly impressive number of witnesses by themselves, without qualification, is misleading. The relevant issue is not *how many* witnesses were interviewed, but rather what *type* of witnesses (i.e., firsthand, secondhand, etc.) these people are and how truthful and accurate their statements are.

Unfortunately, a careful reading of Moore and Berlitz's *Roswell Incident* reveals that despite the impressive claim of having "interviewed more than seventy witnesses," the testimonies of just *twenty-five* people are presented. Out of these twenty-five, only *seven* of them are *firsthand* sources who claim to have *seen* the alleged saucer debris, and one of these accounts is suspect. Of these seven people, however, only *five* of them claim to have actually handled the material personally, and one of them is adamant that it was not from an extraterrestrial spacecraft.[4]

The remainder of the professed "witnesses" cited in *The Roswell Incident* are either *secondhand* sources (whose testimonies constitute hearsay and thus would not be admissible in an American court of law), or are people who saw *no wreckage at all, nor were they ever present* at the "debris field" during the critical time.[5] In other words, they are not actually witnesses in the true sense of the word.

THE EYEWITNESS CAROUSEL OF CONFUSION— FATHER TIME AND FLAWED MEMORIES

While the pro-UFO community and the Roswell authors stress the *number* of witnesses, another factor in their firm belief that Roswell involved the crash of an extraterrestrial spacecraft is the apparent consistency of the eyewitness testimonies.

However, a careful reading of the statements presented in *The Roswell Incident* and elsewhere reveals that there are serious discrepancies among the various accounts which, when analyzed in detail and taken collectively, severely weaken the case.

One undeniable truth that many UFO advocates seem to easily

forget is that when Bill Moore and Stanton Friedman first started interviewing some of the original witnesses regarding Roswell, the recollections of these people had undoubtedly changed. If nothing else, their memories reflected the passage of nearly *thirty-one* years of time, if not more. After all, even the very *first* witness interviewed, Maj. Jesse Marcel, was not questioned by Friedman until 1978, again almost thirty-one years *after* the event.[6]

It is an irrefutable fact that the passage of time erodes the accuracy of one's recollections of an event. Despite this reality, the Roswell authors continue to stress just how "clear and sharp" their witnesses' "memories" are, even though nearly fifty years have now elapsed. Certainly those memories could not have improved.

Perhaps the most absurd attempt to paint the Roswell eyewitnesses and their testimonies as beyond dispute can be found in Randle and Schmitt's popular book *UFO Crash at Roswell,* which was later adapted for television by Showtime®, under the name *Roswell.*

In drawing a parallel between the alleged UFO events at Roswell and the assassination of President John F. Kennedy, Randle and Schmitt state that "The Roswell memories are vivid and detailed, despite the passage of so many years" and constitute a "snapshot memory."[7]

If this is the case, to use Randle and Schmitt's analogy, then these people forgot to load film in their camera, for even the most important "star" witness to Roswell, Maj. Jesse Marcel, when first interviewed, *could not even remember the month of the alleged UFO crash, let alone the year.*[8] Indeed, Marcel's own answer as to when this supposed "snapshot memory" event took place, was simply "in the late forties"!

Nonetheless, if we are to have any hope of trying to determine the truth about the events surrounding Roswell, we must examine in detail the individual testimonies that have been offered for the record in order to try and ascertain their veracity and true meaning. Let us begin by examining the testimonies as they were first revealed for the public record in the book *The Roswell Incident.*

THE WILMOTS

Mr. and Mrs. Dan Wilmot were sitting out on their front porch at night when they both saw an object which looked to them like "two inverted saucers faced mouth to mouth" fly overhead. They observed the craft for approximately forty to fifty seconds and saw that it was heading in a northwest direction.[9]

In *The Roswell Incident,* Berlitz and Moore attempt to connect the alleged UFO that the Wilmots reported with the debris that was later recovered by Mac Brazel at the Foster ranch: "At between 9:45 and 9:50 P.M. on the evening of July 2, 1947, what appeared to be a flying saucer passed over Roswell heading northwest at a high rate of speed, as witnessed by the Wilmots. Somewhere north of Roswell, the saucer ran into the lightning storm witnessed by Brazel, made a course correction to the south-southwest, was struck by a lightning bolt, and suffered severe on-board damage."[10]

While this is an interesting hypothesis, one must remember that it is just that—a hypothesis—with no concrete evidence to support it. Obviously, since the actual material that was later recovered at the Foster ranch is not available for examination, nor was it ever shown to the Wilmots, it is not possible to connect the debris to the object that the Wilmots claim they observed.

Although the Wilmots' professed sighting of "two inverted saucers joined mouth to mouth" remains unexplained because their report was never properly investigated, it is a leap of faith, theory and conjecture, not fact or science, to state with any certainty that the object they claim to have observed later crashed and scattered its debris on the Foster ranch for Mac Brazel to discover.

Finally, the additional claim by Berlitz and Moore that the object was later struck by lightning and made a "course correction" is mere theorizing of no scientific value. In trying to determine the true nature of the events surrounding Roswell, one must concentrate on facts, not open-ended guesswork.

LYDIA SLEPPY

Lydia Sleppy was a teletype operator at radio station KOAT in Albuquerque at the time of the Roswell incident. At approximately 4:00 P.M., on July 7, 1947, Sleppy claims that she received a telephone call from reporter Johnnie McBoyle, who worked at their sister station, KSWS, in Roswell. According to Sleppy, McBoyle told her to "get ready for a scoop" and then went on to claim that the military had recovered a flying saucer and that a farmer [Mac Brazel] had found it. McBoyle also stated that he had "been there and seen it."[11]

While Lydia Sleppy began keying in on the teletype the story that McBoyle was dictating to her via telephone, she claims that her machine suddenly stopped working and after a few minutes started sending her an ominous message instructing her to stop transmitting. She was ordered to "stop communication immediately."[12]

Sleppy claims that she then told McBoyle what had happened and asked him what she should do next. According to Sleppy, McBoyle told her "Forget about it. You never heard it. Look, you're not supposed to know. Don't talk about it to anyone."[13]

Problems with Sleppy's Account

Lydia Sleppy's dramatic statements first debuted in *The Roswell Incident*. The way its authors portray the story, it would appear that some element of the U.S. government not only managed to intercept and stop Sleppy's teletype transmission, but also silenced reporter Johnny McBoyle as well. The question now becomes, is there any credible evidence that this event took place as described?

Unfortunately, there are numerous problems with Sleppy's story, each of which indicate that it is probably not true.

According to Stanton Friedman, the FBI was the agency responsible for eavesdropping and then instructing Lydia Sleppy through her teletype machine to cease her transmission. Friedman claims this came as no surprise, "in view of all the classified work that was going on at that time."[14]

In order to assess the accuracy of Lydia Sleppy's account, as well as try and verify Friedman's FBI-connection claim, I contacted *both* the FBI headquarters in Washington, D.C., and their field office in Dallas, Texas. After repeated inquiries made between August and October 1996, two interesting discoveries were made.

According to *both* FBI offices, the agency had no "wire" in place at the time the alleged events occurred and they were in no position to monitor any news transmissions! Furthermore, the inquiry also revealed that the agency had *never* opened a file on Lydia Sleppy nor had they ever bothered "eavesdropping" on any of the teletype communications of radio station KOAT in Albuquerque. As one agent bluntly put it, "You better believe . . . that with the way J. Edgar Hoover ran things back then someone would have made a report on this. Hell, we've got stuff here on file that goes back to the bureau's very first day of existence. We definitely keep our paperwork around here and there's plenty of it."[15] Although conspiracy buffs will no doubt cry "cover-up," the burden of proof remains on *their* shoulders. Until such evidence is forthcoming, the statements made by the FBI must stand.

While the FBI's failure to find any objective evidence to support Sleppy's story was most intriguing, an even more interesting revelation was disclosed by investigators at the Dallas field office.

In researching the technical aspects of what would be required to place such a "tap" on the kind of teletype machine that Sleppy had to have used at KOAT, it was discovered that the particular model she used had both send and receive capabilities. This discovery seemed to initially support the feasibility of Sleppy's story. However, the credibility of Lydia Sleppy's account began to unravel when the Dallas FBI field office noticed that in order for Sleppy to have *received* a message, the bell on the top of her teletype would have gone off to indicate an incoming transmission. At this point, in order for Sleppy to receive the incoming message and have it print out for her to view, she would have to have then thrown a *manual switch* to put the teletype machine into the "receive" mode![16]

Since Lydia Sleppy claims she was on the phone with reporter Johnny McBoyle at the time of the alleged transmission, is it possible that McBoyle might be able to provide any supportive corroboration? Unfortunately, according to Stanton Friedman,

McBoyle refused to talk and has never substantiated Sleppy's version of events.[17] Thus, if we are to try and understand what really happened around Roswell, New Mexico, in early July, 1947, we need to search elsewhere.

WALT WHITMORE JR.

Walt Whitmore Jr. is the son of the late Walt E. Whitmore, who at the time of the event owned radio station KGFL in Roswell. The elder Whitmore, it is alleged, was the first journalist to interview Mac Brazel and had managed to do so on a wire recorder. KGFL was planning to broadcast Brazel's remarks as a "scoop" to be carried on the Mutual wire service.

According to *The Roswell Incident,* Walt Whitmore Sr. "hid Mac Brazel at the Whitmore home to keep the interview exclusive. At the very moment of the interview, the Army, according to Whitmore, was 'having a fit' because they could not locate the 'rancher who had found the flying saucer.' "[18]

Walt Whitmore Jr. claims that he saw some of the debris that Brazel had brought into town with him. He described it as consisting for the most part of "extremely tough, metallic, foil-like substance and some small beams that appeared to be either wood or wood-like. Some of the material had a sort of writing on it which looked like numbers that had been either added or multiplied." Whitmore Jr. also added that the metal was was extremely light in weight but "could not be torn or cut at all."[19]

Whitmore says that his father, as well as others, attempted to drive out to the crash site but were turned away by the military who had the whole area sealed off. He also claims that he drove out to the location a few days later, after the military had left, and saw a "fan-shaped" area where they had "cleaned it out."[20]

Problems with Whitmore's Account

Walt Whitmore Jr. was first interviewed for the record for *The Roswell Incident.* However, over the years he has been interviewed by countless UFO researchers and has *changed* his story. Whitmore's embellishments have become so great that there is now no way to separate the details of what may actually have taken place in 1947 versus what he now claims is true.

For example, Whitmore states that he saw some of the debris that Mac Brazel had brought into town with him. The problem with this claim is that Whitmore has said he didn't see Mac Brazel until the *evening,* when his father brought Brazel home to stay with them. Whitmore Jr. elaborated on this by specifically stating that he had to sleep on the couch, and let Brazel have his room.[21] This means that Whitmore Jr. didn't meet with Brazel until *after* he had already been to Sheriff Wilcox's office and had met with Maj. Jesse Marcel, the intelligence officer from Roswell Army Air Field who had been dispatched to the sheriff's department in order to examine some of the debris that Brazel had brought in. Thus, in order for Walt Whitmore Jr. to have seen *any* of the debris that Brazel had brought with him to show the authorities, Brazel must have neglected to turn over some of the material to Major Marcel. Yet there is no evidence of this in any of the pro-UFO Roswell books![22]

There is no disputing the fact that when Brazel showed the debris to Marcel he did not know what it was from. Since Marcel thought, like Brazel, that the material might have indeed come from some sort of "flying disc," it is highly unlikely that Marcel would have let Brazel wander off with some of this material. Indeed, according to the pro-UFO Roswell researchers, Marcel took this material to Colonel Blanchard at Roswell Army Air Field.

But Walt Whitmore Jr.'s claims do not end with just having been a mere witness. Indeed, in an interview with UFO researcher Karl Pflock, Whitmore, whose identity Pflock tries to hide by assigning him the pseudonym of "Reluctant," now claims that he has several pieces of the Roswell fragments in his possession! "I still have the material I collected on the [Foster] ranch site in July 1947. It is . . . stored in a safe and secure place." [Ellipses in the original.][23]

Whitmore Jr. also told Pflock a story that blatantly *contradicts* what he is quoted as saying in *The Roswell Incident.* Instead of venturing out to the crash site *after* the military had cleaned out the area as he originally claimed, Whitmore Jr. told Pflock that Brazel had drawn a map for him and that he had managed to get to the crash site to retrieve the precious fragments *before* the military arrived there![24]

Unfortunately, Karl Pflock accepts Whitmore's tale as factual, failing to have noticed the numerous discrepancies and continual changes in his various accounts. Of Whitmore Jr., Pflock writes, "I am confident that what Reluctant has told me about visiting the debris field and what was found there is true and accurate to the best of the witness's recollection."[25]

The only way that Karl Pflock can be right is if both versions of Whitmore's story are true, which is an impossibility. Perhaps it was appropriate for Pflock to name his "witness" Reluctant after all. For until Walt Whitmore Jr. comes forth with his professed collection of Roswell flying disc debris for science to examine, one should be "reluctant" to accept his changing accounts as true.

FLOYD AND LORETTA PROCTOR

Floyd and Loretta Proctor lived eight miles from the Foster ranch and were the nearest neighbors to Mac Brazel at the time of his discovery of the alleged spacecraft debris. Brazel traveled to the Proctors' residence and unsuccessfully tried to get them to come over and view the material that he had found. The Proctors declined to do so because, in the words of Floyd Proctor, "I was tired and busy, and just didn't want to bother going all that way over there right then."[26] In a later interview, Loretta Proctor clarified the reason she and her husband didn't go, adding that "gas and tires were expensive then. We had our own chores."[27]

According to the Proctors, after hearing the description of the material from Mac Brazel, they suggested to him that he contact the authorities and take it to Roswell. Brazel apparently took them up on their suggestion, because according to Floyd, "the next thing we knew he was in Roswell."[28]

The Proctors were first interviewed by Bill Moore in June 1979 while he was doing research for *The Roswell Incident*. Although Floyd Proctor has since passed away, his wife, Loretta, has been interviewed numerous times by UFO researchers and the media. The pro-UFO community and the Roswell authors use Loretta

Proctor's many pronouncements to support the theory that the material Mac Brazel originally discovered was extraterrestrial in nature. Unfortunately, as is the case with many of the Roswell witnesses, there are problems with Loretta Proctor's statements which seem to have escaped the attention of the pro-UFO community entirely, especially the Roswell authors.

The book *Crash at Corona* presents a typical example of one of Loretta Proctor's many public comments:

> [Mac] had this piece of material that he had picked up. He wanted to show it to us and wanted us to go down and see the rest of the debris or whatever, [but] we didn't on account of the transportation and everything wasn't too good. He didn't get anybody to come out who was interested in it. The piece he brought looked like kind of tan, light-brown plastic . . . it was very lightweight, like balsa wood. It wasn't a large piece, maybe about four inches long, maybe just a little larger than a pencil.
>
> *We cut on it with a knife and would hold a match on it, and it wouldn't burn.* We knew it wasn't wood. It was smooth like plastic, it didn't have real sharp corners, kind of like a dowel stick. Kind of dark tan. It didn't have any grain . . . just smooth. I hadn't seen anything like it. [Ellipses in the original, emphasis added.][29]

These remarks by Loretta Proctor were made in July 1990 during a conference on UFO "crashes" sponsored by the Fund for UFO Research in Washington, D.C. While her testimony is intriguing, it blatantly *contradicts* earlier comments she is already on record as having made.

In a taped interview recorded on April 20, 1989, *just fifteen months earlier,* the same Loretta Proctor stated unequivocally, in response to the question if she had ever tried to cut the strange piece she allegedly saw or do anything else with it: "No, we [Floyd and I] didn't. He [Mac Brazel] did."[30]

Unfortunately for the Roswell advocates, Loretta Proctor's statements have become more and more embellished over time. As if this weren't bad enough, there is a legitimate concern as to whether or not Loretta Proctor *ever really saw* even a small piece of the supposed strange "alien" material. In her original interview with Bill Moore in 1979, Loretta Proctor made *no mention at all* of ever having *personally* seen any of the debris Brazel claimed had fallen on the Foster ranch.[31] In fact, Floyd Proctor, who spoke at greater length with Moore than Loretta ever did, *never* indicated that he had seen any of the "mysterious" debris himself. Indeed, Floyd Proctor's testimony, as Moore quotes him in *The Roswell Incident,* makes it very clear that it was *Mac Brazel* who described the strange material to the both of them and had also made the claims about not being able to cut it with his knife![32] The "burning" of the debris was also never mentioned.

The sad truth about Loretta Proctor's statements is that they have changed dramatically over the years, especially since the time of her husband's death. Loretta Proctor has transformed herself from being a simple witness who never indicated that she had seen any debris to now being a "witness" who not only saw a "sliver" of the "UFO" material, but is someone who also tried to "cut" and "burn" it, all to no avail.

Loretta Proctor, in recent years, has also claimed that her son, Dee, was with Mac Brazel when he discovered the alleged UFO debris. This claim is suspicious for three reasons: (1) While her husband Floyd was alive *neither* of them ever mentioned this; (2) Dee Proctor himself has *no recollection of the event;*[33] and (3) Whenever anyone asks Loretta Proctor if she wouldn't mind if her son was interviewed about the event, she intercedes on his behalf and actively *dissuades* researchers from doing so, usually with admonitions like "he says that he's not going to talk to anyone about it."[34]

If we are to try and understand the true nature of the material that fell on the Foster ranch, we must look beyond the ever-changing accounts provided over the years by Loretta Proctor. The only portions of her testimony in which we can put some reasonable credence are those parts which also square with what her late husband said. Unfortunately, the Proctors' statements do not constitute hard evidence that anything "extraterrestrial" was recovered by Mac Brazel, despite the proclamations of the pro-UFO Roswell authors.

It is safe to say, based on the joint testimonies of both Floyd and Loretta Proctor, that Mac Brazel tried to get them to come down to the Foster ranch to view the debris that he discovered. However, there is no credible evidence or corroborative testimony that indicates that Brazel showed the Proctors any material or that they ever saw any. Loretta Proctor's statements remain unsupported, and they have changed over time.

COLONEL BLANCHARD'S WIDOW

It is mentioned in *The Roswell Incident* that Stanton Friedman spoke with Col. William Blanchard's widow about what had happened in 1947. (Blanchard was the commanding officer at Roswell Army Air Field at the time of the incident.) In response to Friedman's inquiries, Blanchard's widow is purported to have said that Blanchard "knew it was nothing made by us. At first he thought it might be Russian because of the strange symbols on it. Later on, he realized it wasn't Russian either."[35]

Unfortunately, as interesting as this testimony may appear, or what it seems to infer, it does not constitute hard, objective evidence one way or another in the Roswell case. Mrs. Blanchard was not present when the Roswell debris was recovered. Moreover, she never saw any of the wreckage. Other than the single quote offered up in *The Roswell Incident* we aren't provided with anything further.

This lack of information concerning Blanchard's widow is not limited to just *The Roswell Incident*. Indeed, Blanchard's widow is mentioned in only one of the other pro-UFO Roswell books. Thus, in order to try and gain some insights into what was recovered near Roswell, we need to examine statements made by others.

MAJOR HUGHIE GREEN

British Maj. Hughie Green was driving through New Mexico in 1947, heading toward the eastern United States. Green heard the numerous radio broadcasts about the U.S. Army having recovered a "flying disc."

Unfortunately, Green's claim about having *heard* the original Roswell radio broadcasts is of no value. No one disputes the fact that there were such broadcasts. Green is simply one of countless people who heard the press reports. Since Green saw no wreckage and has no direct knowledge of anything, he is not a witness as to what was recovered near Roswell and his testimony cannot be used as such.

VERN AND JEAN MALTAIS

Vern and Jean Maltais were first discovered as "witnesses" by Stanton Friedman, whom they approached in October 1978 after a lecture he had given on UFOs at Bemidji State University in Minnesota. Waiting until most of the crowd had left, Vern and Jean walked up to Friedman cautiously and told him about a crashed UFO story they had heard.

According to the Maltaises, a late friend of theirs named Grady L. "Barney" Barnett told them that he was out on the Plains of San Augustin in the late 1940s and had witnessed the recovery of a flying saucer and its dead occupants by the military. Although the location of this particular UFO retrieval was nowhere near Roswell, nonetheless, Berlitz, Moore, and Friedman believed that the Barnett crash story was somehow related. The theory they developed was that lightning had struck the craft and caused it to scatter debris over the Foster ranch. This is the material that Mac Brazel would later discover. Despite shedding some debris, the ship remained airborne for a short time, eventually crashing west of Socorro, on the Plains of San Augustin, where Barney Barnett would stumble upon it.

The Barnett Factor: An Exercise in Faith

Although the Maltaises' story about Barney Barnett is an interesting one, acceptance of it as being factual requires a leap of faith—Barney Barnett died several years before his story came to light, so UFO researchers were never able to interview him.

According to the Maltaises, Barnett told them that he was not the only civilian present at the crash site. Supposedly, a group of archaeologists from the University of Pennsylvania were there as well, and the entire group was later sworn to secrecy after the military arrived.

If this is true, and the incident really happened, it is suspicious that *no one* in the fifty years since this alleged crash took place has ever come forward and provided any verifiable evidence that it ever occurred. In other words, no one from either the military or this supposed group of archaeologists has ever surfaced! Indeed, the "best evidence" that UFO researchers have been able to come up with to date is track down a few friends of Barney Barnett who "vouch" for his credibility. Some of these acquaintances, curiously, recall that Barnett never said anything to them about the event.

Finally, there is the issue of a diary written by Ruth Barnett, Barney's wife. In a series of entries covering the alleged timeframe of the secret recovery, there is no mention in her memoirs about either the UFO "crash" or that Barney Barnett was even on the plains during the days in question.[36]

In summation, the evidence that a UFO once crashed and was secretly recovered on the Plains of San Augustin in July 1947 simply does not exist. The only "proof" for such an occurrence lies in the secondhand story of the Maltaises, who claim that their friend Barney Barnett told them he had witnessed such an event.

BILL BRAZEL JR.

Bill Brazel Jr., William "Mac" Brazel's son, is one of only seven *firsthand* witnesses whose testimony appears in *The Roswell Incident*. Brazel claims that he was entirely unaware that anything "unusual" had even occurred at the Foster ranch until he "picked up a copy of [the newspaper] the Albuquerque *Journal* one evening and saw Dad's picture on the front page."[37]

After reading the account about his father, Brazel drove out to the Foster ranch in order to provide any assistance that might be needed. When he arrived, Brazel Jr. claims that no one was there.

When interviewed by William L. Moore in 1979, Brazel recalled that his father had told him that during the night of a very bad thunderstorm he had heard an odd explosion. The next day, while out in a pasture tending sheep, he noticed some unusual debris scattered over a large area. According to Brazel Jr. his father thought nothing of the matter until a day or two had passed, when he decided to collect some of the material and bring it back to his ranch house.

Later that evening, Mac Brazel drove to Floyd and Loretta Proctor's house, his nearest neighbors, and described the debris to them. Brazel tried to get Floyd to drive back with him to examine the material, but was unsuccessful.

The following evening Mac Brazel traveled to Corona, about an hour from Roswell, to visit a relative named Hollis Wilson. After mentioning what had happened, Wilson and a friend of his who was visiting at the time suggested to Brazel that he might have collected the remains of a flying saucer. UFO reports were sweeping the nation in the media at that time, thus the suggestion that Brazel might have stumbled upon the wreckage of one.[38]

When Brazel was asked by researcher Moore if his father had ever described what he had found, he replied "No, not exactly; but then, he didn't need to since I had some of it myself." Elaborating, Bill Brazel Jr. explained that "after a good rain I would manage to find a piece or two that they had overlooked. After about a year and a half or two years, I had managed to accumulate quite a small collection—about enough that if you were to lay it out on this tabletop it would take up about as much area as your briefcase there."[39]

When Moore then asked Brazel Jr. to describe the material that *he* was now claiming to have found, Brazel gave the following account:

There were several types of stuff. Of course all I had was [*sic*] small bits and pieces, but one thing that I can say about it was that it sure was light in weight. It weighed almost nothing. There was some wooden-like particles I picked up. These were like balsa wood in weight, but a bit darker in color and much harder. You . . . couldn't scratch it with your fingernail like ordinary balsa, and you couldn't break it either. It was pliable, but wouldn't break. Of course, all I had was a few splinters. It never occurred to me to try to burn it so I don't know if it would burn or not.

There were also several bits of a metal-like substance, something on the order of tinfoil except that this stuff wouldn't tear and was actually a bit darker in color than tinfoil—more like lead foil, except very thin and extremely lightweight. The odd thing about this foil was that you could wrinkle it and lay it back down and it immediately resumed its original shape. It was quite pliable, yet you couldn't crease or bend it like ordinary metal. It was almost more like a plastic of some sort, except that it was definitely metallic in nature. I don't know what it was, but I do know that Dad once said the Army had told him that they definitely established it was not anything made by us.[40]

How Accurate Is Bill Brazel's Testimony?

Other than Maj. Jesse Marcel, whose testimony will be examined later in this chapter, Bill Brazel is the Roswell incident's most important witness. While Brazel's statements are, for the most part, consistent with the testimonies given by the other surviving first-hand witnesses in *The Roswell Incident*, unfortunately there are some remarks of his that are demonstrably erroneous, as well as likely to be embellishments.

One example is that Brazel claimed that he first learned about the discovery of the "saucer" debris and his father's alleged plight in Roswell when he "picked up a copy of the Albuquerque *Journal* one evening and saw Dad's picture on the front page." A check in past issues of the Albuquerque *Journal* revealed that while the newspaper had indeed featured a story on the "flying disc" (as did many papers throughout the United States), Mac Brazel's picture *never* appeared in any articles published by the *Journal,* let alone on the "front page" as Brazel claimed.

What's more troubling, however, and far more important to the credibility of certain aspects of Brazel's testimony, are his claims that Air Force personnel made a subsequent trip to the Foster ranch where they asked him to "hand over" the few supplemental fragments that he claimed he had later found.

After telling author William Moore about the bits and pieces of unusual debris that he claimed to have collected, Moore asked Bill Brazel Jr. the logical question, "What ever became of this [wreckage] collection of yours? Do you still have it?"

In response to Moore's inquiry, Brazel gave the following account:

Now that's the curious part of the story. No, I don't have it. One night about two years after Dad's incident, I went into Corona for the evening. While I was there, I guess I talked too much—more than I should have. I know I mentioned having this collection to someone. Anyway, the next day a staff car came out to the ranch from Roswell with a captain and three enlisted men in it. Dad was away at the time; but it turned out they didn't want him anyway. They wanted me. Seems the captain—Armstrong, I think his name was, Captain Armstrong—had heard about my collection and asked to see it. Of course I showed it to him, and he said that this stuff was important to the country's security and that it was most important that I let him have it. . . . I didn't know what else to do, so I agreed. Next he wanted me to take them out to the pasture where I had found this stuff. I said OK and took them there. After they had poked around a bit and satisfied themselves that there didn't appear to be any more of the material out there, the captain again asked me if I had any more of this material or if I knew of anyone else who did. I said no, I didn't; and he said that if I ever found any more that it was most important that I call him at Roswell right away. Naturally I said I would, but I never did because after that I never found any more.[41]

While Brazel's claim about the alleged confiscation of his collection of material makes for interesting reading, there are no other witnesses to verify his story. As Brazel himself stated, "Dad was away at the time." Furthermore, it is doubtful that Brazel is telling the truth, because his sister, Bessie, has gone on record as stating that "We never found any other pieces of it afterwards—after the military was there. Of course we were out there quite a lot over the years, but we never found so much as a shred. The military scraped it all up pretty well."[42] Because Brazel Jr. lacks any witnesses to his story, it would seem that Bessie is the more believable sibling.

One would think that if Brazel's confiscation tale were true that he would have told at least *one* of his family members, friends, or acquaintances about the incident, since he certainly felt at liberty to tell UFO researchers Friedman and Moore. Suspiciously, there is no record of this.

There is an additional problem with Brazel's account. Like many of the original Roswell witnesses, as we shall discover, Brazel has changed his story. In another interview that took place, Brazel told UFO researcher Stanton Friedman that

I was in Corona, in the bar, the pool hall—sort of a meeting place—domino parlor. . . . That's where everybody got together. Everybody was askin' . . . they'd seen the papers (this was about a month after the crash) and I said, "Oh, I picked up a few little bits and pieces and fragments." "So, what are they?" "I dunno."

Then, lo and behold, here comes the military (out to the ranch, a day or two later). I'm almost positive that the officer in charge, his name was Armstrong, a real nice guy. He had a black sergeant with him that was real nice. I think there was two other enlisted men. They said, "We understand your father found this weather balloon." I said, "Well, yeah!" "And we understand you found some bits and pieces." I said "Yeah, I've got a cigar box that's got a few of 'em in there, down at the saddle shed."

And this (I think he was a captain), and he said, "Well, we would like to take it with us." I said, "Well . . ." And he smiled and he said, "Your father turned the rest of it over to us, and you know he's under oath not to tell." "Well," he said, "we came after those bits and pieces." And I kind of smiled and said, "OK, you can have the stuff, I have no use for it at all."

He said, "Well, have you examined it?" And I said, "Well, enough to know that I don't know what the hell it is!" And he said, "We would rather you didn't talk very much about it." [Ellipses in the original.][43]

While Bill Brazel Jr.'s account to Friedman was slightly more melodramatic than the version he told Moore, it is interesting to note that Brazel significantly changed the timeline of the alleged Air Force "confiscation" of his small collection of debris fragments. Originally, Brazel told Moore that it had been some "two years" after his father had first discovered the wreckage, yet he told Stanton Friedman that it had only been "about a month."

There are other issues with Brazel Jr.'s account concerning the purported Air Force personnel. Indeed, a check with Air Force officials revealed that there were *no black sergeants* stationed at Roswell Army Air Field in 1947. Racial segregation was still prevalent in the United States Armed Forces in 1947, even in the Army Air Force.[44]

Furthermore, there is no record of a "Captain Armstrong" stationed at Roswell Army Air Field between the years 1947 through 1949. Yet, in his testimony to author William Moore, Brazel Jr. had claimed that this "Captain Armstrong" had specifically requested for him to contact him at Roswell Army Air Field! Thus, if Brazel was telling the truth, he had to have been grossly in error with regard to both the race of one of the men (an unlikely occurrence), as well as the last name of the other individual who Brazel claimed was not only an officer but "a real nice fellow."

In their book *The Truth about the UFO Crash at Roswell,* Randle and Schmitt make the claim that the military "was still watching" Bill Brazel Jr. and others at the Foster ranch.[45] While this sounds ominous, it is highly unlikely. As mentioned previously, the Foster ranch is over *eight miles* from its nearest neighbor, the Proctors. It is located in the middle of the New Mexico desert with nothing around it. The question becomes *how* would the military in 1947 be able to "watch" Brazel Jr. and others at the ranch? There would be no place for them to hide; it's bare, flat desert terrain for miles. There was no telephone at the house for an intelligence agency to tap into or monitor any outgoing calls and the type of advanced eavesdropping devices that would allow remote conversation recording to take place did not exist in 1947.

Furthermore, if the military had indeed been "watching" Brazel Jr. they would not have had to wait for him to open his mouth and "spill the beans" about his fragment collection—they would have known about it all along, having "spied" on him—and they would have moved in more quickly rather than wait until he told several patrons at a public gathering place in Corona. If security was a real concern, as we are led to believe by Randle and Schmitt, things would haven been handled differently than they supposedly were.

The truth is, a significant portion of Bill Brazel's testimony must be considered suspect. About the only thing we can be reasonably certain of is that foil-like material, very strong in nature, was recovered. We can assume that Brazel Jr.'s description of the material is fairly accurate, since it is consistent with what other witnesses have reported.

BESSIE BRAZEL SCHREIBER

In July 1979, Bill Moore interviewed Bessie Brazel Schreiber, Mac Brazel's daughter, who was just twelve years old at the time her father discovered the debris. In her interview with Moore, Schreiber claimed that

> There was what appeared to be pieces of heavily waxed paper and a sort of aluminum-like foil. Some of these pieces had something like numbers and lettering on them, but there were no words that we were able to make out. Some of the metal-foil pieces had a sort of tape stuck to them, and when these were held to the light they showed what looked like pastel flowers or designs. Even though the stuff looked like tape it could not be peeled off or removed at all. It was very light in weight but there sure was a lot of it.[46]

When Moore asked her what happened after her father had brought some of the material to the authorities in Roswell, Schreiber replied that they were "descended upon by military and news people" the next day. Schreiber also claimed that the family was sworn to secrecy.

Moore asked Bessie Schreiber if the debris she observed could possibly have come from a weather balloon. She indicated that she had seen weather balloons before and was adamant in her reply, "No, it was definitely not a balloon."[47]

Reviewing Schreiber's Account

Although Bessie Schreiber told Moore that the device her father discovered was not a weather balloon, her description of the material isn't exactly what one would expect of an advanced extraterrestrial spacecraft either. About the only thing one can say about Bessie Schreiber's account is that the material she recalls observing has consistent elements with what other witnesses have testified to: aluminum-like foil, wax paper, tape with flowers or pastel designs on it, and some writing. While these are not the usual components of a weather balloon, this does suggest that whatever the device was, it consisted of manmade materials, the type of which one would hardly expect to find an extraterrestrial spacecraft to be made from.

MAJ. JESSE ANTOINE MARCEL

The single, most important eyewitness according to Roswell UFO debris advocates is Maj. Jesse A. Marcel, who was an intelligence officer with the 509th Bomb Group. As the pro-UFO community is often fond of pointing out, the 509th was an "elite" group of military personnel who were stationed at Roswell, the only nuclear air base in existence at that time. Indeed, the pilots who dropped the atomic bombs that ended World War II came from Roswell.

Major Marcel was having lunch on July 6,* when he received a telephone call from Chavez County Sheriff George Wilcox explaining that a rancher had brought to him some material from a device that had fallen on his ranch. Marcel listened to the description of the debris then phoned his commanding officer, Col. William H. Blanchard, who ordered Marcel to go see Brazel and investigate the matter firsthand.

Hours later, Major Marcel and a Counter Intelligence Corps (CIC) officer by the name of Sheridan Cavitt drove in separate vehicles and followed Mac Brazel out to the Foster Ranch. The three men arrived in the late afternoon and didn't get to conduct their first, serious examination of the "debris field" until the next day, July 7.

Major Marcel described the wreckage he had personally observed and handled while at the Foster ranch in response to a series of questions asked by Friedman and Moore during three interviews conducted in 1979, some *thirty-two years* after the event. This was his first public interview regarding the UFO crash.

QUESTION: Do you think that what you saw was a weather balloon?

---

*Although the *The Roswell Incident* claims that Maj. Jesse Marcel first received the phone call about the debris from Sheriff Wilcox on July 7, Bill Moore has subsequently gone on record stating that this is a typographical error by the publisher that appears in the book. Therefore, I have used the date of July 6, 1947, in light of this revelation, of which most UFO and Roswell researchers are simply unaware. (See William L. Moore and Jamie Shandera, "Enough Is Too Much," *Focus,* September 30, 1990, p. 11).

MAJOR MARCEL: It was not. I was pretty well acquainted with most everything that was in the air at that time, both ours and foreign. I was also acquainted with virtually every type of weather-observation or radar tracking device being used by either civilians or the military. It was definitely not a weather or tracking device, nor was it any sort of plane or missile. What it was we didn't know. We just picked up the fragments. It was something I had never seen before, or since, for that matter. I don't know what it was, but it certainly wasn't anything built by us and it most certainly wasn't any weather balloon.

QUESTION: Can you describe the materials that you found on the site?

MAJOR MARCEL: There was all kinds of stuff—small beams about three-eighths or a half inch square with some sort of hieroglyphics on them that nobody could decipher. These looked something like balsa wood, and were of about the same weight, except that they were not wood at all. They were very hard, although flexible, and would not burn. There was a great deal of an unusual parchment-like substance which was brown in color and extremely strong, and a great number of small pieces of a metal like tinfoil, except that it wasn't tinfoil. I was interested in electronics and kept looking for something that resembled instruments or electronic equipment, but I didn't find anything. One of the other fellows, Cavitt, I think, found a black box, metallic-looking box several inches square. As there was no apparent way to open this, and since it didn't appear to be an instrument of any sort (it too was very light weight), we threw it in with the rest of the stuff. I don't know what eventually happened to the box, but it went along with the rest of the material we eventually took to Fort Worth.

As Jesse Marcel described the material for Moore, he claimed that a lot of it looked like parchment and had small numbers with symbols that he called "hieroglyphics" for lack of a better term. Marcel described these as pink and purple in color and looked as if they were painted on.

Major Marcel also claims that he tried to burn the material and some of the wood-like beams with his cigarette lighter but was unsuccessful. He then made the startling claim to Moore that someone had told him that one of the pieces of metal was so unusual that despite its being as thin as aluminum foil, that they couldn't dent it with a sixteen-pound sledgehammer.[48]

There is no disputing the fact that Major Marcel's testimony is extremely compelling. At first glance, it makes any reasonable person genuinely wonder if indeed the debris he collected might have been from an extraterrestrial spacecraft.

Marcel first surfaced in the media during the initial press reports surrounding the original recovery of the debris. However, after the Air Force originally explained the affair away as nothing more than the misidentification of a "weather balloon," Marcel quietly faded away, never to be heard from again outside a small circle of friends until February 21, 1978, when he was eventually interviewed by UFO researcher Stanton Friedman.

Friedman was doing a television interview in Baton Rouge, Louisiana, when, during a coffee break, a director from the station mentioned to him that "The person you really ought to talk to is Jesse Marcel. He handled pieces of one of those (UFO) things."[49] Friedman, always on the trail to blow open the "Cosmic Watergate," (a commendable cause, if such a massive, government-sponsored UFO cover-up indeed exists), telephoned Marcel the next day and subsequently interviewed him.

Throughout the rest of 1978 and 1979, Friedman interviewed Major Marcel repeatedly both by himself, and later with his research associate, Bill Moore, to provide content for what later would be included in *The Roswell Incident*.

While the testimony of Maj. Jesse Marcel as it appears in *The Roswell Incident* is certainly powerful, the relevant question is, can it be trusted? Was Major Marcel telling the truth in his interviews with Friedman and Moore? Unfortunately, the answer is a *definitive* no, and for the first time in any book yet written on the subject of the Roswell UFO "crash" it shall be proven so.

Maj. Jesse Marcel—The Hidden Truth

The first distortions concerning Maj. Jesse Marcel have to do with his background. To put it bluntly, most of what was written about Marcel by Berlitz and Moore just isn't true.

While there is no evidence that the quotes attributed to Major Marcel by both Friedman and Moore in *The Roswell Incident* are inaccurate, unfortunately for pro-UFO buffs and those who consider Major Marcel to be their "star" witness, it appears that Major Marcel *himself* did the confabulating!

To prove this, I obtained a copy of Marcel's entire military service file, which totals nearly 200 pages. The file is extremely incriminating, for it proves beyond a shadow of a doubt that Major Marcel had a penchant for exaggerating things and repeatedly trying to "write himself" into the history books.

For example, in *The Roswell Incident* Berlitz and Moore claim that Major Marcel was a *pilot* and "had been flying since 1928." To buttress their point, the authors further quote Major Marcel directly, citing his claim that he was "familiar with virtually everything that flew."[50]

If Marcel was indeed "familiar with everything that flew," then it was from a hobbyist standpoint only, for his military file clearly establishes that he was *never* a pilot!

Unfortunately, this startling revelation concerning Marcel's background is just the beginning of a long list of embellishments and distortions that the major was guilty of making to Moore and Friedman; embellishments which, until this writing, have gone unchecked and accepted at face value by the pro-UFO Roswell authors.

After making the claim that Marcel was a pilot, Berlitz and Moore write that:

> As one of the few cartographers familiar with both the making and interpreting of aerial maps before World War II, he was sent to intelligence school by the Army Air Force *following Pearl Harbor* and proved to be so capable a student that, upon completion of training, he was retained as an instructor. Fifteen months later, he applied for and was granted *combat duty,* and went to New Guinea, where he became intelligence officer for his bomber squadron and later for his entire group. Flying as a *bombardier, waist gunner, and pilot, he logged 468 hours of combat flying B-24s, was awarded five air medals for shooting down five enemy aircraft, and was himself shot down once (on his third mission).* [Emphasis added.][51]

While Major Marcel's background summary as presented in this excerpt sounds impressive, once again, according to his military file virtually *none* of this is true!

Discrepancies between *The Roswell Incident* and Marcel's record are not confined to his early military career. Berlitz and Moore state:

> In October 1947, just three months after the Roswell Incident, Marcel was suddenly transferred to Washington, D.C. . . . Once there, he was quickly promoted to lieutenant colonel (in December) and assigned to a Special Weapons Program that was busy collecting air samples from throughout the world and analyzing them in an effort to detect whether the Russians had exploded their first nuclear bomb. "When we finally detected that there had been an atomic explosion, it was my job to write the report on it," related Marcel. "In fact, when President Truman went on the air to declare that the Russians had exploded a nuclear device, it was my report that he was reading from."[52]

Moore and Berlitz cite this tale to provide Jesse Marcel with additional credibility. However, as we shall discover, this claim is also untrue.

UFO researcher Robert Todd has done more extensive research into the background claims of Jesse Marcel than any other person. It was Todd who first obtained Major Marcel's complete military file, which excluded only medical information. In interviews with me and in his own privately published statements Robert Todd has expressed his opinions about Marcel as follows:

> Marcel claimed he was an aide to General Hap Arnold, and that it had been Arnold who decided he should go to intelligence school. This claim is false. When Marcel applied for an appointment as a second lieutenant, he was still working for the Shell Oil Company in Houston, Texas. When Marcel accepted the appointment and entered active duty, his very first assignment was as a student at the Army Air Forces Intelligence School (AAFIS) in Harrisburg, Pennsylvania. The decision to send him to intelligence school had been made by the Air Force even *before* Marcel accepted the appointment. . . . It was also decided that, after

completing intelligence school, Marcel would be assigned to a combat unit as a "Photo Interpretation Officer," both decisions undoubtedly based on Marcel's employment at Shell Oil where he made maps from aerial photographs. . . .

Marcel also claimed he had "flying experience" prior to going into the Air Force, and that he had been a "private pilot" who had started flying in 1928. He said he had accumulated 3,000 hours of flight time as a pilot, and 8,000 hours of total flying time. His personnel file, however, does not support these claims. Nowhere on his application for appointment (completed and signed by Marcel in January 1942), or the "Classification Questionnaire for Reserve Officers" (completed and signed by Marcel in February 1942), did he mention *any* experience as a pilot. He didn't even mention that he had flown in aircraft as a passenger, although he did reveal important pieces of information such as his hobbies of amateur photography and amateur radio, and that he had acted in school and community plays, and had sung in a quartet over radio and at parties. . . . The closest he came to indicating any civilian involvement with anything airborne was his description of his work for Shell Oil Company, where he made maps from aerial photographs. If indeed he had a private pilot's certificate in civilian life, he never hinted at it in any of the many official forms and other documents he was required to complete or verify throughout his military career. It doesn't seem likely that modesty prevented him from revealing this information to the air arm of the military services.

Among Marcel's other claims was that he flew in combat as a waist gunner, a bombardier, *and* as a pilot. While his personnel file indicates that he flew *on* combat missions, it does *not* support his more impressive claims. Since Marcel's primary Military Occupational Specialty (MOS) was "Intelligence Staff Officer (Combat)," we may reasonably assume he flew on combat missions to assess bomb damage, and/or to identify possible future targets or targets of opportunity. The records show that, throughout his entire Air Force career, he had no aeronautical rating whatsoever, not as a bombardier, nor in any other crew position. Bombardiers required extensive training, and nowhere in his file does it show he received such training, or that he was even considered for such training. Pilots also required extensive training, and, again, the file shows Marcel did not receive that training, nor was he even considered for such training.

His "Reserve Officer Career Brief," dated 20 November 1947, lists his flying experience as "NONE." In another document in the file, dated 19 August 1948, General Ramey specifically stated that Marcel was *not* a rated pilot, a fact Ramey noted would limit Marcel's career in the Air Force.

Nevertheless, it appears that many World War II bomber pilots allowed each member of the crew (including enlisted personnel) an opportunity to fly the aircraft at least once, so they would be more familiar with the controls should the pilot and copilot become incapacitated. It seems this practice was credited for saving more than one ship and its crew. *If* Marcel piloted *any* aircraft during the war, it surely was [in this capacity]. Had the pilot and copilot actually become incapacitated and had Marcel been called upon to save the ship, you can be certain we would have heard about it. That is the *only* set of circumstances under which Marcel would have been allowed to pilot an aircraft in combat.

As for his claim that he flew as a waist gunner, the records show he had no training for that position either. According to the file, Marcel was scored for his proficiency in the use of firearms, and scored an unimpressive 44 percent with a pistol. The records also show he fired 25 rounds from a Thompson submachine gun, 40 rounds from a carbine, and 20 rounds from a 22-caliber rifle.

According to his service record, that was the full extent of his hands-on exposure to firearms. Furthermore, the position of waist gunner was an enlisted man's position, not an officer's position. Even so, bombardiers and navigators also had training as gunners—but intelligence officers did not. Nowhere does Marcel's service record show he had any training as a gunner.

Given the above facts, it might seem downright incredible that Marcel actually claimed he had been awarded five Air Medals because he shot down five enemy planes while manning the waist gun of a B-24 bomber. The official records, however, show otherwise. These records—some signed by Marcel himself—clearly show he was awarded only two Air Medals (one Air Medal and an oak leaf cluster for a subsequent award of the same medal). Moreover, the citations giving the reasons for the awards make absolutely no mention of Marcel's having shot down even one enemy aircraft. In fact, the citations make it clear the medals were awarded because Marcel had flown on enough combat missions for enough hours to qualify for the awards.

While commendable, two Air Medals are not five. In terms of numbers, Marcel claimed he received 150 percent more Air Medals than he actually received, a significant exaggeration by any reasonable standard. He also grossly misrepresented the circumstances under which the medals were awarded. And once again, there is no innocent explanation for this rather glaring discrepancy.

There may be a grain of truth to his claims of manning a waist gun, to the extent he was allowed to squeeze off a few rounds to see what it was like, but the claim he shot down five enemy aircraft and was awarded five Air Medals as a result is a blatant lie. Five confirmed "kills" (officially called "victories") would have made Marcel an "ace," and his achievement would have been noted in his service record in no uncertain terms. It is not.

Marcel also contributed to a misunderstanding regarding his rank. The military ranking system has changed significantly over the years, becoming less complicated in the process. The crashed-saucer promoters never fail to mention that Marcel attained the rank of lieutenant colonel, as if this automatically bestows credibility on anything he had to say. What they don't say (probably because they don't know it) is that Marcel's active-duty rank never rose above major. When he left active duty in September 1950, the highest rank he had attained while on active duty was still major. Marcel told receptive . . . Roswell "investigators" that he was promoted to lieutenant colonel in December 1947, but that—incredibly—he didn't find out about the promotion until he left the service (presumably meaning when he left active duty), because "They kept me so busy I never even looked at my personal files."

The official records show that Marcel was indeed promoted to lieutenant colonel in December 1947—in the *Air Force Reserve*. Despite his reserve rank, his active-duty rank was still *major*. . . .

As for his claim that he didn't find out about the promotion until after he left the service, it was an outright lie. Not only did he know about the promotion, but he had specifically requested it in a 29 October 1947 letter to the commanding officer of the 509th Bomb Group. By letter dated 20 November 1947, Marcel was informed he had been appointed a lieutenant colonel "in the Officers Reserve Corps," and was further advised that the appointment would be canceled if he did not accept it by signing the oath of office "within a reasonable time." Marcel signed the oath on 1 December 1947, thereby accepting the appointment officially. . . .

It appears Marcel fed the faithful other lies about his background. He told Roswell "investigators" that he had a bachelor's degree in physics from George Washington University in Washington, D.C. Marcel had been stationed in Washington during part of his assignment with the Strategic Air Command (SAC), from 16 August to 9 November 1948: and during his assignment with the Air Force organization responsible for detecting foreign atomic explosions, from 26 December 1948 to September 1950. He also claimed he attended the University of Wisconsin, Ohio State University, New York University, and Louisiana State University (LSU).

The forms Marcel filled out himself prior to entering active duty show that he claimed he attended LSU for one year. On one form he said he had been a "special student" while on another he said he had taken noncredit courses in mathematics, English, and physics. On records dated later, the one year at LSU grew to one and a half years, with no obvious explanation for the discrepancy, aside from the fact that the information had to have come from Marcel himself.

There are no records in the file that show the Air Force made any attempt to verify his attendance at LSU. When I wrote to LSU to verify Marcel's claim, they informed me they could find no record of him, although they did find the records for his son. A second search produced the same results.

Marcel claimed he completed work on his bachelor's degree at George Washington University, and that he had in fact received a degree. Yet, when I wrote to the university, they informed me they could find no record of Marcel. And once again, a second search produced the same results. No attempt was made to contact the other universities he claimed he attended, as there is no indication he ever lived in Wisconsin, Ohio, or New York where he would have had the opportunity to attend these universities in person. When he left active duty in September 1950, he apparently returned to Louisiana where he was self-employed as a television repairman.

None of the records in Marcel's personnel file—with the records dating as late as June 1958 when he was discharged from the Air Force Reserve, long after he left Washington, D.C., and returned to Louisiana—show he attended any college, except for that one and a half years at LSU which Marcel himself had characterized as noncredit.

During a December 1979 interview with Bob Pratt, then a reporter with the *National Enquirer,* Marcel was asked how long he stayed at Roswell following the Roswell incident. He said he was transferred to Washington, D.C., the "latter part of 1947," where he said he was given a lengthy title of some kind. But according to the official records, Marcel was assigned to the 509th Bombardment Wing at Walker Air Force Base (AFB) Roswell, New Mexico, until 16 August 1948, when he was transferred to SAC headquarters at Andrews AFB, Washington, D.C. That was more than a year after the Roswell incident had taken place. . . .

Whatever the cause, the crashed-saucer promoters use Marcel's erroneous statement to suggest that . . . his superiors immediately promoted him and transferred him to a position of even greater responsibility. It sounds good, but the timing is off by about a year.

At SAC, Marcel was given the title of "Chief, Technical Trends & Developments, Alien Capabilities Section, Intelligence Division, Headquarters," presumably the lengthy title he had alluded to during the interview with Bob Pratt. Marcel remained at Andrews AFB until 9 November 1948, when he transferred— along with SAC headquarters—to Offutt AFB, Nebraska, where he held the same title. On 26 December 1948, he was again transferred, from SAC to the 1009th Special Weapons Squadron (part of Headquarters Command) in Washington, D.C., where he was made the officer in charge of the "War Room, Intelligence Branch Operations Division, AFOAT-1." AFOAT-1 (1009th Special Weapons Squadron) was responsible for operating the Long Range Detection Program (LRDP), which was intended to alert the United States to atomic explosions that occurred anywhere in the world, especially in the Soviet Union.

Marcel furnished Pratt (and others) with details of his assignment at AFOAT-1. In fact, he made the rather astonishing (and equally impressive) claim that, when AFOAT-1 detected the first Soviet atomic explosion in 1949, Marcel himself had to write a report on it. "In fact," he claimed, "I wrote the very report President Truman read on the air declaring that Russia had exploded an atomic device." Curiously, President Truman never went on the air to announce the Soviet A-bomb explosion. Instead, the White House issued a written statement. . . . In addition, no documentation has surfaced to support Marcel's claim to fame, while records have surfaced that suggest Marcel inflated his role.

Among the records on the Soviet A-bomb explosion that have surfaced are formerly top-secret records from AFOAT-1 that found their way into President Truman's files. Not surprisingly, Marcel's name does not appear anywhere in these records, including records of the advisory group convened to evaluate AFOAT-1's data and conclusions. . . . But what has also surfaced is a copy of the White House statement itself, complete with corrections. *Nothing* about the typed, one-page statement suggests Marcel had anything whatever to do with it. . . . There is little reason to give Marcel's claim any credence whatsoever. . . .

In his Showtime movie *Roswell*, Paul Davids did his level best to turn Major Marcel into a folk hero who blazed the trail to the "truth" about the Roswell incident. But the truth is that Major Marcel . . . had a problem with the truth. . . .

While there is no credible evidence that Friedman and Moore ever misquoted Maj. Jesse Marcel, their *failure* to discover the serious *falsehoods* this key witness made with regard to his own personal and professional background is inexcusable.

Since Marcel's own military record proves that he had a penchant for embellishing things and distorting his true place in history, one has to now question quite seriously the accuracy of his testimony regarding the alleged "saucer" debris he collected on the Foster ranch.

When Robert Todd wrote to Jesse Marcel Jr. to ask him about the various discrepancies in his father's claims, he received a very revealing response. Not only did Jesse Marcel Jr. fail to refute a single point in Todd's research, he refused to deal with the subject at all![53]

We must consider Major Marcel's statements as trustworthy only if other, independent source confirmation exists.

JESSE MARCEL JR.

Jesse Marcel Jr. was just eleven years old at the time of the Roswell incident. According to Marcel Jr. his father came home late one evening and said he had with him the remains of a flying disc. Major Marcel then went to his car, and brought in some of the material, and spread it out on the kitchen floor of their home for all to look at.

According to Marcel Jr. the debris consisted of pieces of aluminum-like foil with small sticks that looked like kite sticks. He also recalled some unusual looking symbols on the beams of dark wood. To this day, he doesn't know what it was that he saw back in 1947.

The first problem in trying to analyze the testimony of Jesse Marcel Jr. is the fact that he was just eleven years old when he saw the material. Had he been older, his description and recollections of what he claims he saw might have been more complete. As things stand, Jesse Marcel Jr. doesn't really remember many details.

Unfortunately, Jesse Marcel Jr.'s recollections of the debris he briefly saw and handled do not provide us with enough details to know precisely what their true nature was. In order to try and ascertain this, we must look elsewhere.

LT. WALTER HAUT

Walter Haut was Roswell Army Air Field's Public Information Officer at the time of the Roswell incident in 1947. It was Haut who, at the request of the base commander, Colonel William Blanchard, drafted the initial press release announcing the recovery of a flying disc.

Although Walter Haut wrote the press release, he actually saw *no material or debris.* Indeed, Haut's knowledge of the properties of the material that was recovered came only from secondhand or other sources, the primary individual being Maj. Jesse Marcel. Walter Haut's experience with the Roswell affair is severely limited, his testimony provides us nothing as far as gaining any insight into what the debris actually was.

WHAT WE KNOW ABOUT ROSWELL SO FAR . . .

Despite the highly touted number of "witnesses" to the Roswell affair, the testimonies, as we have seen, when examined critically, are not as impressive as claimed. Indeed, it appears that the only thing we can say with any certainty about Roswell at this stage in our investigation is that:

1. An object scattered debris over the Foster ranch. Some of this debris was collected and turned over to the military authorities by William "Mac" Brazel. However, there is no way to know exactly when Brazel found the debris, as accounts vary.

2. The debris consisted, in part, of aluminum foil-like material. The substance was hard to tear, would straighten itself out when folded up, and could not be burnt.

3. There were dark beams of what appeared to be a balsa-like wood. This wood could not be burned and had strange "hieroglyphic"-type writing on it, as did some of the pieces of foil-like material.

4. The strange symbols observed were pink or pastel in color and were not readable.

5. The debris included some thread-like material that could not be torn or broken.

6. All of the material was very light in weight and very strong.

7. No one recognized the material or device as anything he or she had seen before.

8. The material was originally identified as being the remains of a flying disc. Later, this same material was "explained" by military authorities as being from a weather balloon.

While the number of witnesses to the Roswell incident is not as high as has been claimed, nonetheless, the few descriptions that seem to be reliable and independently corroborated are tantalizing just the same. However, as bizarre as the material described appears to have been, the corroborated descriptions fall short of what science demands as sufficient proof to say that this material was extraterrestrial in origin. We must remember that two key factors are missing here: (1) No one has ever described the remains of an intact ship, airborne vehicle, or any sort of fuselage; and (2) No "alien" bodies were ever described by any of the *primary* eyewitnesses. At best we can say the object and its debris remain unexplained. Indeed, in order to gain further insight into what it was that scattered debris over the Foster ranch we need to look at additional testimonies if we are to be successful.

In order to try and understand just what happened at Roswell, we must look elsewhere. There are, after all, according to researchers Kevin Randle and Donald Schmitt, "hundreds" of more witnesses whose testimonies we can examine.

NOTES

1. Stanton T. Friedman, personal interviews with Kal K. Korff, Union City, California, May 1980, and Portland, Oregon, March 1996.

2. Kevin D. Randle and Donald R. Schmitt, *The Truth about the UFO Crash at Roswell* (New York: Avon Books, 1994), p. 215.

3. Friedman interviews with Korff, May 1980. Also, William L. Moore, personal interview with Kal K. Korff, Fremont, California, December 1980.

4. Charles Berlitz and William L. Moore, *The Roswell Incident* (New York: Berkeley Books, 1988), pp. 36–37.

5. Ibid., pp. 81, 95.

6. Stanton Friedman and Don Berliner, *Crash at Corona: The U.S. Military Retrieval and Cover-Up of a UFO* (New York: Paragon House, 1992), pp. 8–9.

7. Kevin D. Randle and Donald R. Schmitt, *UFO Crash at Roswell* (New York: Avon Books, 1991), p. 8.

8. Friedman and Berliner, *Crash at Corona,* p. 9.

9. Berlitz and Moore, *The Roswell Incident,* p. 23.

10. Ibid., pp. 99–100.

11. Ibid., p. 15.

12. Ibid., p. 16.

13. Ibid.

14. Friedman and Berliner, *Crash at Corona,* p. 12.

15. Kal K. Korff, personal phone conversation with representatives of the Federal Bureau of Investigation, Washington, D.C., and Dallas, Texas, August 1, 1996, through October 15, 1996.

16. Ibid.

17. Berlitz and Moore, *The Roswell Incident,* p. 17.

18. Ibid., p. 97.

19. Ibid., pp. 98–99.

20. Ibid.

21. Randle and Schmitt, *The Truth about the UFO Crash at Roswell,* p. 64.

22. Berlitz and Moore, *The Roswell Incident.* See also, Friedman and Berliner, *Crash at Corona,* and Randle and Schmitt, *UFO Crash at Roswell* and *The Truth about the UFO Crash at Roswell.*

23. Karl Pflock, *Roswell in Perspective* (Mt. Ranier, Md.: Fund for UFO Research, 1994), p. 87.

24. Ibid.

25. Ibid.

26. Berlitz and Moore, *The Roswell Incident,* p. 92.

27. Randle and Schmitt, *The Truth about the UFO Crash at Roswell,* p. 32.

28. Berlitz and Moore, *The Roswell Incident,* pp. 93–94.

29. Friedman and Berliner, *Crash at Corona,* p. 72.

30. Kevin D. Randle, *Roswell UFO Crash Update* (New Brunswick, N.J.: Global Communications, 1995), p. 163. See also Randle and Schmitt, *UFO Crash at Roswell,* p. 148.

31. Berlitz and Moore, *The Roswell Incident,* pp. 92–95.

32. Ibid., p. 93.

33. Randle, *Roswell UFO Crash Update,* p. 166.

34. Ibid.

35. Berlitz and Moore, *The Roswell Incident,* p. 47.

36. Randle and Schmitt, *The Truth about the UFO Crash at Roswell,* p. 190.

37. Berliner and Friedman, *Crash at Corona,* p. 83.

38. Berlitz and Moore, *The Roswell Incident,* pp. 83–87.

39. Ibid., p. 87.

40. Ibid., pp. 87–88.

41. Ibid., pp. 89–90.

42. Ibid., p. 97.

43. Friedman and Berliner, *Crash at Corona,* p. 85.

44. Kal K. Korff, phone conversations with United States Air Force historical personnel, Pentagon, Washington, D.C., September 10, 1996.

45. Randle and Schmitt, *The Truth about the UFO Crash at Roswell,* p. 37.

46. Berlitz and Moore, *The Roswell Incident,* p. 96.

47. Ibid., p. 97.

48. Ibid., pp. 73–74.

49. Friedman and Berliner, *Crash at Corona,* p. 8.

50. Berlitz and Moore, *The Roswell Incident,* p. 68.

51. Ibid.

52. Ibid., p. 77.

53. Jim Moseley, *Saucer Smear* 43, issue 5 (March 1996), posted on <http://www.mcs.com/~kvg/smear/v42/22950605.htm>.

3

The New Roswell "Witnesses"

This work [the book *The Truth about the UFO Crash at Roswell*]
will rise or fall on the research we did, on the credibility of our
investigation and the accuracy of our reporting. Don't let others
drag you from the path that is important by clouding the issues
and muddying the water. When the dust settles, you'll find that
we were right . . . again. [Ellipses in original.][1]

After the initial publication in 1980 of *The Roswell Incident*,
William L. Moore and Stanton Friedman continued their quest to
learn more about the alleged Roswell UFO crash of 1947. Through
their persistent efforts, additional people were located, while others
came forward voluntarily.

Throughout the 1980s, Friedman and Moore kept the UFO
community and the media informed about the progress of their
investigative efforts through a series of privately published papers,
interviews, and lectures given at various UFO-related meetings and
conventions.

In the fall of 1988, the Center for UFO Studies (CUFOS) in
Chicago, Illinois, decided to throw their own hat into the Roswell
arena. Donald R. Schmitt, then director of special investigations for
CUFOS, teamed up with UFO researcher Kevin D. Randle to start

a fresh inquiry.[2] According to Randle and Schmitt, Moore and Friedman's original investigation was "incomplete," because "many of the primary witnesses had not been interviewed systematically or in depth." Randle and Schmitt also faulted Friedman and Moore because the "actual site of the crash had not been studied." Randle and Schmitt would later boast that "CUFOS planned to remedy both these problems."[3]

In September 1989, approximately one year after Randle and Schmitt started conducting their renewed investigation, the popular NBC television series "Unsolved Mysteries" opened its new fall season with a half-hour segment devoted to the Roswell UFO crash. Seen by over twenty-six million people, the episode became one of the top-rated shows that week for television.[4] Friedman and Randle were hired as consultants for the episode, much to the consternation of William L. Moore.*

As is customary during a typical episode of "Unsolved Mysteries," a plea went out to all viewers soliciting any new information that might help "solve" the purported Roswell UFO crash of 1947. According to Stanton Friedman, "scores of [viewers] called a special telephone number to offer assistance."[5]

In 1991, Randle and Schmitt published their first treatise detailing the results of their new investigation. Titled *UFO Crash at Roswell,* the book was later adapted for a television special by Showtime® and simply titled *Roswell.*

Not to be outdone, in 1992 Stanton Friedman coauthored *Crash at Corona: The U.S. Military Retrieval and Cover-Up of a UFO* with aviation writer Don Berliner.

In 1994, due to the commercial success of their earlier work,

---

*Friedman's activities concerning the NBC "Unsolved Mysteries" segment have been the subject of controversy for a number of years. According to a publication released by William L. Moore, Friedman "deliberately undermined Bill [Moore] and took credit for everything." Moore's publication also claims that Friedman "knew if the producers talked with Bill that they would use him instead of Stanton. And Stanton didn't want that—he wanted all the credit for himself; so he cut Bill out." Because of this and other bizarre incidents between them, Friedman and Moore effectively ended their professional collaboration and personal friendship, a rift that continues as of this writing. (See *Focus,* vol. V, 31 December 1990, pp. 17–22, and Friedman and Berliner, *Crash at Corona,* p. 46.)

Randle and Schmitt teamed up a second time to release *The Truth about the UFO Crash at Roswell,* a book designed to "correct errors in the original manuscript,"[6] and update readers on their continuing investigative efforts. According to the authors, *Truth* presents "the complete story of an alien spacecraft recovered outside of Roswell, New Mexico, in the summer of 1947."[7]

Finally, in 1995 Randle authored (by himself) *Roswell UFO Crash Update: Exposing the Military Cover-Up of the Century.* The book was published by Global Communications in New York by UFO sensationalist Timothy Green Beckley, who has a reputation for printing some of the wildest saucer-related tales ever known.[8]

The significance of mentioning the brief history of both the Randle–Schmitt and Friedman–Berliner books, as well as the "Unsolved Mysteries" episode, is the profound impact these events have had on the database of alleged Roswell evidence.

The "Unsolved Mysteries" program, for example, brought forth several purportedly important "witnesses," just as continuing investigations by Friedman, Randle, and Schmitt have produced what the public has been told are still more. In fact, Randle and Schmitt boast of having "conducted more than two thousand interviews with more than five hundred people" during their investigation into Roswell.[9] While this sounds impressive at first glance, the relevant issue once again is *not* the *number* of statements or "witnesses," but whether their testimonies are *credible!*

In order to try and determine the facts, let us examine critically the remarks and testimonies that are now on record as having been made by the following individuals: Ruben Anaya, Gerald Anderson, Sgt. Melvin E. Brown, Glenn Dennis, Maj. Edwin Easley, Gen. Arthur Exon, Pappy Henderson, Frank Kaufmann, Jim Ragsdale, Frankie Rowe, the Franciscan nuns, Corp. E. L. Pyles, and M.Sgt. Lewis S. Rickett.

It should be noted that some or all of these people have been widely endorsed, with their testimonies featured at great lengths in either Friedman and Berliner's book, or in Randle's and Schmitt's various works.

RUBEN ANAYA

Ruben Anaya, a political activist for the 1947 Lieutenant-Governor of New Mexico, Joseph Montoya, claims that around the time of the Roswell incident, he received a telephone call from Montoya, who, according to Anaya, was frantic and pleaded with him to "Get your car, Ruben, and pick me up. Get me the hell out of here [off Roswell Army Air Field]."[10]

Anaya claims that he drove to his brother Pete's house, and after explaining the unusual phone call from Montoya, he and his brother, along with a friend of theirs, Moses Burrola, drove immediately to Roswell Army Air Field.

Following the instructions he was given, Anaya claims that the three men arrived on the base and picked up Montoya on the east side, just past the water tower near the airplane hangars. Anaya says that he noticed that Montoya was "very pale, almost white, and he was shaking." Claiming that Montoya was "very, very scared," Anaya also stated that Montoya had told him once again to "Get me the hell out of here, I want to go." Anaya, his brother, and Moses Burrola then sped off the base with Montoya in the car.[11]

According to Anaya, the four men returned to Pete Anaya's house and Montoya was "still shaking." Anaya tried to calm the lieutenant governor, noting that Montoya was so distressed that he gave him some scotch and whiskey. "The man took half a quart, just boom, boom, boom. He was very scared," Anaya recalled.[12]

Ruben Anaya then told an elaborate tale about how Lieutenant Governor Montoya had seen four alien bodies and the wreckage from the UFO brought onto Roswell Army Air Field. Montoya purportedly told Anaya that there were numerous officials there, from doctors to ordinary soldiers.

Montoya then claimed that he wanted to return to Albuquerque, and asked that Anaya take him back to Roswell Army Air Field where he was to catch a military flight that had been scheduled to leave for Kirtland Army Air Field. Anaya claims that Montoya slept for a short while, and then the four men returned him to Roswell via car.

Anaya's testimony was first featured at length in Randle and Schmitt's *The Truth about the Roswell UFO Crash*. According to

Anaya, Montoya told him that they had better not talk to anyone about the incident or the "FBI would do away with them."[13]

Anaya's Account Collapses

While there's no denying that Ruben Anaya's account is a rather dramatic one, the relevant question is whether any credible evidence to support his story exists. As it turns out, there are several problems with his account that make it improbable.

The key to determining the credibility of Anaya's story is ascertaining the whereabouts of his famous witness, then-Lieutenant Governor of New Mexico, Joseph Montoya. Did he actually visit Roswell Army Air Field at the time of the incident and if so, what does this necessarily tell us?

Since Montoya was a high-profile figure, being the lieutenant governor, his whereabouts would have been covered by the media. However, a check through newspaper archives located in Albuquerque, Corona, Los Alamos, Roswell, and Socorro, reveals that there is *no record* of Lieutenant Governor Montoya traveling during the first two weeks in July 1947. Moreover, there is no mention of any visit for the *entire month* of July 1947 to Roswell Army Air Field.

In addition, a detailed check of the official visitor's logs for Roswell Army Air Field for the *entire month* of July 1947 also revealed that then-Lt. Gov. Joseph Montoya did *not* visit the base.

The Roswell Army Air Field's visitors logs are significant for two reasons: (1) They establish that Anaya's account is at odds with the known facts—Montoya did not visit the base, and (2) Their contents also reveal that despite the initial excitement over the officially announced recovery of a "flying disc," there was *no increase or abnormal deviation* in either the number or types of visitors to the base! This find is extremely revealing, for if the Roswell incident truly involved the recovery of debris from an extraterrestrial spacecraft, the expected increase or deviation that should be present regarding personnel entering and leaving the base simply isn't there. This incriminating fact does not bode well for the advocates of the Roswell affair.

Returning to the issue of the credibility of Anaya's story, a check with the governor's office of the State of New Mexico *confirmed* that then-Lieutenant Governor Montoya was in *Albuquerque* during the early part of July 1947.[14]

Another problem with Anaya's account is the fact that he has *changed* his story. For example, in interviews with Randle and Schmitt, Anaya claimed that only he, his brother, and Moses Burrola had driven to Roswell Army Air Field to pick up Montoya.[15] However, in an interview with UFO researcher Karl Pflock, Anaya not only gave a slightly different account, but also said that yet another individual drove with them in their car to the base, a man named Ralph Chaes.[16]

Finally, the claim by Anaya that the FBI would "do away" with him, his brother, and his friend(s) if they ever talked about this affair is absurd. It's also obvious that these professed threats have not been taken seriously by Anaya, or he would not have voluntarily stepped forward as a supposed "witness," telling anyone who would listen about the alleged incident.

In summation, there is no objective evidence that Ruben Anaya's story is credible. Anaya's various accounts are inconsistent and his claimed "facts" don't check out. It is a shame that Randle and Schmitt, who first foisted Anaya into the public spotlight on a grand scale, didn't bother conducting even the most rudimentary of investigations into verifying his claims. If they had bothered doing so they would have discovered that his story isn't credible. Unfortunately, this is not the the only time in their book that Randle and Schmitt are guilty of blindly endorsing the tall tales of individuals without proper investigation.

GERALD ANDERSON

One of the professed witnesses to come forth after the airing of the Roswell segment on "Unsolved Mysteries" was Gerald Anderson, who claims that while just five years of age he and his family happened upon a crashed flying saucer near the Plains of San Augustin—the old site resurrected straight from the Barney Barnett tale mentioned in chapter 2.

Anderson telephoned the toll-free number for "Unsolved Mysteries" and claimed that he had "seen it all." He was subsequently interviewed separately by both Stanton Friedman and Kevin Randle. Friedman believed Anderson but Randle had doubts.[17] This would not be the first time that Friedman and Randle would quarrel over the credibility of each other's "witnesses."

Anderson claims that he and his family, all of whom were conveniently dead by the time he told his story, had stumbled across the crashed saucer on the Plains of San Augustin while out searching for moss agate. After hearing his brother yell "Them's Martians," Anderson stated that he observed four alien beings: two dead, one badly injured having difficulty breathing, and another that appeared to be fine providing first aid to the injured alien.[18]

Anderson's account to both Friedman and Randle was extremely detailed. It was so detailed in fact that it is outright *amazing* that Friedman could have been duped so easily into accepting it as legitimate. As mentioned previously, Anderson was only five years of age at the time of the alleged encounter. It is a fact that five-year-olds simply cannot remember events in extreme detail, especially when they are recounted for the first time some *forty-three years after the fact!*

Over the course of a dozen pages Anderson's account and photos of he and Friedman together are splashed throughout the book *Crash at Corona*. Anderson had been the marquee "witnesses" whom Friedman and Berliner had showcased in their treatise, but the honeymoon would soon be over. Unfortunately, for readers of the book, it ended after *Crash at Corona* had sold out and was in additional printings.

Anderson's Credibility Woes

Perhaps the most suspicious aspect of Gerald Anderson's account is the level of incredible detail he provided to Stanton Friedman. Anderson appeared to be the "perfect" witness, filling in all the blanks.

Among the "facts" supplied by Gerald Anderson were that he apparently saw not only Barney Barnett at the crash site, but he even named the archaeology professor who he claimed was also present, a man he initially identified as Adrian Buskirk, but was later shown to be Winfried Buskirk.[19] There was one problem with this identification: During the time in question, Winfried Buskirk, by his own admission, was nowhere near the Plains of San Augustin. Buskirk spent from late June 1947 until September of that year at the Fort Apache Indian Reservation working on his doctoral thesis.[20]

As time progressed and Anderson was busy granting countless interviews to a wide variety of news media because of the exposure he had received thanks in part to Stanton Friedman, he began to *change* his story, adding further details. Anderson would eventually produce a diary, allegedly written by his Uncle Ted, the contents of which he said were written at the time of the event in 1947. Theoretically, the diary was an important piece of corroboration for the fact that a flying saucer had crashed on the Plains of San Augustin. However, forensic examination by Dr. Richard Brunelle of the diary Anderson submitted to Friedman for testing proved it to have been written sometime after 1970 because of the ink that had been used. The diary also contained errors in its content which would not likely have occurred if it had been written at the time of the alleged UFO crash of 1947.[21]

Since Anderson was the only surviving "witness" to the event he claimed took place, he is suspected of having faked the diary. While this has never been proven, there was one other document Gerald Anderson did fake which would further erode his credibility.

While being interviewed by Kevin Randle about the flying saucer crash he claims to have observed, Anderson told others about his conversation and when doing so claimed that he had spoken to Randle for only twenty-six minutes on the telephone. Randle, who had taped the interview, knew better. While Anderson's sticking by his twenty-six-minute claim was not significant in itself, what he did afterward was.

When Randle pressed Anderson on the issue of the length of their phone call, Anderson continued to deny that the actual conversation was twice as long as he had claimed. To "prove" it, Anderson supplied a phone bill showing that his conversation with Randle had lasted only twenty-six minutes. There was only one problem, the phone bill turned out to be a forgery, a fact verified by phone company records, and Gerald Anderson had created it![22] If

Anderson could fabricate a document such as a phone bill, then he could certainly also forge a diary.

As the months dragged on Anderson continued to change elements of his story. While Stanton Friedman, more than anyone, repeatedly rose to Anderson's defense on numerous occasions, eventually Anderson's credibility collapsed like a house of cards in the wind. Indeed, even Friedman was eventually forced to concede that his previously highly touted "witness" had no credibility whatsoever—a fact that should have been obvious from the beginning.

In a collective attempt to save face, in the paperback version of their fabled *Crash at Corona* (now mislabeled by their publisher as "The Definitive Study of the Roswell Incident"), in a special preface to the paperback edition, Friedman and Berliner wrote: "In the case of Gerald Anderson, the primary witness to the details of the crash at the Plains of San Augustin, problems have arisen. He has admitted falsifying a document, and has changed his testimony. Even though some of his testimony has been corroborated by others, the authors no longer have confidence in his description of the crash scene and the aftermath."[23]

With this single paragraph, Friedman and Berliner washed their hands of Gerald Anderson. Despite their sheepish disclaimer, however, the sections concerning Anderson in *Crash at Corona* were left in the reprints of their treatise. It was as if the authors were saying just ignore those parts of the book, the rest of it is still valid.

SGT. MELVIN E. BROWN

According to *Crash at Corona, UFO Crash at Roswell, The Truth about the UFO Crash at Roswell,* and *Beyond Roswell,* Sgt. Melvin E. Brown was present at the first debris site, saw the alien bodies, and helped guard them while they were en route to the base at Roswell.

The earliest published statement concerning what Melvin Brown supposedly saw appears in UFO researcher Timothy Good's book, *Alien Contact: Top Secret UFO Files Revealed.* According to Good, Brown was reading an article in the [London] *Daily Mail* in the late 1970s about Roswell when he suddenly blurted out to his family, "I was there!"[24]

While remarking that the story in the *Daily Mail* was, for the most part, "true," Brown added that he had been ordered out to the location where the alien bodies had been found and was told to "form a ring around whatever it was they had to cover, and everything was put on trucks." Brown, it is also reported, was instructed "not to look and to take no notice, and . . . sworn to secrecy."[25] While Brown purportedly followed his orders, he is said to have wondered why "refrigerated trucks" were being used.

At some point during the day, Brown and another soldier were told to climb into one of the trucks loaded with ice and accompany the vehicle back to Roswell Army Air Field where he was "to take this stuff to a hangar." While Brown was sitting in the back of the truck, we are told that he lifted up a tarp and "saw two, or possibly three [alien] bodies."[26]

Problems with the Brown Account

The first difficulty with the alleged account by Sgt. Melvin Brown is that it is *not firsthand testimony!* Indeed, the remarks attributed to Brown come from only one source; his daughter, Beverly Bean.

Melvin Brown died in 1986. Bean's claims regarding her father's alleged involvement in the Roswell UFO crash came to light only *after* his death, in a series of interviews conducted with UFO researchers Timothy Good in 1988, Stanton Friedman in 1989, and Randle and Schmitt in 1990 and 1991. Thus, *all* the testimonies attributed to Melvin Brown are *secondhand* information at best and constitute hearsay. This is an important distinction.

Despite this fact, some of the Roswell authors cite Brown's "statements" in their attempt to "prove" that aliens were involved in the Roswell affair. Moreover, in what are blatant examples of what I will politely call journalistic license, Randle and Schmitt write phrases in their books such as "*Brown said* that [the crate] had been prepared for shipment [of the alien bodies] out that night" and "*According to him* [Brown], [the aliens] were smaller than humans and had a skin that was yellowish-orange and like that of a lizard, meaning it was leathery and beaded, but not scaly."[27]

Obviously, since Brown was *never interviewed by anyone* and had died roughly four years *before* Randle and Schmitt were told about his purported "remarks" from his daughter, *one does not know* with any certainty that "Brown said" anything, contrary to what the authors claim.

Indeed, a more honest way for Randle and Schmitt to convey Brown's alleged testimony in their books would have been to preface their dogmatic declarations with simple phrases such as: "According to Beverly Bean, Brown's daughter, he said. . . ." Instead, Randle and Schmitt's presentation, as written, is misleading if not followed carefully by the discerning reader. As we shall see, these are not the only examples in Randle and Schmitt's books where such journalistic liberties and other distortions are taken.

Another pair of Roswell authors who also get conveniently sloppy in their presentation of what are supposed to be the "facts," are Friedman and Berliner in *Crash at Corona*. In introducing the "testimony" of Melvin Brown, Friedman and Berliner start by saying "Another man who saw bodies was Sgt. Melvin E. Brown. . . ."[28]

Since Friedman and Berliner's source is, once again, Beverly Bean, there's *no way to be certain* that Brown saw any alien bodies, let alone near the Foster ranch, as all of these authors claim. Again, it would have been more accurate for Friedman and Berliner to write instead that "According to Beverly Bean, her late father, Sgt. Melvin E. Brown . . ." reported whatever.

Now that we have established that Melvin Brown never went on record presenting any firsthand testimony, and therefore cannot be considered a true witness, despite the Roswell authors' claims; what about the remarks attributed to him by his daughter, Beverly? Do her comments constitute credible evidence for the presence of aliens in the Roswell stewpot of claims? Unfortunately, there are problems with several aspects of Bean's various accounts which cast doubt on their veracity. Like many other so-called witnesses to Roswell, Bean has changed her story over the years.

In her first interviews, conducted with British UFO researcher Timothy Good between January and March 1988, Bean stated that her father first told her about his involvement with the alien bodies after reading the British newspaper the *Daily Mail* in the late 1970s. According to Bean, Brown shouted excitedly after reading the article, "I was there!"

However, in 1989, in her interview with Stanton Friedman, Bean told a significantly different story. Instead of her father having first told her about his involvement with the recovery of the aliens after reading the article in the *Daily Mail,* Bean told Friedman: "When we were young, he [Brown] used to tell us stories about things that had happened to him when he was young. We got to know those stories by heart and would all say together, 'Here we go again!' "

"Sometimes, but not too often, he used to say that he saw a man from outer space. That used to make us all giggle like mad."[29]

Not once during Bean's published interview with Friedman is there any mention of the *Daily Mail* article, nor the "burst of excitement" Bean says her father exhibited after reading the story. Instead, Bean was now claiming that she had heard the "alien tale" when she was a kid.

Finally, in interviews conducted in 1990 and 1991 by Randle and Schmitt, Bean changed her story once again, this time claiming that her father was watching the Apollo moon landings in 1969 when he suddenly blurted out that he had seen aliens at Roswell.[30]

In addition to these discrepancies, which have gone unreported until this writing, there is another problem with Bean's account. According to Sgt. Melvin Brown's official military file, his job duties in the service were limited to that of being a cook. While his file notes that he had "three months cooks and bakers school," and received a rating as an "expert" with an M1 Carbine rifle, Brown's career in the United States Army was severely limited because he had only an eighth-grade education.[31]

While stationed at Roswell, Brown was assigned to Squadron K of the same bomb wing in which Maj. Jesse Marcel served. While Brown may have known Marcel, he was never a military police officer, nor was he ever in intelligence or counter-intelligence. Once again, Brown was simply a cook.

When one considers the extreme secrecy in which military officials are said to have cloaked the Roswell operation during the recovery of the alien bodies and the spaceship (according to the pro-UFO Roswell authors), it seems highly improbable that Melvin Brown would have been chosen to carry out the all-important task of "escorting" the recovered extraterrestrials back to the base at Roswell. Of the thousands of personnel stationed at Roswell Army

Air Field in 1947, there were simply too many others who would have been chosen for this task.

Finally, as the pro-UFO Roswell researchers will admit when pressed, Beverly Bean is the *only person* in the Brown family who has made these claims about her father. Bean's sister and her own mother have never confirmed her account.[32]

While this revealing insight has been rationalized by Bean and Randle and Schmitt under the "explanation" that the Brown family "think the government can still do something to [Brown] or his records,"[33] such a notion is highly unlikely. As noted earlier, Sergeant Brown passed away in 1986, nearly eleven years ago. Since Brown is no longer alive, and in fact had been dead for at least *two years* before Bean's earliest interviews, how could the military or the United States government possibly "do anything" to him?

Obviously, Bean's stated "concerns" for her father's posthumous well-being and professed fears of government retribution cannot be too great. Otherwise, it stands to reason that she would never have mentioned her father's involvement in the alleged alien recovery operation in the first place!

Nonetheless, the uncritical acceptance of Bean's statements is yet another example of just how desperate some of the UFO authors are in order to build their "extraterrestrial" case for Roswell. To claim that Sergeant Brown was an actual "witness" to the recovery of alien bodies near Roswell is pure speculation. To state it as fact is inexcusable, if not deliberately misleading.

It is interesting to note how some of the pro-UFO Roswell authors attempt to force-fit Beverly Bean's account so that it will mesh nicely with the other "witnesses" who have come forward in recent years claiming to have observed alien bodes. When these authors aren't trying to force fit the details, they simply *omit* those descriptions that are troublesome.

For example, in *Crash at Corona,* Friedman and Berliner write, once again quoting Beverly Bean, that Sergeant Brown "had a quick look under the covering [the tarp] and saw two dead bodies . . . alien bodies." [Ellipses in the original.]

What Friedman and Berliner deliberately omit in their quotation of Beverly Bean, through the use of ellipses in their book, is her description of what she claims the skin of the aliens looked like.

According to Bean, she claims her father told her that the skin of the dead aliens was yellowish-orange in color, looking like that of a lizard, leathery but not scaly.

Friedman and Berliner make no mention of this little detail because it does not "jive" with the descriptions of their other "witnesses," who have consistently stated that the aliens' skin was *gray*. The truth is, Bean's descriptions blatantly *contradict* these other accounts. Yet on the very next page of their book, Friedman and Berliner write, rather comically, that "The descriptions of bodies are not merely highly consistent, but agree in most respects with those given by persons suspected of having been 'abducted' by presumed aliens."[34]

GLENN DENNIS

Glenn Dennis was a twenty-two-year-old mortuary officer with the Ballard Funeral Home at the time of the Roswell incident. The Ballard Funeral Home had a contract with Roswell Army Air Field at the time to handle mortuary and other funeral-related affairs.

Dennis claims that at approximately 1:30 P.M. on the afternoon of July 5, 1947 (July 9 or 10 according to Berliner and Friedman[35]), he received a telephone call from the base mortuary officer at Roswell Army Air Field inquiring as to "what size, what type of caskets, and how small [were the] caskets that we could furnish that could be hermetically sealed." Dennis also claims that regarding caskets, he was also asked by the base mortuary officer "What's the smallest size we [the Ballard Funeral Home] could get?"[36]

Dennis answered the questions put to him and thought nothing further about the matter until approximately thirty to forty minutes later when he received a second telephone call from the same mortuary officer at Roswell Army Air Field. This time, the inquiry was about how to prepare deceased bodies. As Dennis put it, "He [the base mortuary officer] was asking me about our preparations . . . preparing a body that had been laying out in the elements . . . how we treated burnt bodies or the very traumatic cases . . . I went through the steps on how we treated the bodies" [ellipses in the original].[37]

"The next question," Dennis claimed, "was what would you do

where you wouldn't change any of the chemical contents, you wouldn't destroy any blood, you wouldn't destroy anything that might be important down the road. What . . . chemicals [do] you use [that] would change the chemical contents [of the blood]?"

Dennis also claims that he was asked "about the chemical composition of blood, about the breakdown of tissue, what happened to tissue when it is laid out [in the sun] for several days." Other curious questions put to Dennis were such things as "what's this going to do to the blood system, what's this going to do to the tissue?"[38]

After answering the numerous questions that were put to him, Dennis got curious and both asked and offered to help out. According to Dennis, the mortuary officer from Roswell Army Air Field declined his offer, saying that the numerous questions he had just asked were merely "for future reference."[39]

At approximately six or seven in the evening, Dennis claims that he drove an injured airman to the base infirmary at Roswell Army Air Field. The infirmary and the base mortuary were in the same building. After escorting the injured airman and parking his ambulance around the back of the building, Dennis claims he went inside and while there he encountered Naomi Maria Selff, a nurse who was a friend of his. Dennis had stopped to say "hello" to her and after observing that "there was quite a lot of activity going on," she came up and asked him in a panicked voice, "How in the hell did you get in here?" Replying that he "just walked in," Dennis claims that his nurse friend then suddenly told him "My God, you are going to get killed!"[40]

Dennis says that while he was walking back toward a soda machine to purchase the two of them a drink, suddenly a red-haired colonel started yelling at him and said, "What's that son-of-a-bitch doin' here?" Dennis then explained that the colonel "hollered at the MPs and . . . these two MPs grabbed me by the arms and carried me clear outside, they carried me to the ambulance, I didn't walk, they carried me! And they told me to get my ass out of there!"[41]

According to Dennis, he was escorted by the military all the way back to the Ballard Funeral Home.

Approximately two or three hours after returning, Glenn Dennis claims that he received yet another phone call from Roswell Army Air Field, only this time he was not asked for advice, he was given it: "You open your mouth [about the incident] and you'll be so far back in the jug they'll have to shoot pinto beans [into you] with a bean shooter!" he was told.

"Go to hell!" Dennis shot back.[42]

While Dennis claims he laughed off the threat, it had made enough of an impression on him that he became extremely curious. The next day, he established contact with his nurse friend, who asked if he could come to Roswell Army Air Field to see her. Dennis agreed, and the two of them met at the officer's club for lunch.

When Glenn saw her he said she looked frightened, and "was about to go into shock. She looked so different," he recalled.

According to Dennis, Naomi told him that there were three alien bodies, all dead, two of which were badly mutilated. "Until they got those bodies frozen, the smell was so bad you couldn't get within a hundred feet of them without gagging," she told him.[43]

Glenn Dennis claims that Naomi drew some sketches on a prescription pad detailing what the aliens looked like. She then gave him her drawings and admonished Dennis to keep them a secret. According to Berliner and Friedman, Dennis "guarded them carefully."[44]

After they finished their conversation, Dennis claims he dropped Naomi off at her barracks because she appeared to be on the verge of a nervous collapse. It would be the last time that Glenn Dennis would ever see her again.

In subsequent attempts to contact his friend, Dennis was told that she was "away at a seminar," and later that, "she had been transferred to England." Dennis claims he tried writing, and after receiving an initial reply letter from her promising to "explain everything at a later date," his second letter was returned by the post office bearing the ominous marking of "Deceased" stamped on it.[45]

Death-Knells for Dennis's Testimony

Glenn Dennis's testimony plays an important part in the Roswell mythology because his account is endorsed by nearly every pro-UFO Roswell author, including Don Berliner, Stanton Friedman, Michael Hesemann, Philip Mantle, Karl Pflock, Kevin Randle, and Don Schmitt. In their books these authors devote considerable space to Dennis's claims. However, despite these ringing endorsements, the relevant question remains, is Dennis's startling account an accurate portrayal of the demonstrable facts? Unfortunately, there are several reasons for being suspicious of Dennis's story. The reality is, his tale cannot be trusted.

The first curious (and suspicious) aspect of Dennis's story has to do with the *timing* of it. Glenn Dennis is a close friend of Lt. Walter Haut, the very person who wrote the original Roswell press release under the orders of Colonel Blanchard announcing the initial recovery of the flying disk by Maj. Jesse Marcel. According to Haut, Glenn Dennis never said anything at all about his knowledge and happenstance involvement in the Roswell incident until late 1988 or early 1989![46]

The question now becomes, why did Glenn Dennis *wait* some forty to forty-one years to come forward with his story, when everyone around him (including his friend Haut) was busy talking their heads off as early as 1979? Why the ten-year delay?

In order to try and resolve this issue, I telephoned Dennis to try and ask him this very question. He refused to take my phone calls. Curiously, no other researcher seems to have cross-examined Dennis over this issue, and if the pro-UFO Roswell authors ever did, there's no record of it.

Another factor that casts doubt on the credibility of Dennis's story has to do with the fact he has changed his story repeatedly, adding new details over the years. For example, when Dennis originally recounted his story for Stanton Friedman, which Friedman faithfully reproduces in *Crash at Corona,* he stated that the officer who had yelled at him was a red-haired colonel. However, when Dennis later recounted his story to other researchers such as Karl Pflock and Kevin Randle, suddenly, the officer was a red-haired *captain!*[47] Moreover, Dennis then claimed that it wasn't just the captain/colonel that had threatened him, but now it was a "black sergeant" who mentioned to Glenn Dennis that he would "make good dog food."[48]

As noted earlier in chapter 2, there were no black sergeants stationed at Roswell Army Air Field in 1947.

In another interview, Dennis stated that the Air Force visited the Ballard Funeral Home and "took all the baby-size or youth-size caskets we had."[49] Yet in his various retellings of his story to UFO researchers Friedman, Pflock, Randle, and Schmitt, Dennis stated that no Air Force personnel came to Ballard, instead they had simply called him and inquired about child-size caskets![50]

Stanton Friedman claims that Glenn Dennis carefully guarded the precious sketches that his deceased nurse friend had given him of the supposed aliens that were at Roswell Army Air Field. Yet when Friedman went to look through Dennis's office with him at the funeral home to try and find them they had been conveniently "thrown out."[51]

Regarding Glenn Dennis's nurse friend, he is on record as having given two *contradictory* accounts as to what allegedly happened to her. As mentioned previously, Dennis indicated that she had *died* shortly after being transferred to England. He also stated that she died in an airplane crash and this is why his second letter to her had been returned by the post office and marked "deceased." However, in an interview conducted by UFO researcher Anne MacFie on December 31, 1991, Dennis told a distinctly different story. When MacFie asked Glenn Dennis if his nurse friend was still alive, he replied "I don't know. I heard she died several years ago [1988], but that's only hearsay."[52]

MacFie then asked Dennis if he had ever bothered contacting the nurse "to see if she would talk now that others have." Glenn Dennis then answered "I never did try and contact her. She did join an order [became a nun] after she got out of the Army. But I don't think she would [talk]. She was so disciplined that if her superior told her to walk across fire, she probably would have done it."[53]

In order to try and determine whether or not the nurse ever existed, I checked with the National Personnel Records and Information Center (NPRIC) in St. Louis, Missouri. According to Air Force records, there were five nurses stationed at Roswell Army Air Field in 1947 and *none* of them was transferred that year. Furthermore, there was *no record* indicating that any of them had died in an aircraft-related accident in 1947.[54] In fact, in order to research Glenn Dennis's claim that his nurse friend had died in an aircraft accident shortly after being transferred to England, I searched through past issues of the *New York Times, Stars and Stripes,* and checked with the Federal Aviation Administration and the Royal Air Force in England for any mention of any airplane disasters involving U.S. Army Air Force nurses in 1947. After repeated inquiries since early 1995, no records have ever been found to support Glenn Dennis's story.[55]

During an interview with UFO researcher Karl Pflock, Glenn Dennis provided the name of the nurse he claims later died/became a nun/was transferred to England: Naomi Maria Selff. After learning of this development, I checked once again with the NPRIC in St. Louis. According to existing Air Force records, there has never been a person with the name of Naomi Maria Selff who has ever served in the U.S. Army Air Force!

MAJ. EDWIN EASLEY

Edwin Easley was Roswell Army Air Field's Provost Marshall in charge of the military police at the base in July 1947. If the Roswell incident truly involved the military blocking the roads and sealing off the crash site from the public as the pro-UFO Roswell authors would have us believe, then Edwin Easley would have been the individual (along with his superiors) who oversaw the planning and execution of such a covert operation.

According to the Randle and Schmitt book *The Truth about the Roswell UFO Crash,* Easley is supposed to have confirmed to Randle that there were indeed alien bodies and spacecraft debris present at the crash site located near the Foster ranch. If what Easley purportedly told Randle is true, then Easley's testimony is powerful support for advocates of the extraterrestrial nature of the Roswell debris.

The Easley Misrepresentations

Kevin Randle interviewed Maj. Edwin Easley shortly before his death. After initially refusing to confirm to Randle that he was even there at Roswell, Randle claims that Easley on his deathbed eventually confessed that not only had he "been there," but that he had also seen alien bodies. Indeed, the authors write, "Easley was reluctant to talk of bodies, but finally, before he died, said that he had seen them. He had been close enough to them to know they weren't human. He called them 'creatures.' "[56]

There's a problem with Randle's claim about Easley's alleged deathbed statements. To be blunt about the matter, Kevin Randle was not present when Easley was dying, only his family members were.[57] This means that Kevin Randle is not in a position to comment about what Easley supposedly said because he wasn't there.

The truth of the matter is that there is no evidence other than Kevin Randle's "word" that Major Easley either said or did the things that Randle claims. And because Major Easley is deceased, he cannot now be questioned on the accuracy of Randle's comments.

When I checked with the Center for UFO Studies, where Randle and Schmitt claim that all of the interview tapes and documentation for their research are archived, it turned out that there are no tapes or forms of independent documentation or verification on file proving that Easley indeed had made the statements Randle posthumously attributes to him![58] Researchers Robert Todd and Stanton Friedman have also tried to obtain similar supportive evidence for many of Randle's other claims regarding his research into Roswell but have been unsuccessful.[59]

Even if Kevin Randle is telling the truth regarding what Easley told him, there is a very valid reason to call into question any remarks that Easley might have made. According to Easley's family, he was quite advanced in age when he spoke with Randle. His memory was failing him and Easley had a tendency to place himself in events at which he was not present.[60]

Randle has made other claims, such as Easley having told him there were five extraterrestrial bodies recovered near Roswell.[61] Once again, until Kevin Randle is ever able to provide evidence and/or documentation to back up his statement, Easley's alleged deathbed remarks cannot be considered as credible evidence for the extraterrestrial nature of the Roswell incident.

BRIG. GEN. ARTHUR EXON

The testimony of Arthur Exon first became known to the public when it was prominently featured in Randle and Schmitt's *UFO Crash at Roswell*. Exon is the former commanding officer of Wright-Patterson Air Force Base in Ohio, where some of the Roswell debris was sent for analysis in a secret flight ordered by Gen. Roger Ramey, after Ramey had told the press that the flight had been canceled.

To read the Randle-Schmitt book, it appears that Exon *corroborates* the Roswell UFO recovery by providing impressive-sounding testimony that appears to be firsthand. "We heard the material was coming to Wright Field. . . . It was brought into our material evaluation labs. I don't know how it arrived but the boys who tested it said it was very unusual." Exon described the material: "[Some of it] could be easily ripped or changed . . . there were other parts of it that were very thin but awfully strong and couldn't be dented with very heavy hammers. . . . It was flexible to a degree," and, according to Exon, "some of it was flimsy and was tougher than hell and almost like foil but strong. It had them pretty puzzled."[62]

To almost anyone reading this, it would appear that based on the Randle-Schmitt portrayal of Exon he was a *firsthand* source who was present and personally saw what he describes. However, this is not true. Although Exon was *stationed* at Wright-Patterson Air Force Base in 1947 when the Roswell debris was flown in for examination, Exon was *not* a firsthand witness to the event.

Apparently, Exon himself agrees, for in a letter dated November 24, 1991, he blatantly told Kevin Randle, "Further, you both [Randle and Schmitt] likely recall on many occasions during my visits with you in person and on the phone . . . that *I did not know anything firsthand.* Although I believe you did quote me accurately, I do believe that in your writings you gave *more credence and impression of personal and direct knowledge* that my recordings would indicate on their own! I felt that throughout the portions where my name was used." [Emphasis in the original and added.]

There is no excuse for how Exon's "testimony" is misrepresented in the Randle-Schmitt book. It is blatant fiction on the part of the authors, with Randle and Schmitt once again distorting the facts. Exon was relating hearsay to Randle and Schmitt concerning rumors he had heard, not information he knew through firsthand experience to be true. Randle and Schmitt were deceptive in their presentation of both Exon's recollections and his supposed "involvement" in the Roswell affair.

PAPPY HENDERSON

Pappy Henderson is a legendary World War II pilot who was stationed at Roswell Army Air Field during the time of the Roswell incident. According to *Crash at Corona* and Randle and Schmitt's works, Henderson allegedly flew at least one planeload of debris (along with possible alien bodies) to Wright-Patterson Air Force Base in Ohio for secret government examination.

Pappy Henderson Reality Check

Although Pappy Henderson is touted as a "witness" and active participant in the alleged cover-up of the Roswell incident, in reality he cannot be considered as such for one simple reason: Pappy Henderson was *never interviewed* about his purported involvement by UFO investigators (Stanton Friedman, Bill Moore, Kevin Randle, and Donald Schmitt included) while he was alive! Since this is an indisputable fact, the question now becomes *why* is Pappy Henderson touted by the pro-UFO Roswell authors as a "witness"?

Unfortunately, the only "proof" that Henderson was even involved in the Roswell recovery comes from rumors and scuttlebutt courtesy of some of the surviving members of his family and a few acquaintances. In other words, like the Sgt. Melvin Brown affair, there is no firsthand evidence anywhere to be found that Henderson was involved in any capacity. Indeed, it is curious that neither Maj. Jesse Marcel or even Brigadier General DuBose ever mentioned Henderson, let alone that he purportedly flew the debris and saw alien bodies. One would think that if Henderson *really* had been involved as has been claimed, because he was by far the most famous pilot stationed at Roswell Army Air Field,[63] one would think that at least DuBose or Marcel would have at least mentioned him.

Possible Source of the Henderson Myth

Pappy Henderson was noted for having a tremendous sense of humor. Like many expert, daredevil-type pilots from the World War II era, Patterson played hard and lived life to the fullest. One of the things that Henderson was noted for, according to those who knew him, is the fact that he loved to tell good story. Since Roswell was rife with rumors about an "alien" spaceship having been recovered and subsequently covered up, such scuttlebutt played right into the hands of someone like Pappy Henderson whose sense of humor could exploit such gossip.

Pappy Henderson also had among his prized possessions some fragments from a Nazi V-2 rocket* he obtained while he was stationed overseas.[64] Henderson took advantage of many opportunities to show his souvenir off to friends, and in his later years would claim that the pieces were from a "crashed UFO."[65] Henderson was probably pulling a practical joke on his unsuspecting friends, but the fact that he did this has only managed to confuse the issue.

Pappy Henderson died in the late 1980s. According to *Crash at Corona,* the saucer fragment Henderson allegedly possessed is still somewhere out there just waiting to be found. However, according to Berliner and Friedman, Henderson's widow won't permit them to search through her husband's belongings in order to try and find it.[66]

To claim that Pappy Henderson was a "witness" to the Roswell incident and personally flew both the saucer debris and deceased extraterrestrials is speculation at best. Until any credible evidence emerges to verify this, Henderson's connection to the Roswell incident is tenuous at best.

FRANK KAUFMANN

Frank Kaufmann's numerous claims about his "extensive involvement" in the Roswell incident are featured at length in both Randle-Schmitt books. According to them, Kaufmann is the central character in what took place and is "Roswell's" most important witness. While Randle and Schmitt endorse Frank Kaufmann as credible, Stanton Friedman does not.[67]

---

*The V-2 rocket or "buzz bomb" was invented and used primarily against the British by the Nazis during World War II. The V-2 was the world's first large-scale rocket that carried a high explosive payload. The rocket was unmanned and both the U.S. and Soviet governments captured several of them for study after the war.

In what is a somewhat misleading and downright confusing portrayal, Randle and Schmitt in their two books present Kaufmann as *three different people!* Using various names that Randle made up (literally) such as Joseph Osborn and Frank MacKenzie,[68] the authors present the numerous accounts of Kaufmann and weave them throughout their narrative as if they're the actions of separate people. In truth, it's all Frank Kaufmann as the source.[69]

According to Kaufmann, on July 2, 1947, while stationed at Roswell Army Air Field, he received a telephone call from Brig. Gen. Martin Scanlon of the Air Defense Command to proceed immediately to the military radar facilities at White Sands, New Mexico. For slightly over a day, a UFO had been tracked by "both officers and the enlisted technicians" over southern Mexico and had also violated the restricted air space above the White Sands Proving Ground.

In the book *The Truth about the Roswell UFO Crash,* Randle and Schmitt write about Kaufmann's assignment from General Scanlon by saying, "MacKenzie could not leave the radar room unattended. In fact, once he had his watch established, he set up a system of mirrors so that he could see a warning light even when he needed to use the latrine."[70]

Kaufmann claims that no less than two additional radar sites tracked the strange object at the same time. These other facilities were at located in Alamogordo and Roswell. Kaufmann says he observed the UFO on the radar screen for more than twenty-four hours straight before he finally reported back to Scanlon the status of the object and was ordered back to Roswell Army Air Field.

On the evening of July 4, 1947, at approximately 11:20 P.M., Kaufmann claims that while observing the UFO on one of the radar sets it "Brightened like a sunburst and disappeared from the screen." Kaufmann says that they could tell the object had been struck by lightning or had exploded and they were able to triangulate its location.[71]

Kaufmann then claims that he and his special team of military elite traveled north of Roswell and located the crash site. Kaufmann says he saw five alien bodies scattered in and around the craft. All of them were dead.

The alien corpses were taken back to Roswell Army Air Field and flown out in a series of secret flights first to Andrews AFB and later to Wright-Patterson AFB in Ohio. The reason for the stop at

Andrews was so that the Army Chief of Staff and future President of the United States, Dwight Eisenhower, along with Secretary of War Robert Patterson, could view them. The alien bodies were then taken to Washington, D.C.[72]

Frank Kaufmann has the distinction of being the only "witness" to have participated in virtually every aspect of the Roswell incident. He observed the UFO on radar as a member of a secret military elite unit. He was there observing on the radar screen the very moment the UFO crashed and its location was triangulated. Kaufmann was ordered out to the crash site where he saw both the spaceship and five dead extraterrestrials. But wait, there's more! Frank Kaufmann was a privileged member of an elite UFO recovery team, "The Unholy 13," that still exists today![73]

UFO researcher Karl Pflock has written extensively about the ongoing saga and tales of Frank Kaufmann. To put it politely, they are voluminous; a whole book could be written about them and nothing else. Kaufmann can show you drawings of both the craft and the aliens. He can also tell you which technologies of modern science are a direct result of reverse-engineering the technology of the crashed UFO. Kaufmann can also show you still-classified and secret government documents concerning Roswell. Kaufmann can sketch out various components of the inner workings of the saucer. Dubbed by writer Arthur S. Levine as "the Zelig of Roswell," Kaufmann has literally seen and done it all.[74]

Frank Kaufmann: Sense and Nonsense

As mentioned previously, the tales concerning Roswell by Frank Kaufmann can fill an entire book. So can a refutation of those claims. To put it mildly, Frank Kaufmann has a credibility problem. For example, Kaufmann claims that he was originally ordered by Brig. Gen. Martin Scanlon out to the White Sands radar facilities. This is highly unlikely, because at that time in July 1947 Martin Scanlon was *the public relations officer* for the Air Defense Command.[75] It is highly improbable that he would have the authority to order Kaufmann around.

According to Kaufmann, he could tell that the UFO had been struck by lightning because of the way it "flashed" on the radar screen. Unfortunately, the truth is that because of technology limitations at the time, those first, primitive radar units of 1947 were *not capable* of detecting an object when it was struck by lightning.[76]

Kaufmann claims that the strange craft was being tracked on radar sets at three locations at the time, in Albuquerque, Roswell, and White Sands. This is impossible. In 1947, radar installations of the type Frank Kaufmann talks about were just becoming operational. While there were indeed a few radar stations in place, their ability to track aerial objects hundreds of miles away in all directions simply did not exist. The radar units at White Sands, for example, *did not have the range* to track any objects hovering near or over Roswell because it was too far away.

Another real problem that trips up Kaufmann's account is the fact that the Capitan Mountains (with an elevation of more than 10,000 feet) lie between the three radar installations, making such alleged trackings impossible![77]

Kaufmann claims that he was part of a secret, elite UFO recovery team in 1947 and still is to this very day. The name of the group, it will be recalled, is the "Unholy 13." If this team indeed exists and is so secret, and Kaufmann is still an active member and under a security oath, then *why* is he telling anyone who will listen all the details about this group? For a man who claims to be under an oath of security he certainly is telling the very secrets he's supposed to keep! Indeed, Kaufmann has supplied everything from sketches of the aliens to diagrams that show how their technology works, and has even shown old photos of himself with other members of his alleged secret recovery team.[78]

Kaufmann says that he was stationed at Roswell Army Air Field in July 1947 when General Scanlon called him about the UFO. However, Kaufmann would later admit that he was *discharged* from the service in 1945, some two years before![79] If Kaufmann was no longer in the military by the time of the Roswell incident, then why and how could General Scanlon have ordered him to go anywhere or do his bidding?

Frank Kaufmann has gone on record as claiming to have seen several prominent people involved in the Roswell incident view the alien bodies at Roswell Army Air Field. Some of the names he has mentioned have included the famous aviator Charles Lindbergh,

Dr. Werner Von Braun, President Harry Truman, and then-Army Chief of Staff and later President of the United States, Dwight D. Eisenhower.[80] This is impossible, since it can be shown that none of these people were in Roswell visiting the base at the time.

Kaufmann and the Randle Factor

Frank Kaufmann's greatest supporter among the pro-UFO Roswell authors is Kevin Randle. Randle, more than anyone, has written Frank Kaufmann into the history of the Roswell legend.

Kevin Randle is also responsible for creating one of the most blatant examples of fiction passed off as fact concerning Roswell and Frank Kaufmann. In his *The Truth about the Roswell UFO Crash,* Randle mentions that Kaufmann (whom he calls "MacKenzie" in the book to "protect" his source) had constructed a labyrinth of mirrors at his station so that he could watch the radar scope from the latrine. However, when pressed about this claim, Randle later admitted (but only after repeated questioning) that *no such event had ever taken place!* In what would amount to one of the most bizarre apologies ever uttered in the field of UFOlogy, Randle lamely explained that he had accidentally "confused" a scene from a *science-fiction movie* with this portion of Kaufmann's testimony! In other words, the inventive radar/mirror/latrine scene never occurred.

The numerous Roswell-related tales of Frank Kaufmann are just not credible. The burden is on Kaufmann and his supporters to submit verifiable evidence that holds up to scrutiny. Until this happens, their statements cannot be taken seriously.

JIM RAGSDALE

Jim Ragsdale is another "witness" discovered by Randle and Schmitt who claims that while he was out camping at night with his girlfriend, Trudy Truelove, he heard a large explosion. Driving over to see what caused the noise, Ragsdale told Randle and Schmitt that he and Truelove saw a craft that had smashed into the side of a cliff dwelling. Ragsdale would tell Randle "I'm sure that [there] were bodies, either bodies or dummies."[81]

Because this was late at night, and the only source of light available to the couple at the time was a flashlight that had weak batteries, Ragsdale claims that he and Truelove arose early the next morning and returned to the location where they got a closer look at the craft and alien bodies.

While Ragsdale and Truelove were busy collecting some debris fragments from the extraterrestrial spaceship, they suddenly heard the sound of a military convoy that came screeching in nearby. Not wanting to be discovered, they hid behind some trees and went unnoticed by military authorities. Ragsdale claims that he and his girlfriend then quietly drove away.[82]

Ragsdale Loses Credibility

Although Jim Ragsdale's testimony was widely touted by Randle and Schmitt in their Roswell books, after a short period of time he began to *change* his story.

Ragsdale had initially reported to Randle that he had seen alien bodies scattered around the wreckage of the craft. However, over the next few months Ragsdale began to tell a more elaborate story of having actually gone down to the hull of the spaceship, where he now said there were four bodies. Not stopping there, Ragsdale started claiming that he had gotten close to the bodies and even tried unsuccessfully to remove a helmet off one of the aliens.[83] Indeed, before Ragsdale died, his tale had grown to include the claim that he had removed eleven gold helmets and had buried them in the desert![84] Of course, these valuable helmets have never been found.

Despite his claim that he and his girlfriend had collected debris samples from the spacecraft, Ragsdale never produced any fragments to support his claim.

To put it bluntly, Ragsdale's account is simply unbelievable.

FRANKIE ROWE

Frankie Rowe's father, Dan Dwyer, was a fireman with the Roswell Fire Department in July 1947. According to Rowe, her father and the men in his firefighting unit responded to a telephone call requesting that they come out to the location where the spaceship had crashed. Rowe claims that her father saw two body bags into which the aliens had been placed. She also says that later her father observed that one alien had *survived* the crash and was put inside an ambulance and taken to Roswell Army Air Field.

Rowe says that when she was visiting her father's fire station a few days later, a New Mexico state trooper came into the facility and showed her and some others who were present a small piece of metal from the UFO that he had retrieved from the crash site.

Frankie Rowe claims that she got to examine the "strange" piece of metal and noted that it weighed almost nothing. She also stated that the fragment could not be torn, cut, or burned.

Within two or three days, Rowe claims that members of the military later showed up to her house and threatened her and her family with death and internment in a concentration camp if they ever told anyone about what they knew.[85]

Where Rowe's Boat Springs Leaks

When considering Frankie Rowe's testimony, there are several problems that arise, the first of which is the fact there are no records anywhere indicating that the Roswell Fire Department made a run outside of town anytime during the month of July 1947!

In 1947, the city of Roswell had only *two* fire trucks. Because of this limitation, the city at that time rarely dispatched firefighters outside the town limits because it would leave the rest of the town vulnerable and unprotected.[86] Rowe would have us believe that a fire truck was dispatched anyway, despite the fact that the location to the alleged UFO crash site she claims her father visited was more than *thirty miles* away!

A second problem with Rowe's account has to do with the fact that according to her and the Roswell advocates, the entire recovery of the alleged extraterrestrial spacecraft was carried out under the strictest secrecy. If this is true, then why would the military have called a *civilian* fire department when they had their *own personnel* on the base to use?

Also, if Dwyer's fire company was actually called out to the crash site, and there was indeed the subsequent threats of death and other nefarious activities that indicate that a high-level cover-up was in progress, then why was the fire crew not sworn to secrecy right on the spot by the military? If Rowe is telling the truth, why would the military let several days go by before coming out to threaten and intimidate her family?

Another example of how Rowe's account just doesn't make sense is her claim about a New Mexico state trooper. According to Rowe, a trooper stopped by her father's fire department and showed them a piece of the UFO that had crashed. The trooper specifically told Rowe that he didn't know how long he would be able to hold on to the fragment and whether or not he would be able to keep it if and when the military found out that he had it.[87]

If what Frankie Rowe says is true, the question becomes, if this trooper was so concerned over this issue, why did he flash around his precious souvenir for everyone to see as if he wanted the whole world to know he had it? If he really valued it, *why* would he then allow everyone present to try and destroy the fragment by attempting to burn, cut, or tear it up?

Frankie Rowe's story does not hold up under critical evaluation. Until evidence emerges that supports her claims, her account must be considered highly suspect.

THE FRANCISCAN NUNS

In *The Truth about the UFO Crash at Roswell*, authors Kevin Randle and Donald Schmitt make the claim that "In Roswell proper at St. Mary's Hospital, Franciscan Catholic nuns Mother Superior Mary Bernadette and Sister Capistrano making routine night observations, saw a brilliant light plunge to earth, due north of their location. They believed it to be a disabled aircraft of some kind and recorded its passage in their logbook. The entry noted the sighting was late on the night of July 4, between 11:00 and 11:30 P.M."[88]

Randle and Schmitt present the nuns' alleged observations in an attempt to make the case that they saw the spacecraft before it crashed. However, there are two problems with this hypothesis: (1) The object purportedly observed by the two nuns could have been anything, including a meteor, since the descriptions of it are sufficiently vague; (2) Despite repeated requests to produce the original logs that contain the written entries by these nuns, neither Kevin Randle or Donald Schmitt has ever done so.[89] Until they do, there is no credible evidence that either the logs or the nuns even exist, as my own investigation revealed nothing.

CORP. E. L. PYLES

Randle and Schmitt state in *The Truth about the UFO Crash at Roswell* that Corp. E. L. Pyles was yet another witness who, like the Franciscan nuns, observed the spaceship that flew over the town of Roswell before it crashed.

The problem with the representation of the Pyles sighting by Randle and Schmitt is that it is *wishful speculation* on their part. When Pyles recounted his story, *he was uncertain of both the date and time* that he observed the star-like object. Indeed, Pyles's recollection of the event was so vague because of the near forty years that had elapsed since the incident that he wasn't even certain of his exact location at the time of his observation![90]

Because of this fact, any attempt to link him to the event at Roswell is pure speculation at best. The truth is Pyles's "UFO" sighting is simply too vague and contains too few details to determine what, if anything, he may have actually observed.

LEWIS S. RICKETT AND DR. LINCOLN LAPAZ

M.Sgt. Lewis S. Rickett was the Counter Intelligent Corps agent who, with Sheridan Cavitt, drove out to the Foster ranch to investigate Brazel's claim that the remains of a flying disc had come down.

Although Rickett's testimony never appeared in the original *Roswell Incident* book, it was featured in Randle and Schmitt's two books and in *Crash at Corona.*

Rickett tells an elaborate tale of how several trips were made out to the Foster ranch to collect the debris. He also claims that a large military cordon was in place and that the metal that was recovered could not be bent or dented. But of all the claims that Rickett has made to Roswell researchers, it's his involvement with Dr. Lincoln LaPaz that is most revealing.

Lewis Rickett and a Tall Tale

Lewis Rickett says that Dr. Lincoln LaPaz, a famous scientist in New Mexico who specialized in studying meteors, was not only involved in the Roswell incident, but that he undertook several UFO investigations in the summer of 1947 accompanied by Rickett. One of these outings was to pinpoint the trajectory of the object that had crashed near Roswell.[91]

There is no disputing the fact that Dr. Lincoln LaPaz both had an interest in UFOs and investigated several cases firsthand. It is also possible that Rickett may have actually been assigned for a short while to assist LaPaz in some of these field investigations for UFO reports that may have been of interest. However, it requires a leap of faith to state that LaPaz was involved on a firsthand basis in the Roswell incident.

Lewis Rickett was in his eighties when he was interviewed about his experiences at Roswell, and, according to Sheridan Cavitt, he loved to tell stories.[92] One example of Rickett's unreliability involves LaPaz's knowledge of languages. According to Rickett, LaPaz spoke Spanish and was able to talk with many of the Mexican natives who lived throughout New Mexico about their alleged UFO sightings. However, acquaintances claim that LaPaz did not speak Spanish.[93] Apparently, Rickett's Roswell "remembrances" are a synthesis of both real and unreal events.

If UFO investigators had managed to reach Lewis Rickett at a much earlier time, perhaps his testimony could be considered credible and actually be of some value providing insight into what it really was that Mac Brazel discovered crashed on the Foster ranch. But too much time elapsed and Rickett's testimony cannot be relied upon. To present it any other way simply is not accurate.

VARIABLE ALIEN BODY COUNTS

One of the arguments that I have repeatedly heard by pro-UFO researchers at various UFO conventions over the years is that the witnesses in the Roswell incident are remarkably consistent with regard to the number of alien bodies reportedly recovered. However, a careful examination of the books by the Roswell authors does not support this contention. Indeed, if aliens actually were recovered near Roswell in 1947, the purported "witnesses" to this event do not even agree among themselves. For example, Gerald Anderson claimed to have seen four aliens: two dead, one injured, and one uninjured. Glenn Dennis saw three aliens, all of whom were dead. Jim Ragsdale and Ruben Anaya each saw three bodies, but Anaya also saw one live extraterrestrial. The list goes on, but this is enough to demonstrate the wide variety of alien body counts.

CONCLUSION

As we have seen, the testimonies from the so-called new witnesses are either overblown and exaggerated by the pro-UFO Roswell authors or they are blatant confabulations. Still other highly touted "witnesses" by the pro-UFO Roswell authors are not really witnesses at all, except by the standards of their own vocabulary.

If we are to try and determine what it was that really scattered debris over the Foster ranch and was later recovered by the Army Air Force in July 1947, we must look elsewhere for these answers. Unfortunately, the overhyped number of seemingly credible "witnesses" to the Roswell affair aren't really all they are cracked up to be.

Our search now turns to the *physical* evidence that exists in the Roswell incident.

NOTES

1. Kevin D. Randle and Donald R. Schmitt, *The Truth about the UFO Crash at Roswell* (New York: Avon Books, 1994), p. 223.
2. Kevin D. Randle and Donald R. Schmitt, *UFO Crash at Roswell* (New York: Avon Books, 1991), pp. 125–26.
3. Ibid.
4. Bob Kiviat, television producer for "Unsolved Mysteries," personal interview, Burbank, California, November 17, 1994.
5. Stanton T. Friedman and Don Berliner, *Crash at Corona: The U.S. Military Retrieval and Cover-Up of a UFO* (New York: Paragon House, 1992), p. 46.
6. Randle and Schmitt, *The Truth about the UFO Crash at Roswell*, p. xiii.
7. Ibid.

8. Kevin D. Randle, *Roswell UFO Crash Update, Exploring the Military Cover-Up of the Century* (New York: Global Communications, 1995), p. 191.

9. Ibid., p. 129.

10. Randle and Schmitt, *The Truth about the UFO Crash at Roswell,* pp. 22–23.

11. Ibid., p. 23.

12. Ibid.

13. Ibid., p. 25.

14. Kal K. Korff, personal phone conversations with personnel at the office of the Governor of New Mexico, October 7–8, 1996.

15. Randle and Schmitt, *The Truth about the UFO Crash at Roswell*, p. 23.

16. Karl Pflock, *Roswell in Perspective* (Mt. Rainier, Md.: Fund for UFO Research, 1994), p. 110.

17. Friedman and Berliner, *Crash at Corona,* pp. 89–90 and 185–91.

18. Ibid., p. 9.

19. Kevin D. Randle, *A History of UFO Crashes* (New York: Avon Books, 1995), pp. 40–41.

20. Ibid., p. 41.

21. Ibid., pp. 47–48.

22. Ibid., pp. 53–54.

23. Friedman and Berliner, *Crash at Corona,* p. xvi.

24. Timothy Good, *Alien Contact: Top Secret UFO Files Revealed* (New York: William Morrow and Company, 1993), p. 99.

25. Ibid.

26. Ibid.

27. Randle and Schmitt, *The Truth about the UFO Crash at Roswell*, pp. 15, 82–83.

28. Friedman and Berliner, *Crash at Corona,* p. 128.

29. Ibid.

30. Randle and Schmitt, *The Truth about the UFO Crash at Roswell*, p. 214.

31. Sgt. Melvin E. Brown, *Enlisted Record and Report of Separation Honorable Discharge,* United States Army.

32. Randle and Schmitt, *UFO Crash at Roswell,* p. 270.

33. Ibid.

34. Friedman and Berliner, *Crash at Corona,* p. 129.

35. Ibid., p. 115.

36. Randle and Schmitt, *The Truth about the UFO Crash at Roswell,* p. 14, and Friedman and Berliner, *Crash at Corona,* p. 115.

37. Randle and Schmitt, *The Truth about the UFO Crash at Roswell,* p. 14.

38. Friedman and Berliner, *Crash at Corona,* pp. 115–16.

39. Randle and Schmitt, *The Truth about the UFO Crash at Roswell,* p. 14.

40. Friedman and Berliner, *Crash at Corona,* p. 116.

41. Ibid., p. 117.

42. Ibid.

43. Ibid., p. 118.

44. Ibid.

45. Ibid., p. 119.

46. Philip J. Klass, *Skeptics UFO Newsletter,* (Internet version posted on http://www.wufoc.tripnet.com.klass.ns), issue 31, January 1995, p. 1.

47. Randle and Schmitt, *The Truth about the UFO Crash at Roswell,* p. 20.

48. Ibid.

49. Philip J. Klass, *Skeptics UFO Newsletter,* p. 1.

50. Randle and Schmitt, *The Truth about the UFO Crash at Roswell,* p. 14. See also Karl Pflock, *Roswell in Perspective,* p. 93, and Friedman and Berliner, *Crash at Corona,* p. 115.

51. Friedman and Berliner, *Crash at Corona,* p. 118.

52. Philip J. Klass, *Skeptics UFO Newsletter,* p. 3.

53. Ibid.

54. Kal K. Korff, personal phone conversations with several personnel at the National Personnel Records and Information Center, St. Louis, Missouri, September 10–12, 1996, October 21–25, 1996.

55. Kal K. Korff, archive record searches through past issues of the *New York Times, Stars and Stripes,* records of the Federal Aviation Administration, and the Royal Air Force in England.

56. Randle and Schmitt, *The Truth about the UFO Crash at Roswell,* p. 174.

57. Stanton T. Friedman, *Open Letter to Kevin Randle,* November 10, 1995, p. 4, posted on <http://www.medianet.nbnet.nb.ca/kdrfals2.txt>.

58. Robert Todd, "Randle Dumps—and Dumps On—Schmitt," *Cowflop Alert,* September 22, 1995, p. 2.

59. Friedman, *Open Letter to Kevin Randle,* p. 4. See also Robert Todd, *Cowflop Alert,* p. 2.

60. Kal Korff interview with Dr. Harold Granich, Easley's physician, July 16, 1994.

61. Kevin D. Randle, *A History of UFO Crashes,* p. 127.

62. Randle and Schmitt, *UFO Crash at Roswell,* pp. 109–10.

63. Friedman and Berliner, *Crash at Corona,* p. 125.

64. Randle and Schmitt, *The Truth about the UFO Crash at Roswell,* pp. 147–48.

65. Kal K. Korff, personal interview with Jonathan Smith (who served with Pappy Henderson), San Jose, California, March 15, 1995.

66. Friedman and Berliner, *Crash at Corona,* p. 126.

67. Friedman, *Open Letter to Kevin Randle,* pp. 3–7. See also Randle and Schmitt, *The Truth about the UFO Crash at Roswell,* pp. 147–48.

68. Dava Sobel, "The Truth about Roswell" (internet posting on http://www.vjentr.com), p. 6. See also Pflock, *Roswell in Perspective,* p. 41.

69. Arthur. S. Levine, personal phone conversation with Kevin D. Randle, October 1996, for MSNBC article, transcribed by Kal Korff.

70. Randle and Schmitt, *The Truth about the UFO Crash at Roswell,* p. 6.

71. Ibid., p. 6.

72. Ibid., pp. 14–16.

73. Pflock, *Roswell in Perspective,* p. 50.

74. Arthur S. Levine, special report to MSNBC, "Roswell: Truth or Fiction?" October 31, 1996, posted on <http://www.MSNBC.com/news/35568.ASP>.

75. Pflock, *Roswell in Perspective*, p. 44.

76. Kal K. Korff, personal telephone conversation with officials at White Sands, New Mexico, November 13, 1996.

77. Kal K. Korff, personal telephone conversation with the New Mexico Institute of Mining and Technology, Socorro, New Mexico, November 13, 1996.

78. Pflock, *Roswell in Perspective*, pp. 46–55.

79. Stanton T. Friedman, *An Open Letter to Kevin Randle,* p. 3.

80. Pflock, *Roswell in Perspective*, pp. 46–55. See also Dava Sobel, "The Truth about Roswell."

81. Kevin Randle, "The Ragsdale Letter, Part II" (unpublished letter), p. 1.

82. Randle and Schmitt, *The Truth about the UFO Crash at Roswell,* p. 8.

83. Kevin Randle, "The Ragsdale Letter, Part I," p. 1.

84. Arthur S. Levine, "Roswell: Truth or Fiction?" (MSNBC internet article), October 31, 1996.

85. Randle and Schmitt, *The Truth about the UFO Crash at Roswell,* pp. 20–21; Pflock, *Roswell in Perspective,* p. 107. See also Randle and Schmitt, *The Truth about the UFO Crash at Roswell,* pp. 88–89.

86. Kal K. Korff, personal phone conversation with Roswell city officials and Roswell Fire department personnel, November 12, 1996.

87. Pflock, *Roswell in Perspective*, p. 107.

88. Randle and Schmitt, *The Truth about the UFO Crash at Roswell,* p. 148.

89. Friedman, *Open Letter to Kevin Randle.* See also Fred Whiting, letter to Kevin Randle, April 12, 1995.

90. Friedman, *An Open Letter to Kevin Randle.* See also Pflock, *Roswell in Perspective,* p. 37.

91. Randle and Schmitt, *The Truth about the UFO Crash at Roswell,* pp. 143, 171.

92. Kal K. Korff, personal interview with Sheridan Cavitt.

93. Kal K. Korff, personal telephone interview with physicist Al Kaufmann (one of LaPaz's coworkers), November 5, 1996.

4

The "Alien" Materials Recovered at Roswell

> The disc that crashed, [near Roswell] had collided with a meteor in orbit of Terra [Earth], and was attempting to compensate it's [*sic*] flight vector, but because of the collision, the inter-atmospheric propulsion system malfunctioned, and the occupants sent out a distress signal to their companions on Mars. The [alien] "launchship" commander made the decision to authorize an attempted soft-landing on the New Mexican desert. At the same time, the inter-atmospheric propulsion system had a massive burn-out, and the disc was soon virtually helpless.[1]

Of the more curious aspects of the alleged Roswell UFO crash of 1947 are the numerous claims by individuals who purport to have either seen or handled the supposed "alien" debris. Without fail their descriptions are always the same: metal that looked a lot like tin foil, yet (1) couldn't be torn, cut, or burned; (2) couldn't be bent; (3) would straighten itself out after being crumpled up and couldn't be permanently creased or dented.

To the Roswell advocates, the consistency of these testimonies is a researcher's dream come true. However, dreams and reality are often two different things entirely. Why is it, for example, that none of the descriptions by any of the witnesses ever deviates from that which was originally reported by Moore and Berlitz in their original *Roswell Incident* book of 1980? Can't any of these "witnesses" add anything *new* to the description stockpile that already exists?

If a person were to take an object, especially one that was so *unlike* anything anyone had seen before, and hand it to twelve different people for examination, one would expect both a wide variety of descriptions, plus some commonalities. On the other hand, if all twelve descriptions were *identical* almost down to the very words used, as numerous court trials have demonstrated, then there would most likely be something wrong. In fact, this would probably indicate either collusion among the witnesses or at least some copycatting taking place.

Add to this scenario the fact that these twelve people are free to "beat up" the object by trying to burn, cut, fold, dent, and tear it (or any other thing they can think of), and the number of descriptions should increase even further. Yet we do not find this perfectly normal, expected result when it comes to the testimonies of the alleged "witnesses" who claim to have handled the Roswell alien debris.

More importantly, despite the numerous witnesses who now claim to have seen and handled the "alien" metallic foil, *none* of them appears to have ever kept a piece of this metal as a souvenir if nothing else. This is despite the fact that several of these "witnesses" claim that they *knew* the metal they were holding was "extraterrestrial" at the time they first handled it in 1947!

While there are a couple of people, as we discussed in chapter 3, who claim to have "pocketed a piece," conveniently, and suspiciously, *none of them* has ever managed to produce for scientific examination any of the fragment(s) he claims to possess. Until this happens, the testimonies of those who claim to have such samples cannot be considered credible.

As the Roswell UFO craze has gained in popularity over the past few years, it was predictable that "anonymous" individuals would step forward, claiming to have actual pieces of the alien metal. While such claims must be regarded with caution, at least any purported fragments offered by sources (even anonymous ones) can be scientifically tested and quantified in a laboratory. If a genuinely verifiable piece of material that proved to be technically beyond what could be manufactured on Earth, or at least to not have originated on Earth, were ever revealed, then at last the pro-UFO community would have its long sought after "smoking gun" blowing open the Roswell "cover-up" once and for all.

ART BELL AND THE "ROSWELL" FRAGMENT

Art Bell is a nighttime radio talk show personality who hosts "Coast to Coast" and "Dreamland." Enormously popular, Bell's syndicated programs are carried by more than 210 stations and heard by countless millions of people.

On April 18, 1996, Bell received a letter written by an anonymous individual who claimed to be serving in the U.S. military and whose father was part of the secret "recovery team" at Roswell.* Accompanying the letter to Bell were pieces of metal said to be some of the actual extraterrestrial material collected by the military. The following is the complete text of the letter Bell received:

April 10, 1996

Dear Mr. Bell,

I've followed your broadcasts over the last year or so, and have been considering whether or not to share with you and your listeners some information related to the Roswell UFO crash.

My grandfather was a member of the Retrieval Team sent to the crash site just after the incident was reported. He died in 1974, but not before he had sat down with some of us and talked about the incident.

I am currently serving in the military, and hold a Security Clearance, and do NOT wish to "go public," and risk losing my career and commission.

Nonetheless, I would like to briefly tell you what my own grandfather told me about Roswell. In fact, I enclose for your safekeeping "samples" that were in the possession of my grandfather until he died, and which I have had since his estate was settled. As I understand it, they came from the UFO debris, and were

---

*This letter has been posted on the Internet at various websites, including <http://www.artbell.com> and also <http://www.wufoc.com/ uknewdx.htm>.

among a large batch subsequently sent to Wright-Patterson AFB in Ohio from New Mexico.

My grandfather was able to "appropriate" them, and stated that the metallic samples are "pure extract aluminum." You will note that they appear old and tempered, and they have been placed in tissue paper and in baggies for posterity.

I have had them since 1974, and after considerable thought and reflection, give them to you. Feel free to share them with any of your friends in the UFO research community.

I have listened to many people over the years discuss Roswell and the crash events, as reported by many who were either there or who heard about it from eyewitnesses.

The recent *Roswell* movie was similar to my grandfather's own account, but a critical element was left out, and it is that element which I would like to share.

As my grandad stated, the Team arrived at the crash site just after the AAF/USAF [Army Air Force/United States Air Force] reported the ground zero location. They found two dead occupants hurled free of the disc.

A lone surviving occupant was found within the disc, and it was apparent its left left leg was broken. There was a minimal radiation contamination, and it was quickly dispersed with a water/solvent wash, and soon the occupant was dispatched for medical assistance and isolation. The bodies were sent to the Wright-Patterson AFB for dispersal. The debris was also loaded onto three trucks which finished the on-load just before sunset.

Grandad was part of the Team that went with the surviving occupant. The occupant communicated via telepathic means. It spoke perfect English, and communicated the following:

The disc was a "probeship" dispatched from a "launchship" that was stationed at the dimensional gateway to the Terran Solar System thirty-two light years from Terra. They had been conducting operations on Terra for over 100 years.

Another group was exploring Mars and Io [one of the moons of Jupiter].

Each "probeship" carried a crew of three. A "launchship" had a crew of (100) one hundred.

The disc that crashed had collided with a meteor in orbit of Terra and was attempting to compensate its flight vector, but because of the collision, the inter-atmospheric propulsion system malfunctioned, and the occupants sent out a distress signal to their companions on Mars. The "launchship" commander made the decision to authorize an attempted soft-landing on the New Mexican desert. At the same time, the inter-atmospheric propulsion system had a massive electrical burn-out, and the disc was soon virtually helpless.

There was another option available to the occupants, but it involved activating the Dimensional powerplant for deep space travel. However, it opens an energy vortex around the disc for 1,500 miles in all directions. Activating the Dimensional powerplant would have resulted in the annihilation of the states of New Mexico, Arizona, California, and portions of Mexico. Possibly even further states would have been affected.

Thus, the occupants chose to ride the ship down and hope for the best. They literally sacrificed their lives rather than destroy the populations within their proximity.

The Dimensional powerplant self-destructed, and the inter-atmospheric propulsion system was also deactivated to prevent the technology from falling into the hands of the Terrans. This was done in accordance with their standing orders in regards to any compromise with contact experiences.

Grandad spent a total of twenty-six weeks on the Team that examined and debriefed the lone survivor of the Roswell crash. Grandad's affiliation with the "project" ended when the occupant was to be transported to a long-term facility. He was placed on-board a USAF transport aircraft that was to be sent to Washington, D.C.

It may interest you that three fighter aircraft, dispatched to investigate a distress call from the transport, experienced many electrical malfunctioning systems failures as they entered the airspace of the transport's last reported location. No crash or debris of the transport was ever found. The Team was disbanded.

Well, I realize I have likely shocked you with this bizarre and incredible account, and seeking to remain "unknown" likely doesn't do anything for my credibility . . . eh? And the metal "samples" only will likely add to the controversy. [Ellipses in the original.]

But, I know you will take this with a "grain of salt," and I don't blame you, Mr. Bell. I just hope that you can understand my reasons and my own desire to maintain my career and commission.

I am passing through Southern California with an Operational Readiness Mobility Exercise, and will mail this just prior to this exercise, possibly from the Charleston area.

I will listen to your broadcast to receive any acknowledging [*sic*] or confirmation that you have received this package.

This letter and the contents of the package are given to you, with the hope that it helps contribute to discussion on the subject of UFO phenomena.

I agree with Neil Armstrong, a good friend of mine, who dared to say, at the White House no less, that there are things "out there," which boggle the mind and are far beyond our ability to comprehend.

Sign me,

A Friend

As expected, when Bell received the "mysterious" letter, he promptly announced it on the air with all the excitement and hyperbole for which his show is noted. Much to Bell's credit, however, he made arrangements to have the pieces of metallic debris scientifically analyzed.

Immediately after Bell's startling announcement, the Internet and computer-based online services were "a buzz" with stories about "Roswell UFO fragments" having finally been found. Expectations ran high, with the UFO faithful keeping their collective fingers crossed. Perhaps the Roswell case would be settled once and for all, with irrefutable proof having at last been found.

While the metallic samples were starting to undergo scientific testing, Bell received a *second* letter from the mysterious source.* This second letter, which was dated April 22, 1996, read as follows:

Dear Mr. Bell, at great risk, I am writing you in regards to the package sent your way. I had opportunity to listen to a tape recording of the radio broadcasts, when I returned home after having participated in the Readiness Mobility Exercises.

My son, a senior in college, recorded them for me.

I must say that I was somewhat surprised by the negative and close-minded responses directed your way, by some of your own listeners.

You seemed to indicate that receiving the package has vastly upset your life, and in this I would like to say that wasn't my intention, and I offer my apologies.

*This letter was also posted on the Internet for public perusal.

Further information regarding the Roswell Crash, and my grandfather's affiliation, would likely be potentially beneficial in your efforts at correlation and verification.

In this regard, I can only say, based on past conversations on the subject with Grandad, that the Retrieval Team consisted of three segments: the On-site Team, the In-House Team, and the Security Team. The credentials of the team members weren't only military related. There were individuals with backgrounds from the University of Colorado, Office of Naval Research, AAF/USAF and U.S. Army, UCLA and Atomic Energy Commission, and National Advisory Committee on Aeronautics, and Office of Scientific Research and Development. Additionally, there were consultants from England, France, and Russia involved.

Grandad stated their own analysis of the sample indicated it as pure extract aluminum, as a conductor for the electromagnetic fields created in the propulsion systems. However, critically needed data was "eliminated" by the self-destruct mechanisms on the disc vehicle itself. Furthermore, the occupant-survivor of the crash refused to disclose technical information, despite a series of interrogative attempts to extract technological data. No means could be found to secure the information.

There were always two Security Team members present at every face-to-face meeting with the survivor. The survivor had the ability to deduce thoughts and questions, prior to them being asked. Sometimes it became frustrating.

The disc itself was literally dissected, and it was discovered that the propulsion system had actually fused together the many components. There were control-type devices forged in the shape of the alien hand which were assumed to be control and activation surfaces.

What is today fiber-optic technology was part and parcel of the alien technology within the control panels, albeit fused and melted when the self-destruct mechanism was activated.

There were Westinghouse-affiliated persons on the Team, and Grandad always thought some of them had gone back with the knowledge and incorporated it into the future research with the phone systems.

Of course the military was concerned as to the ability of the aliens to enter our atmosphere at will, undetected, and thusly they recommended to the President that a space program be set into motion, and that a system of satellites be placed into orbit by

1957, and this satellite system be patched into the then DEW Line early warning system . . . which became later NORAD. [Ellipses in the original.]

Grandad stated that it was his opinion that NORAD was formed not only to track possible ICBMs from hostile nations, but as a established detection system for UFO craft. That is why the NASA space agency has been "incorporated" by and large with our armed forces, and there are so many "classified" missions.

This is my opinion, but Grandad prophesied such occurring as far back as 1971.

Well, I am scheduled to travel back to Charleston AFB and then Pope AFB. I'll mail this from somewhere in [South Carolina].

I'll not likely communicate again. My wife is concerned, as am I, that the intelligence agencies will put two and two together, so it is inadvisable to further communicate this information. I hope you understand my position.

I could likely face a court martial or sedition charges for stating some of this information and [these] opinions.

You would be surprised at the extent of internal policies on this subject, and the consequences for current commissioned officers talking about UFO phenomena. . . .

I wish you all the best, and will be listening.

I commend your courage and integrity.

I hope your listeners understand that the subject of Roswell has great potential at extrapolating the truth on UFOs, and what has come to be known as a Cosmic Watergate is only the tip of an iceberg.

Grandad said that when the truth does come out, humanity will be changed beyond comprehension. He also said many on the In-House Team lobbied to release the information to the public. Not all of them were paranoid in trusting the public with the truth.

Sign me, Still

A Friend

On May 19, 1996, Art Bell featured UFO researcher Linda Moulton Howe, whom he had hired to report on the metallurgical and scientific analyses that were being conducted on the mysterious pieces of metal that Bell had received. Howe is noted for her study of alleged UFO-related cattle mutilations and crop circles. She is also a believer of the infamous Eduard "Billy" Meier hoax in Switzerland and has a reputation for not always being entirely objective.*

Howe took the metal specimens and made arrangements for a colleague of hers to test them. Although she refused to divulge the scientist's name, for fear of ridicule she claimed,[2] the results of the tests were released nonetheless over a series of broadcasts Howe submitted via tape to Art Bell.

In short, the electron dispersion spectroscopy revealed that some of the samples were almost pure aluminum. The other items, various odd-shaped pieces of metal, consisted of silicon granules (i.e., sand), iron, manganese, calcium, bismuth, and zinc.[3]

Nowhere, among *any* of the samples Art Bell had received, was there any indication that the items were *extraterrestrial* in nature or had not been manufactured on Earth.

Furthermore, these alleged "Roswell" metal samples did not behave according to the numerous witnesses who are on record as having supposedly handled the material. *None* of the samples bore any resemblance to the thin, lightweight aluminum foil-like metal that Jesse Marcel and others claimed would straighten itself right back out after being folded up. Instead, all of the metallic specimens Bell had received were hard, sharp pieces of metal (they looked somewhat like pieces of scrap metal actually), some of which were as thick as four millimeters.[4]

---

*At the 1995 MUFON Annual Symposium in Seattle, Washington, Howe approached me and had the temerity to chastise me for my research exposing the Meier case as a hoax! Howe accused me of being "closed-minded," and admonished me not to dismiss the case entirely. This was the first time I had ever met Howe in person. Surprised, I asked Howe if she had ever been to Switzerland or had ever bothered conducting any firsthand investigation of her own into the Meier case as I had. Howe admitted that she had *not!* I then asked Howe if she had read my book *Spaceships of the Pleiades* and she replied that she had not. I then asked her how she could comment on my research when she had not bothered reading it. Howe, of course, had no answer. I then assured her that while I have never claimed to have disproven *all aspects* of the Meier case (this is impossible for anyone to do), I simply maintain that the so-called evidence offered up by Meier and his proponents is either grossly misrepresented or fraudulent. Howe did not know quite how to respond, so she advised me to keep an "open mind." While I always do, I found the hypocrisy of her advice extremely ironic.

In truth, there is no evidence whatsoever to connect the fragments Bell had been sent to the incident at Roswell, other than the "anonymous" letter that had accompanied them claiming that they were from the famous 1947 incident. If the letter and fragments are genuine, then the Roswell "UFO crash" involved an ordinary man-made object. However, given the weight of the evidence we have examined so far, it appears that the letter and "spaceship fragments" sent to Art Bell are simply a hoax. For the Roswell faithful, their hopes and dreams of finally blowing open the case were dashed once again.

ANOTHER "ROSWELL" FRAGMENT

Around the time of the Art Bell hyperbole/disappointment roller-coaster, the Roswell International UFO Museum and Research Center, one of three dedicated UFO museums that now exist in the town of Roswell, reported that they had received a piece of metal from the famous UFO crash of 1947 from a man named Blake Larsen.

Shortly after receiving the metal, arrangements were made to test the material scientifically. Max Littell, a museum official, summed up the research center's position by saying "If some metal-lurgist says there is nothing in the book like this [i.e., the material is unidentifiable], and he has got all his degrees and is an expert source, then we are home free. This is it."[5]

Shortly after the museum's receipt of the metallic specimen, the media began to cover the story that a possible Roswell flying saucer fragment had been located.

Physicist David E. Thomas, who was watching a television news story about the subject, immediately contacted Charles B. Moore, a professor emeritus of atmospheric physics at the New Mexico Institute of Mining and Technology in Socorro. Moore, intrigued by the metal described by Thomas, telephoned museum board member Miller Johnson, who accepted Professor Moore's offer to help scientifically test the fragment.[6]

On March 29, 1996, the specimen was studied in a preliminary examination at the Bureau of Mines at New Mexico Tech. Chris McKee, the department manager, conducted the analysis, while no less than Roswell's chief of police, Raymond Mounts, made recordings documenting the event.[7]

X-ray fluorescence measurements revealed that the metal was approximately 50 percent copper and 50 percent silver on what was dubbed the "front side" of the specimen, and 87 percent silver and 12 percent copper on the back side. The other 1 percent consisted of various trace elements.

Once again, not the slightest shred of evidence that the specimen was extraterrestrial in origin had been detected. The sample also suffered from the same problem as the one turned into Art Bell and analyzed by Howe's source—it was very rigid and did not straighten itself out when folded. In fact, it could not be folded at all, unless quite a bit of force was applied, and then it would break![8]

While no evidence that the fragment was extraterrestrial had been detected, another test would be needed in order to determine its planet of origin. After all, it was either created on Earth or it was not. Since spectrographic analyses of various stars and galaxies throughout the universe prove that the same elements that are found on Earth exist elsewhere, then isotopic study using mass spectrometry would definitively settle the issue of the fragment's origin once and for all.

The element copper, which comprised at least fifty percent of the specimen, was used as a control. While most isotopes of copper (Cu) decay relatively quickly, two are known to be stable: Cu-63 and Cu-65. As physicist David Thomas put it "No matter where copper is found on Earth, it always consists of the same percentages of these isotopes.* But heavy elements like copper are forged by a variety of thermonuclear events in red giants and supernovae [types of stars], and thus the ratios of various isotopes will most likely vary from star to star."[9]

In other words, the Earth and all its elements have an isotopic fingerprint which can be measured and used as a control when examining the alleged Roswell specimen, or any other one. If the isotopic ratios of copper in the fragment, for example, deviated significantly from those of other control copper samples from Earth, then the piece of metal would definitely be extraterrestrial in origin.

---

*Isotopes are two or more forms of an element having the same number of protons in the nucleus but having different numbers of neutrons.

On August 1, 1996, an isotopic analysis on the fragment was conducted at Los Alamos National Laboratory (LANL) in New Mexico. The study took two days, and was performed by E. Larry Callis of the Chemical Metallurgical Research Division. The examination procedure was recorded and photographed by both LANL personnel and Miller Johnson.

At the LANL facility, both the fragment and a second piece which had been turned in were placed inside a mass spectrometer and carefully measured. The Cu-63 readings results for both pieces turned out to be 69.127 percent and 69.120 percent. As a control, a piece or ordinary, refined copper was measured. Its Cu-63 reading measured 69.174 percent, the scientifically accepted value for Cu-63.[10]

Physicist David Thomas summed up the results of the copper readings succinctly by noting that "the copper was not found to deviate significantly from earthly isotopic ratios."[11]

Since the other element present in the sample was silver, it, too, was measured in the mass spectrometer. The results revealed that for the silver (Ag-107) isotopic ratios, readings of 48.160 percent and 51.840 percent were obtained, well within their earthly norms. In other words, this was conclusive proof that the sample originated from *this planet,* and was *not* the product of extraterrestrial technology!

After the test results were complete, they were published by various media. One of the people who heard about them was *Albuquerque Journal* reporter John Fleck, who had seen an article in the newsletter *New Mexicans for Science and Reason Reports,* a publication produced by a group of the same name, of which physicist David Thomas is a vice president and communications officer.

Fleck wrote an article for the *Albuquerque Journal* on August 13, 1996, which was read by artist Randy Fullbright in St. George, Utah. Fullbright, it turned out, is a jewelry artist and he immediately recognized the alleged "Roswell fragment" as one of his creations! Fullbright had given the piece of metal to the owner of a gallery, and informed him that it was pieces of "scraps from his own artwork."[12]

The gallery owner then gave it to Blake Larsen, who at the time was in the process of leaving St. George, Utah, and moving to Roswell, New Mexico. The gallery owner had told Larsen that the piece of metal was "found near Roswell in 1947" after learning that Larsen was headed there![13]

On September 6, 1996, the *Albuquerque Journal* published a front page exposé of the Roswell fragment saga. The story was written by Fleck and titled "Artist: Fragment is Bogus."

While this alleged "saucer fragment" turned out to be a hoax, just like the metallic debris mailed anonymously to Art Bell, the Roswell International UFO Museum and Research Center nonetheless deserves kudos for not only promptly analyzing the material, but making sure that the personnel and steps to document all procedures were processed in the correct manner. The museum spent $725 of its own money to analyze the fragment for isoptic content alone.[14] Obviously, the gallery owner who pulled the hoax on them had to be aware that the material was bogus. While hoaxes sometimes can make money for those who are behind them, this time it *cost* innocent, well-intending individuals their money and their valuable time.

As of this writing, there has yet to materialize any genuine debris or metallic fragments from the so-called Roswell UFO crash of 1947—despite the claims of various individuals who profess to have such material in their possession. Until such artifacts, whose origin can be scientifically proven to be extraterrestrial, are forthcoming, then the "alien case" for Roswell remains pathetically weak.

So what was it then that crashed and was recovered by Mac Brazel, Jesse Marcel, and Sheridan Cavitt at the Foster ranch? The definitive exposé, and the solution to this fifty-year-old mystery, are presented in the next chapter.

NOTES

1. Kevin D. Randle and Donald R. Schmitt, *The Truth about the UFO Crash at Roswell* (New York: Avon Books, 1994), p. 223.

2. Art Bell, "Analysis of New Metal from Roswell—Report on Preliminary Scientific Examination of Art Bell's Roswell Debris," transcript of Linda Moulton Howe's comments on "Dreamland," broadcast Sunday, May 12, 1996, Art Bell's Website, <http://www.artbell.com>, p. 2.

3. Art Bell, "Art's Parts Scientific Report," Art Bell's Web page, pp. 1–3.

4. Ibid., p. 4.

5. David E. Thomas, "The 'Roswell Fragment'—Case Closed," *Skeptical Inquirer* (November/ December 1996): 5.

6. Ibid.

7. Ibid.

8. Kal K. Korff, personal phone conversation with the International UFO Museum and Research Center, Roswell, New Mexico, October 29, 1996.

9. Thomas, "The 'Roswell Fragment,' " p. 5.

10. Ibid.

11. Ibid.

12. Ibid.

13. Ibid.

14. Ibid.

5

The Air Force Cover-Up:
What the Roswell Object Really Was

> Marcel and [Brigadier General] Ramey left for the map room and
> while they were gone, someone carried the [UFO] wreckage out,
> replacing it with the weather balloon long before any reporters
> were allowed into the office.[1]

> Oh Bull! That material was never switched! . . . They're [Fried-
> man, Randle and Schmitt] full of it! That's no damn weather bal-
> loon! There wasn't one there.[2]

Now that we have uncovered the sad truth behind many of the testimonies concerning the recovery of alleged "flying saucer" debris
near Roswell, where does this leave us? With no known, scientifically verifiable *physical* remnants to study, is there any way that we
can possibly determine the true nature and origin of the actual
wreckage that was collected? Fortunately, the answer is yes, but in
order to do so we must first examine additional evidence.

As mentioned in chapter 1, Colonel Blanchard ordered Lt.
Walter Haut to issue a press release announcing the recovery of a
"flying disc." Haut alerted the local press and radio stations, which
promptly featured his statement.

As expected, Haut's declaration created a worldwide sensation.

Roswell Army Air Field was bombarded with telephone calls, so many of them in fact that Blanchard himself could not get an open line to place his own outgoing calls.[3]

With reporters telephoning both Roswell Army Air Field and Washington, D.C., about the understandably exciting announcement by military officials that the remains of a flying disc had been found, the next phase of the Roswell episode began.

After receiving word of the official declaration of the flying disc recovery, Lt. Gen. Hoyt S. Vandenburg, then Deputy Commander of the U.S. Army Air Forces, telephoned Brig. Gen. Roger S. Ramey, who at the time was the commanding general of the Eighth Air Force at Fort Worth Army Air Field in Fort Worth, Texas. The 509th Bomb Group, under Colonel Blanchard's command, was part of the Eighth Air Force. Ramey was Blanchard's superior officer.

According to the book *The Roswell Incident,*

> Ramey at once called Colonel Blanchard and made known his extreme displeasure as well as that of General Vandenberg for Blanchard's having initiated the press release. He then directed that the Roswell portion of the wreckage be immediately loaded aboard a B-29. With two generals "breathing down his neck," Colonel Blanchard lost no time in ordering Major Marcel personally to fly this material to the general's headquarters at Carswell Air Force Base,* Fort Worth, Texas, for his examination before flying it on to Wright-Patterson Field in Dayton, Ohio, where it would undergo the "further analysis" prescribed for it by General Vandenberg himself.[4]

Berlitz and Moore's account is essentially correct, except for one important detail: obviously, Marcel was *not* ordered by Blanchard "personally to fly" the wreckage himself to Carswell because, as we have already established in chapter 2, Marcel was *never a pilot!* While Major Marcel did accompany the debris flight to Carswell, he did *not* fly the plane *himself* because he did *not know how to.* Unfortunately, Berlitz and Moore's "source" for this

---

*Carswell Air Force Base is also known as Fort Worth Army Air Field. This is where the Eighth Air Force was headquartered and Ramey was in command.

part of the Roswell yarn was Major Marcel himself, who was confabulating and exaggerating his role in the affair once again.[5]

THE BOND JOHNSON FACTOR

James Bond Johnson was a police beat reporter and back-up photographer for the newspaper the Fort Worth *Star-Telegram* at the
time of the Roswell incident. Johnson was in his office when city
editor Cullen Greene told him that the recovered flying saucer
debris announced by the 509th was due to arrive shortly at Fort
Worth Army Air Field.

Greene had gotten his information from an Associated Press
news wire story, and told Johnson to "Get out to General Ramey's
office. They've got a flying saucer and they're bringing it from
Roswell."[6]

When Johnson arrived, he was admitted into Ramey's office
where he saw the debris strewn out on the floor for display. After
looking over the material, he was not impressed. Johnson noted that
there were bits of what appeared to aluminum foil, some balsa
wood sticks, and he distinctly recalled the smell of foul, burnt
rubber. Johnson described the saucer wreckage as "just a bunch of
garbage anyway." Despite his disappointment, Johnson began
taking pictures.[7]

"[Ramey] had a big office, as most of them [generals] do. And
he walked over and I posed him [Ramey] looking at it, squatting
down, holding on to the stuff. . . . At that time I was briefed on the
idea that it was not a flying disc as reported but in fact was a
weather balloon that had crashed. . . . Almost the first thing that
Ramey had said was, 'Oh, we've found out what it is, and you
know, it's a weather balloon.' "[8] [Ellipses in the original.]

While Johnson was busy taking his pictures (he would end up
shooting a total of four) a telephone call was placed from General
Ramey's staff to the base weather officer, Warrant Officer Irving
Newton. Newton was instructed to report to General Ramey's
office, but he refused at first to do so because he was the only
weather officer on duty at the time and did not want to leave his
post unattended.[9]

Shortly thereafter, the telephone rang again where Newton was stationed. This time it was General Ramey himself calling. "Get your ass over here in ten minutes. If you can't get a car, commandeer the first one that comes along—on my orders."[10]

Newton immediately left for Ramey's office.

When Newton arrived, he was informed that "These officers from Roswell think they found a flying saucer, but the general thinks it's a weather balloon. He wants you to take a look at it."[11]

Newton then examined the debris scattered on the floor in Ramey's office and promptly identified it as a weather balloon with a regular Rawin (pronounced Ray•Win) sonde.*[12] Shortly after posing for a picture with the balloon remnants, Newton was dismissed, and returned to his post.

General Ramey announced to the press that the whole flying saucer affair surrounding Roswell was all a mistake. "The special flight to Wright Field has been canceled, gentlemen. This whole affair has been most unfortunate, but in light of the excitement that has been stirred up lately about these so-called flying discs, it is not surprising. Now let's all go home and call it an evening."[13]

With Ramey's sudden announcement, the Roswell "flying disc" story was effectively dead. Since newspapers across the country, and even in Europe, had run the original recovery story announced by the 509th Bomb Group, a retraction or correction would now have to be issued.

Johnson returned to his paper at Fort Worth, developed his pictures, and they were transmitted to newspapers worldwide.

THE AIR FORCE COVER-UP BEGINS

The beginning of the Air Force cover-up concerning the true nature of the object recovered by Maj. Jesse Marcel started with Marcel's arrival at Carswell Air Force Base and Ramey's subsequent announcement that the debris was a misidentified weather balloon.

As was discussed in chapter 2, Marcel maintains that the Roswell debris was from a flying saucer, and that the weather bal-

---

*Rawin sondes are thin, foil-covered balsa frames attached to balloons that can be tracked by radar (the radar beam reflects off the foil target).

loon "explanation" provided by General Ramey was a convenient cover story.

Although Marcel's credibility as a truthful witness in the Roswell saga has been impeached, there is no disputing the fact that he accompanied the wreckage to Carswell and was present in General Ramey's office with him when the weather balloon explanation was given. But was there a cover-up, as Marcel claims, and was the weather balloon story part of that cover-up?

According to Col. Thomas J. DuBose, who was General Ramey's assistant, the weather balloon story was indeed part of the cover-up, designed to get the press "taken off [Ramey's] back in a hurry."[14]

DuBose was first interviewed by William L. Moore for the book *The Roswell Incident* on September 9, 1979. According to the book,

> Speaking from a comfortable margin of thirty-two years after the event, [DuBose] observed that there had been received "orders from on high to ship the material from Roswell directly to Wright Field by special plane." He added that the general (Ramey) was in complete charge and the rest of the officers and men involved "just followed orders." The general was most concerned that the large number of press reporters present be "taken off his back in a hurry." The weather balloon story was a fabrication designed to accomplish that task and "put out the fire" at the same time. He did not recall who first suggested the weather balloon explanation, but thinks it may have been Ramey himself."[15]

If the Roswell incident did not involve the retrieval of wreckage from a genuine flying saucer, then why was the weather balloon story given out as an "explanation," and what was the reason for the cover-up? What was there to possibly hide, since the debris Marcel himself had helped recover was on display in Ramey's office?

FLYING SAUCER OR WEATHER BALLOON?

According to the pro-UFO Roswell authors, specifically Friedman, Randle, and Schmitt, the debris photographed inside General Ramey's office is *not* the material Jesse Marcel and Sheridan Cavitt recovered at the Foster ranch. Instead, it is the remnants of a weather balloon that is said to have been brought in as a cover story to *hide* the true nature of the Roswell incident! In other words, the *real* "flying saucer" material that was transported on board the B-29 and escorted by Major Marcel was kept tightly under wraps.

Unfortunately for the pro-UFO Roswell advocates, the source of the claim that the wreckage in Ramey's office was substituted for that of a weather balloon is none other than, once again, Jesse Marcel. Marcel first made these claims to Stanton Friedman, as noted in chapter 2, and they later appeared in an expanded form in Berlitz and Moore's book, *The Roswell Incident*. Since it is an undisputed fact that Marcel has lied, could it be that he was telling the truth this one time?

The key to understanding (and unraveling) the truth behind Marcel's "bait and switch" claim in the Roswell enigma is a clear understanding of the items shown in the photographs that were taken in General Ramey's office by J. Bond Johnson and others. Either the photos show the *real* debris that Marcel collected and claims was part of a flying saucer, or they do not. And if the photos do not show genuine flying saucer wreckage, then they must depict a weather balloon, because that's what General Ramey said the material was. On the other hand, if the photos show neither item, then there was indeed a cover-up and General Ramey lied.

Clearly, *both* Jesse Marcel and General Ramey cannot be right, since the *same material* appears in *all* the known photos taken in Ramey's office that day. (See figures 2 through 6.)

In order to determine definitively the truthfulness of Major Marcel's substituted wreckage claim, I have analyzed in detail both the photos and the testimonies of the only other people who were in General Ramey's office when the debris was photographed. They are Colonel DuBose and Irving Newton. In a pattern that has sadly become all-too-familiar by now, it appears that Major Marcel was once again confabulating.

THE TESTIMONY OF BRIG. GEN. THOMAS J. DUBOSE

As mentioned earlier, Col. Thomas Jefferson DuBose, who later retired as a brigadier general, was present when the wreckage was

Fig. 1. (Top) The original *Roswell Daily Record* story covering the military's announcement that they have recovered a "flying disc." (Bottom) Within twenty-four hours, the Army Air Force claimed it was all a mistake; what had originally been identified as the remains of a flying disc turned out to be merely a weather balloon. (Courtesy *Roswell Daily.*)

Fig. 2. (Left) Maj. Jesse Marcel, who was dispatched to retrieve the UFO debris on behalf of the military, poses with some of the material he collected. **Fig. 3.** (Right) Despite the fact that Major Marcel claimed that the UFO debris had been switched and replaced with weather balloon wreckage for some photos, a simple visual examination proves that the same material is pictured throughout. (Photos courtesy Special Collections Division, The University of Texas at Arlington Libraries, Arlington, Texas.)

Fig. 4. Brig. Gen. Roger Ramey poses with the debris that Major Marcel mistakenly claimed was part of a "flying disc." (Photo courtesy Special Collections Division, The University of Texas at Arlington Libraries, Arlington, Texas.)

Fig. 5. (Left) The weather balloon "bait and switch" claimed by Marcel and disproved by these photos has led to the myth perpetuated by pro-UFO authors that the "saucer" wreckage was secretly substituted and spirited away by the government. (Photo courtesy Special Collections Division, The University of Texas at Arlington Libraries, Arlington, Texas.) **Fig. 6.** (Right) Since it has been proven that the debris photos show the actual material recovered near Roswell, was the object a weather balloon, or something else? (Photo courtesy UPI/Corbis-Bettman.)

Fig. 7. Unbeknownst to Major Marcel, the debris was actually the remnants of a highly classified military spy device known as Project Mogul. This picture shows one of the radar reflectors from Project Mogul up close. Compare it to the debris pictured in figures 2 through 6 and notice it is identical. (Photo courtesy U.S. Air Force.)

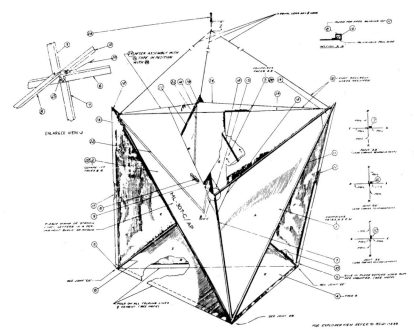

Fig. 8. An engineering specification drawing of a typical Project Mogul radar reflector.

Fig. 9. A close-up photo of the balsa wood frame and foil covering of a Mogul radar reflector.

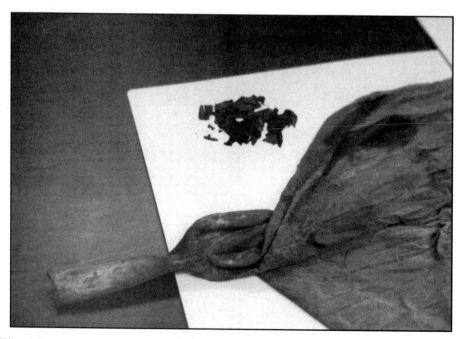

Fig. 10. A close-up view of a Mogul balloon that has been exposed to sunlight for several days. Notice that it looks like the dark material pictured in figures 2 through 6. (Photo courtesy U.S. Air Force.)

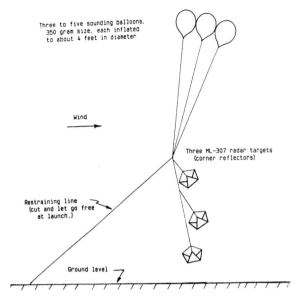

Three to five sounding balloons, 350 gram size, each inflated to about 4 feet in diameter

Wind

Three ML-307 radar targets (corner reflectors)

Restraining line (cut and let go free at launch.)

Ground level

Fig. 11. This drawing shows a Project Mogul balloon array in flight and how the multiple radar reflectors, which were used for tracking purposes, would appear when suspended in the air. (Photo courtesy U.S. Air Force.)

Fig. 12. An actual Project Mogul device after launch. (Photo courtesy U.S. Air Force.)

Fig. 13. Major Marcel's performance was reviewed by his commanding officers just after the Roswell incident. Marcel's tendency to exaggerate things was specifically noted. (Courtesy U.S. Air Force.)

Fig. 14. Marcel's career in the Air Force ended abruptly and unceremoniously when his sister asked him to resign and take over care of their mother because she was unable to do so any longer. (Courtesy U.S. Air Force.)

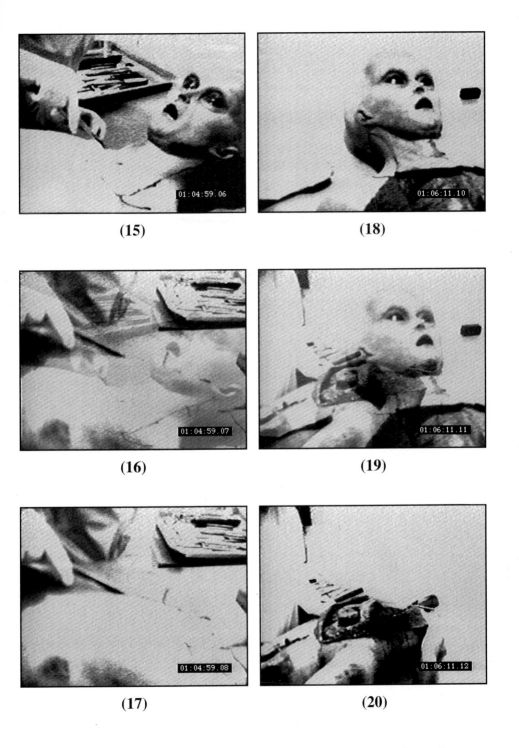

Figs. 15-20. These are stills from the infamous alien autopsy hoax footage. Evidence of abrupt "jump cutting" and other anomalies prove that the film has been heavily edited, contrary to the claims of promoters.

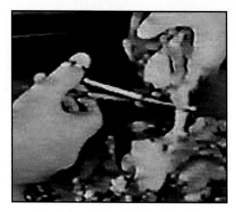

Figs. 21-22. One of the many problems with the autopsy film is that the activities it shows are inconsistent with a real autopsy. A good example is how the alleged pathologist holds the scissors—incorrectly. Figure 22 (Right), which is from a real U.S. Army autopsy, shows the correct position of the fingers, with the forefinger used to steady the scissors. (Figure 22 courtesy U.S. Army.)

Fig. 23. The film canister labels from the alien autopsy film, according to Ray Santilli, the film's chief promoter. The eagle stamp is from the Department of Defense, which did not exist in June and July 1947.

Fig. 24. The alleged cameraman who supposedly shot the alien autopsy footage. Whether he exists or not (this could be an actor), a global search is underway to find and identify him. Anyone who thinks he or she can identify this person is encouraged to notify the author, who will then contact the appropriate legal authorities. A reward has been posted for the arrest and prosecution of those behind the alien autopsy hoax.

brought into General Ramey's office. There's no disputing this fact, because DuBose *himself* met the B-29 when it arrived at Fort Worth from Roswell carrying the debris that Major Marcel had collected. DuBose had received his orders to meet the incoming plane via a telephone call directly from Gen. Clements McMullen in Washington. Prior to this, McMullen had phoned Colonel Blanchard and ordered him to send the debris on to General Ramey.[16]

DuBose not only greeted the incoming plane, but *hand carried the wreckage remnants* in a sealed canvas mail pouch, immediately escorting it to General Ramey's office.

In a revealing interview he granted to UFO researcher and television producer Jamie Shandera, DuBose put to rest the "mystery" of the so-called substituted wreckage and has exposed it for what it is—another Major Marcel myth! The initials "JHS" stand for Jamie H. Shandera, and the initials "GTD" denote Gen. Thomas DuBose:

> JHS: There are two researchers (Don Schmitt and Kevin Randle) who are presently saying that the debris in General Ramey's office had been switched and that you men had a weather balloon there.
>
> GTD: Oh Bull! *That material was never switched!*
>
> JHS: So what you're saying is that the material in General Ramey's office was the *actual debris brought in from Roswell?*
>
> GTD: That's absolutely right.
>
> JHS: Could General Ramey or someone else have ordered a switch without you knowing it?
>
> GTD: I have damn good eyesight—well, it was better back then than it is now—and I was there, and I had charge of that material, and it was *never switched.* [Emphasis added.][17]

In a second interview with Jamie Shandera, General DuBose was asked a series of questions again regarding the debris that was on the floor in Ramey's office. This time, in advance of this second interview, DuBose was mailed photographs of the debris that J. Bond Johnson and others had taken to see if it bore any resemblance to the material he remembers personally observing. Here was General DuBose's reply:

JHS: Did you get a chance to read the material and look at the pictures?

GTD: Yes, and I studied the pictures very carefully.

JHS: Do you recognize that material?

GTD: Oh yes. *That's the material that Marcel brought into Ft. Worth from Roswell.* [Emphasis added.][18]

In a third interview conducted a couple of weeks later by Shandera while visiting DuBose's home in Florida, the general related the following details:

JHS: Now, as to this Roswell business—let's begin with when Jesse Marcel came over from Roswell with this material.

GTD: Yes. Well, as best I can recall, I met the airplane that came in from Roswell and I took a canvas mail pouch with this debris in it over to General Ramey's office. . . .

JHS: Did you see additional debris on the plane?

GTD: No, I was just handed this canvas mail pouch with the stuff in it, and [I] headed *straight to Roger's [General Ramey's] office.* [Emphasis added.]

JHS: Now again, these other researchers (Schmitt, Randle, and Friedman) are saying that you guys switched this stuff and that this stuff was some kind of a weather balloon, and that you did that to fool the press and the press never saw any of the real stuff.

GTD: Nah.[19]

It is important to remember again that General DuBose was handed the material directly in a *sealed pouch* when it was unloaded from the B-29 that had flown in from Roswell. Once in DuBose's custody, the debris was marched *immediately* to Ramey's office and laid out on the floor for everyone to see. As DuBose put it in one of his interviews with Shandera, "it was a bunch of trash. We unbuckled it [the mail pouch] and laid it out on the floor. It was cold potatoes as far as I was concerned."[20]

THE TESTIMONY OF IRVING NEWTON

As mentioned earlier, Warrant Officer Irving Newton was summoned by General Ramey to provide his input on what the material that Major Marcel had recovered on the Foster ranch was. The following statement is from a signed, personal affidavit (obtained from Air Force records) that Irving Newton made on July 21, 1994.

As I recall it was July 1947, I was then a Warrant Officer with seven years service. I was the only weather forecaster on duty in the Fort Worth base weather and flight service center. The base weather covered only the base, the flight service center covered most of the southwest states. I received a call from someone in General Ramey's office who asked that I go to the general's office. I informed him that I was the only forecaster on duty and could not leave. Several minutes later General Ramey himself called and said "Get your ass over here if you don't have a car take the first one with a key."

I was met at the general's office by a lieutenant colonel or colonel who told me that someone had found a flying saucer in New Mexico and they had it in the General's office. And that a flight had been set up to send it to Wright-Patterson Air Force Base, Ohio, but the General suspicioned [*sic*] that it might be meteorological equipment or something of that nature and wanted it examined by qualified meteorological personnel.

The colonel and I walked into the General's office where this supposed flying saucer was laying all over the floor. As soon as I saw it, I giggled and asked if that was the flying saucer. I was told it was.

Several people were in the room when I went in, among them, General Ramey, a couple of press people, a major I learned to be Major Marcel and some other folks. Someone introduced Major Marcel as the person who found this material.

I told them that this was a balloon and a Rawin target. I believed this because I had seen many of these before. They were normally launched by a special crew and followed by a ground radar unit. They [the balloon devices] provided a higher altitude winds aloft [reading]. We did not use them at Fort Worth. However, I was familiar with them because we used them and their products on various projects in which I was involved. These were used mostly on special projects and overseas.

The balloon was made out of a rubber-type expandable material and when launched was about six to eight feet across. When the balloons got to altitude they expanded to twenty feet or more.

The target was used for radar reflections and I believe each leg of the target was approximately 48 inches. It resembled a child's jack (like a child's ball and jacks set) with a metallic material between the legs. The legs were made of material appearing to be like balsa wood kite sticks but much tougher.

While I was examining the debris, Major Marcel was picking up pieces of the target sticks and trying to convince me that some notations on the sticks were alien writings. There were figures on the sticks lavender or pink in color, appeared to be weather faded markings with no rhyme or reason. He did not convince me these were alien writings.

I was convinced at the time that this was a balloon with a Rawin target and remain convinced.

I remember hearing the general tell someone to cancel the flight, the flight to Wright-Patterson.

While in the office several pictures were taken of Major Marcel, General Ramey, myself, and others.

I was dismissed and went to my office to resume my normal duties.

During the ensuing years I have been interviewed by many authors, I have been quoted and misquoted. The facts remain as indicated above. I was not influenced during the original interview, nor today, to provide anything but what I know to be true, that is, the material I saw in General Ramey's office was the remains of a balloon and a Rawin target.[21]

Randle and Schmitt quote an interview with Irving Newton, who remarks on how Jesse Marcel was trying to make it seem like the weather ballon explanation wouldn't fit: "But Marcel did point to portions of the balloon and asked if Newton if was sure that these features would be found on a normal balloon. Newton said that he thought Marcel was trying to save face and not seem to be a jerk who couldn't tell the difference between a balloon and something extraordinary."[22]

While this is a significant revelation by Newton about Major Marcel and should not be taken lightly, Randle and Schmitt nonetheless dismiss it entirely. Indeed, by the time their sequel book,

The Truth about the UFO Crash at Roswell, was released, the authors make a brazen attempt to make an excuse for Major Marcel in describing this same scene:

> But according to Newton, "The major kept pointing to portions of the balloon to ask if I thought it would be found on a regular balloon." Newton said he had the impression the major was trying to save face and not appear to be a fool who couldn't tell the difference from a normal balloon and something from outer space.
>
> It is not clear if this major was Marcel or Maj. Charles Cashon, the PIO [Public Information Officer]. Newton knew neither man. Cashon, as part of his job, might have been trying to sell the balloon explanation to the press. Marcel, as an officer trained in radar operations, and the group air intelligence officer, should have been able to identify a balloon, even one as ripped up as the one in Ramey's office. In fact, forty years after the report, weather casters at various TV stations were able to identify the wreckage of the balloon from the photos taken in Ramey's office.[23]

While it may not have been clear to Randle and Schmitt to whom Newton was referring, it was certainly obvious to Newton. As he indicates in his sworn affidavit, Newton was talking about Major Marcel, *not* Major Cashon.

Randle and Schmitt's additional claim that "Marcel, as an officer trained in radar operations, and the group air intelligence officer, should have been able to identify a balloon," is a blatant attempt by the authors to make Jesse Marcel's version of events appear credible.

Obviously, Randle and Schmitt *never bothered reviewing* Major Marcel's military file like UFO researcher Robert Todd and I have. If they had done so, it would have been obvious to them that Major Marcel was *never* trained in the identification of weather balloons, especially those with radar reflectors, the remnants of which Marcel himself is shown holding up while displaying an awkward look on his face in two of the photographs that were taken in Ramey's office! (See figure 2.)

Randle and Schmitt's last statement, that "weather casters at various TV stations were able to identify the wreckage of the balloon from photos taken" is pure window dressing and irrelevant. Just like weather casters today can easily identify satellites and personal computers, Randle and Schmitt conveniently forget that the Roswell incident took place in *1947*. If anything, it was *less likely* fifty years ago that weather balloons could be identified as such. There is no way to credibly compare the weather forecasters of today, with their modern knowledge, training, and technologies, with what Jesse Marcel *thinks* he knew back in 1947, based on his boastful interviews. The Randle/Schmitt comparison is simply absurd.

Finally, those who wish to independently research the Randle/Schmitt claim that modern meteorologists were able to identify the balloon from the photos are unable to do so. All the authors say in their notation is "Based on the review of [the debris in] the photographs from Ramey's office by various weather forecasters."[24] Conveniently, Randle and Schmitt never identify who these "weather forecasters" are, nor do they provide any other information. We are just assured that they exist, which makes it even more ironic that they should use such a "reference" to buttress their argument in their attempt to save Marcel's credibility.

Now that we have observed that the testimonies of DuBose and Newton are at odds with the account provided by Maj. Jesse Marcel, where does this leave us? Is it possible that the Roswell hysteria was really over nothing more than a misidentified weather balloon? Could Jesse Marcel actually have made the kind of mistake that seems to be indicated here?

THE TESTIMONY OF SHERIDAN CAVITT

In addition to DuBose and Newton, CIC Agent Sheridan Cavitt, who was with Maj. Jesse Marcel during the recovery of the debris at the Foster ranch, was also contacted in 1994 and deposed by Air Force officials (who released him from his national security oath). Although Cavitt was *not* in General Ramey's office, he was shown J. Bond Johnson's photographs and was asked if he thought they depicted the material that he and Major Marcel collected.

In a signed, sworn statement, dated May 24, 1994, included in Pentagon Air Force files, Cavitt was very specific about what his recollections were. These remarks by Sheridan Cavitt have *never been never published* in any of the pro-UFO Roswell books. In fact, in an ironic twist, Cavitt made the following sworn affidavit after viewing copies of Johnson's photographs in Randle and Schmitt's book *UFO Crash at Roswell*!

> I was a Counterintelligence Corp (CIC) Special Agent for the U.S. Army Air Force who was initially assigned to Roswell Army Air Force following my graduation from CIC school at Ft. Holabird, MD, in late June or early July, 1947.
>
> Shortly after arriving at Roswell, New Mexico, in that time frame I had occasion to accompany one of my subordinates, M.Sgt. Lewis Rickett, CIC, and Maj. Jesse Marcel, Intelligence Officer of the 509th Bomb Group, to a ranchland area outside of Roswell to recover some material. I think that this request may have come directly from Major Marcel. I do not know who may have made the report to him. To the best of my knowledge, the three of us traveled to the aforementioned ranch land area by ourselves (that is, no other persons, civilian or military, were with us). I believe we had a military jeep that Marcel checked out to make this trip.
>
> When we got to this location we subsequently located some debris which appeared to me to resemble bamboo type square sticks one-quarter- to one-half-inch square, that were very light, as well as some sort of metallic reflecting material that was also very light. I also vaguely recall some sort of black box (like a weather instrument).
>
> The area of this debris was very small, about 20 feet square, and the material was spread on the ground, but there was no gouge or crater or other obvious sign of impact.
>
> I remember recognizing this material as being consistent with a weather balloon. We gathered up some of this material, which would easily fit into one vehicle. There certainly wasn't a lot of this material, or enough to make up crates of it for multiple flights. What Marcel did with this material at the time was unknown to me, although I know now from reading about this incident in numerous books that it was taken to Eighth Air Force headquarters in Fort Worth where it was subsequently identified as a weather balloon, which I thought it was all along.
>
> I have reviewed the pictures in the 1991 book by Randle and Schmitt on the *UFO Crash at Roswell* wherein Marcel and

Ramey are holding up this material and it appears to be the same type of material that we picked up from the ranch land.

I did not make a report on this incident to my headquarters since I felt that the recovery of a weather balloon was not a big deal that did not merit a written report. In the same referenced book by Randle and Schmitt I was reputed to have told Rickett (on page 63) that we were never there and this incident never happened. The book seems to imply this was in some sort of conspiratorial tone; however it is more likely I told him not to mention it to our head-quarters because we had wasted our time recovering a balloon.

I only went to this area once and recovered debris once and to the best of my knowledge there was [sic] no other efforts to go back there. If there were, they did not involve me.

There was no secretive effort or heightened security regarding this incident or any unusual expenditure of manpower at the base to deal with it. In fact, I do not recall the incident being mentioned again as being any big deal and I never even thought about it again until well after I retired from the military when I began to be contacted by UFO researchers.

Many of the things I have mentioned to these people have either been taken out of context, misrepresented, or just plain made up. I did know both Jesse Marcel and Lewis Rickett very well (both are now deceased). I considered them to be good men, however both did tend to exaggerate things on occasion.

With regards to claims that we tested this material by hitting it with sledgehammers without damaging it, I do not recall any of us doing so. I also did not test this material for radioactivity with a Geiger counter (or anything else).

I do not recall attempting to burn any of this debris but my wife tells me she recalled that Jesse Marcel, his wife and son, did have a small piece that they held over the fire when we had a cookout.

In short, I did help recover some debris near Roswell, New Mexico, in the summer of 1947. I thought at the time and think so now, that this debris was from a crashed balloon.

I am not part of any conspiracy to withhold information from anyone, either the U.S. Government or the American public. . . .

My bottom line is that this whole incident was no big deal and it certainly did not involve anything extraterrestrial.[25]

Now the we have examined the testimonies of three people who actually saw the material that Marcel recovered and have established that the J. Bond Johnson photographs depict that material, was the whole Roswell episode caused by something as simple as the mistaken identification of a weather balloon? If so, then why wasn't anyone able to identify it as such back at Roswell Army Air Field and avoid what later turned out to be a potentially embarrassing situation? The 509th, after all, was the only nuclear air base in the world. Surely they should have been able to distinguish a simple weather balloon from a supposed flying saucer, right?

First off, one must remember that the material recovered by Marcel and Cavitt was only seen by a handful of personnel before being shipped off to General Ramey in Fort Worth. This was limited to Colonel Blanchard, his staff, Jesse Marcel, Sheridan Cavitt, and Lewis S. Rickett. Sheriff Wilcox and Mac Brazel also saw the debris of course, but in terms of trained military personnel whom one might think would be able to identify a weather balloon as such, we are limited to a few of the officers of the 509th.

Secondly, as we shall now discover, although the debris recovered by Marcel and Cavitt did indeed belong to a balloon, this was no ordinary weather balloon. There was indeed a cover-up by Gen. Roger Ramey and the Air Force to hide the specific purpose of this balloon.

DETERMINING THE TRUE IDENTITY OF THE ROSWELL OBJECT

Project Mogul was a super-secret operation in 1947 that involved the use of constant-level balloon trains* that were equipped with various instruments for intelligence-gathering purposes. Project Mogul was a classified operation begun by the United States government after the end of World War II to secretly spy on the former Soviet Union to try and determine the status of the Russian attempts to build a nuclear weapon. Project Mogul was so secret and sensitive in fact that it had a national security rating of "Top Secret A-1," equal to the original Manhattan Project (the effort to build the world's first nuclear bomb)![26] The project was so classified and compartmentalized that even Professor Charles B. Moore, the indi-

---

*Constant level balloon trains are clusters of balloons that are balanced by size, shape, and the gasses they are filled with so that they can float at a fairly consistent altitude and not continually rise up into the atmosphere.

vidual who launched most of the Mogul devices, was unaware of the operation's name himself until informed of it in 1992![27]

In a sworn affidavit, Professor Moore, now a professor emeritus at the New Mexico Mining Institute in Socorro, provided an overview of Project Mogul and specifically those features of it which certainly explain and match the descriptions of the "flying saucer" debris as testified to by the Roswell witnesses.

I was the Project Engineer for the [New York University] NYU balloon project during the 1947 time frame. I was not aware that the project had the name Mogul until 1992 when I was contacted by an individual [UFO researcher Robert Todd] who was working on some research related to the "Roswell Incident" and the relationship to the NYU balloon project.

Our only purpose for the NYU group was to develop constant level balloons. In the early flights at Alamogordo, starting in June 1947, we used radar targets to track the balloons (not all the balloons had targets). Some of the targets were apparently manufactured by a toy or novelty company. Ed Istvan was the procurement officer. . . . The early balloons were made of neoprene. . . .

The neoprene balloons were susceptible to degradation in sunlight turning from a translucent milky white to a dark brown. Some of the material would almost look like dark gray or black flakes or ashes after exposure to the sun for only a few days. The balloon material and radar target material would be scattered after returning to the earth depending on the surface winds. The balloon material also had a peculiar acrid odor due to plasticizers and anti-oxidants.*

There is a recollection from another procurement person (Peterson) that he had obtained radar reflectors from a toy manufacturer. I have a specific recollection of reinforcing tape applied to the seams of the reflectors that had some symbols such as arcs, flowers, circles, and diamonds. These were pinkish in color.

To my knowledge, there were no radar reflectors in New Mexico in 1947 like the ones we used until the NYU group arrived. The Columbia group was primarily involved in developing low frequency microphones for long range detection of

---

*Plasticizers strengthen the material and anti-oxidants prevent the balloon material from becoming brittle in the atmosphere.

explosions. There was intense pressure for these developments, the constant altitude balloons and the microphone gear. . . .

Concerning the make up of the balloon trains, we used braided or twisted nylon lines—there were no monofilament lines [rope made from a single strand of fiber] during the 1947 time frame. Some of the balloons in early June carried radar targets for tracking purposes since we did not have radiosonde receivers [which could pick up information transmitted via radio waves] with us. Some also carried sonobuoys for detecting the pressure waves where we didn't have the Watson Lab microphone gear.* All the radiosondes were covered in white painted cardboard; I don't recall the color of the sonobuoys but I believe they were covered in metal.

On review of the photos in the Randle/Schmitt book, the material looks like one of our balloon and target assemblies. The wooden beams were made of balsa wood that had been coated in an Elmer's-like glue. The targets had eyelets where the various strings were attached. . . .

I think that Flight #4 was the flight that was launched from Alamogordo on June 4, 1947. This is based on Dr. Crary's actual diary of the launch and other events. This is also one of those events where we went to multiple radar targets because we were not having good success with single targets. This flight was with multiple balloons and targets and may have had a sonobuoy. . . .

The Watson Lab gear was the microphone equipment specifically for Mogul. The idea was proposed in a 1945 letter from Dr. Ewing . . . to Glen Spaatz that we might be able to detect nuclear blasts via pressure waves and low frequency microphones. This was developed from a study of the 1883 Krakatoa explosion where pressure waves circled the earth seven times. . . .

In December 1946, Dr. Crary was sent to Alamogordo to run the field stations for Mogul. There were several ground microphone sites for detecting blasts (bombs) detonated off the New Jersey coast. He also initiated activities off Bermuda and Panama. Dr. Crary and Dr. Peoples were the advance people and scientific monitors for our project. Dr. Peoples told us to use the cover story of meteorology and to enforce the need-to-know†—

---

*Watson Laboratories held contracts which related to Project Mogul.

†"Need-to-know" refers to a security compartmentalization policy. For example, two scientists can have the same security clearances working on two dif-

in fact I have been reluctant to discuss any of this until only a few years ago. Your letter [from the Secretary of the Air Force granting amnesty to any and all persons who wished to discuss the events surrounding Roswell] is the first official document I've seen that says this is declassified. . . .

Our new hires were not even aware of the purpose. They thought they were just handling meteorological equipment. Any of the flights that had "tags" would have stated, "Research Balloon Flight, Request Return to NYU." The "service flights" for Dr. Peoples were specific ones carrying the microphone gear. The radar test flights were not recorded. There was a lot of pressure to develop the constant level balloons. The tracking was to be done by the Watson Labs radar for the V-2 launches, etc. Starting in early June, 1947 the 307(B) targets came from NYU. We also launched TNT on some of the balloons to simulate airbursts for detection. All of these balloons were accounted for. These and the radar test flights had no tags—we did not want these to be associated with our project and the explosive ones would all be destroyed with pressure switches.* To my knowledge, the NYU group were the only ones using balloons in New Mexico during this time but others were involved in other activities so debris from rockets, aircraft dropsondes,† etc. may have been found throughout this area. Initially we did not coordinate any of our balloon launches with the Civil Aeronautics Administration. We had no contact with any of the Roswell [Army Air Field base] personnel—although Drs. Crary or Peoples may have. There were two July 8th press releases: in the earlier release, Col. J. D. Ryan stated that radar reflectors were being used to track balloons for wind information. July 8th is the same day the NYU group returned to NYU, so we had no contact with the Roswell personnel when the announcement was made concerning having

---

ferent projects. However, because of security classification procedures, one person may not know what the other is working on unless they have a "need to know" or it is pertinent to their job. The need to know classification even allows officers of lower rank to withhold information from superiors who do not have a legitimate security reason to know certain facts.

*Pressure switches are switches that are triggered once the balloons reach a pre-set altitude or barometric level.

†Dropsondes are radiosondes which are dropped to the ground as opposed to launched in the air.

found the "debris." When we heard the news back in New York, we joked that they probably found one of our balloons. From this time up until about 1980, no one, officially or otherwise, made any contact with me concerning possible association between Mogul and the "Roswell incident" (it was in about 1980 that William Moore contacted me and asked questions about balloons making "gouges" in the earth). The July 10th *Alamogordo News* article shows a demonstration of some of our multiple balloons and target trains. We had no one there so it was surprising to see this. It almost appears that there was some type of "umbrella cover story" to protect our work with Mogul.

I can think of no other explanation for Roswell than one of our early June service flight balloons. If one of our balloons went down there was no shroud of secrecy about it. We would attempt to recover the flight gear when possible, but the reflectors, balloons, and microphone equipment was [*sic*] expendable.

We went to no great effort to recover the equipment and we certainly would not cordon off an area where one of our balloons went down. We would sometimes send out 3–4 men to recover the equipment if we knew where it went down. The July 10th *Alamogordo News* report was a good cover—it does not appear to be a coincidence—I don't know who may have initiated it. [Adm. Albert] Trakowski [Project Mogul officer] does not recall being involved in a cover story in one of my conversations with him.

In New Mexico during 1947, all of our balloon operations were launched from Alamogordo [Army Air Field].[28]

It should be noted that Professor Moore's descriptions of the various components of the Project Mogul balloon arrays are *virtually identical* to what many of the Roswell witnesses, with the exception of Jesse Marcel, have described.

In her sworn, personal affidavit of September 22, 1993 (available from the Fund for UFO Research), Bessie Brazel Schreiber described the material her father had recovered at the Foster ranch:

The debris looked like large pieces of a balloon which had burst. The pieces were small, the largest I remember measuring about the same as the diameter of a basketball. Most of it was kind of a double-sided material, foil-like on one side and rubber-like on the other. Both sides were grayish silver in color, the foil more silvery than the rubber. Sticks, like kite sticks, were attached to some of the pieces with a whitish tape. The tape was about two or three inches wide and had flower-like designs on it. The "flowers" were faint, a variety of pastel colors, and reminded me of Japanese paintings in which the flowers are not at all connected. I do not recall any other types of material or markings, nor do I remember seeing gouges in the ground or any other signs that anything may have hit the ground.

The foil-rubber material could not be torn like ordinary aluminum foil can be torn. I do not recall anything else about the strength or other properties of what we picked up.[29]

For those who seriously believe that the Roswell Incident involves a crashed UFO, the question now becomes what type of supposedly "extraterrestrial" flying saucer would be built from kite sticks, tape with symbols on it, and aluminum foil? The answer is probably none, but these are the precise components of a Project Mogul device!

In an interview conducted on June 8, 1994, by Capt. James McAndrew, Professor Charles Moore elaborated on specific aspects of Project Mogul and how they relate to the Roswell incident as it is known today.

Q: They [UFO researchers] talk in terms of the material, being able to crumple it and releasing it, and it would unfold by itself and not leave any creases. This material looks like it could almost be like aluminum foil, would crease and remain creased.

A: It [the material] does have this paper laminate, and the paper, I think, was maybe a bit tougher than on the earlier [versions of Project Mogul]. But I have no explanation for the fact that it couldn't be bent with a sledge hammer, as one of the people said, and couldn't be . . .

Q: Burned?

A: I think some of the balsa wood was dipped in something like Elmer's glue, and as a result had some sort of a glue coating on which it would make it somewhat resistant to burning.

Q: I know in discussions with Sheridan Cavitt, [the interviewers] talked about the aspect of burning. He did not recall burning anything, but then his wife indicated that there had been one night they'd been out and had a barbeque and had a few beers and that Jesse Marcel just took a piece and stuck it in the barbeque and then pulled it out. So if that's what they're using to say it wouldn't burn, that's not what we consider typically testing a material for burning or not.

Going back to the reinforcing tape and things, there were descriptions concerning unusual symbols and almost like hiero-glyphics—purple, pinkish in nature, that sort of thing.

A: Robert Todd, who has been a person very interested in trying to get to the truth of this, asked me to make a sketch of what I remember. A couple of years ago, or a year or so ago, I made this sketch, and this is my memory of what was there. [See page 248 for sketch.]

I do remember every time I prepared one of these targets for flight, I always wondered why these figures were on the tape. There was always a question of why they were there. When this purplish-pink marking on the debris came up, I immediately remembered that sort of marking. Other people, I have a letter here from one of my technicians, who says oddly he remembers the same marking. You, perhaps, have talked to Albert Trakowski . . .

Q: We have tried to reach Colonel Trakowski, and he has not returned our calls. We've left messages on his answering machine, and there's been no response. . . .

A: Anyway, Albert Trakowski was the Watson Laboratory pro-ject officer on this. When I raised this question to him he said he had talked to John Peterson, one of Colonel Duffy's procurement men, and they were joking about these markings on the tape. I have a letter that I can give you a copy of in which I quote Trakowski in saying, "What do you expect when you have targets made by a toy factory in Manhattan [New York City]?"

Q: So, essentially, the original targets were made by a toy com-pany?

A: Well, it's either a toy company or . . . it was a novelty company. I talked to Ed Istvan who was another one of the Air Force liaison office people who stayed in. Istvan . . . got involved with them because they made radar chaff. In the early days of this effort, there were a number of different targets made. I don't have them here, I have them downstairs. . . . These are balloon fragments, things that held balloons [up] after they'd been exposed to the sun.

Q: (Examining the balloon fragments) Is this the neoprene type or the . . .

A: That's the neoprene type. I have the polyethylene type . . .

Q: Is this from the '47 era?

A: That's a balloon probably from the '50s . . . and that's the way they look after they've been out in the sun. That's about three weeks' exposure to sunlight here in New Mexico.

Q: So the polyethylene really is degraded by sunlight.

A: That's neoprene. All that's neoprene.

Q: This almost looks like ashes of paper.

A: That's right. And there's a big point in some of the recovery that the material was black.

Q: So it appears as though you, yourself, have done some extensive research into this particular incident.

A: Until two years ago, I was quite convinced one of our polyethylene balloons we didn't recover caused it. Then I got this newspaper, [UFO researcher Robert] Todd sent me this, and I immediately saw there's no way that [the Roswell object] could be a polyethylene balloon. . . .

Q: . . . Going back to Brazel, you state that you think it could not be one of the polyethylene balloons. He indicates in this newspaper article that he actually found the debris in mid-June, however it didn't subsequently come out until July.

A: You're right. That is in one of the polyethylene balloons, you're correct. I fall back on my plea that my memory isn't . . .

Q: (interrupting) It comes into depending on what Brazel was speaking about.

A: . . . He [Brazel] talks about the smoky gray rubber . . .

Q: (interrupting) Which these samples here, as you say, if they'd only been out for a short time, a matter of days, smoky gray, that's a very good description of what they looked like.

A: And when you first retrieve it, it has a bad odor. And people talked about there being a burned odor [in General Ramey's office].

Q: The reinforcing tape on these balloons, these polyethylene balloons, we were told this is a type of acetate. It had none of this symbology, is that correct?

A: None at all.

Q: So the symbology on the tape was only related to the radar reflectors.

A: That's correct. Here is a later model polyethylene balloon, and it's a little thinner than the ones we were flying, but there's a polyethylene balloon.

Q: Obviously, you could tear this.

A: This was four mil [millimeters thick]. These balloons that we had . . . (pause) That's [Mogul] Flight 8. These are the little balloons here that are seen from the air.

Q: From a B-17?

A: I think this was a C-54. We did, indeed, have B-17s attached to us, and C-54s. But I think this was trying to chase Flight 8 down [to recover it]. This was one of the candidate flights I thought might have been, until two years ago, I thought might have been an explanation for what occurred [in Roswell].

Q: Why did you change your mind at that point?

A: Because of that newspaper report right there.

Q: Because of [Brazel] saying that he actually found the material in mid-June?

A: No, because he said it was balsa sticks and smoky rubber and had those curious markings on that. That's a very vivid memory I have of these markings on the radar targets we flew.

Q: You said you often wondered why those markings were there. Had you ever resolved that for yourself?

A: Only what Albert Trakowski told me, that our friend John Peterson, [one of] the procurement [men], was just joking, "What else do you expect when you have your targets made by a toy factory?"

Q: Speaking of nylon line, were these braided type lines or were they monofilament type lines?

A: Neither. I think initially we used either parachute cord, which was braided. I don't remember the details of what we used, but . . . the radiosonde cord we used was not strong enough at all to hold the forces that came, so we went to what was called lobster twine. We used a lot of lobster twine that was twisted, a laid line that was used in lobster nets.

Q: There were discussions about what appeared to be unbraided or unstranded fiber type lines. It's been alluded to that [the materials that were found] were the precursor to what we use for fiber optics today. . . . That's why I asked about the monofilament line.

A: A lot of what we used early was a linen cord, not twisted, and it was indeed a brown, dull brown color. But because it was designed just for radiosonde balloons, and we rapidly exceeded its strength. So very quickly, and I don't know when, but we very quickly went over to this twisted lobster twine.

To answer your question, there are three flights that are missing [from your list] here—two, three, and four. I've identified Flight 4. Flight 4 was a flight we made, and you don't have it there, but Flight 4 we made in Alamogordo something like June 2nd or 3rd of 1947. The reason I have it identified is I have Albert Crary's diary. The scientific end of the group was heavily based from Columbia University. It was Dr. James Peoples who was an employee of Watson Laboratory, and there was an Albert Crary who had been a graduate student under Dr. Ewing.

Q: Of course the issue of the large [debris] area has been different in different reports. Different people have stated . . . 200 yards, Cavitt . . . described it in terms of his living room, which is not that large.

A: Even a single target, if it came down, wouldn't have filled a single living room, but a multiple target, being dragged sideways and then blown transversally by any later winds could have filled a reasonable area.

Q: And left pieces of debris everywhere. Depending on . . .

A: (interrupting) What the wind did.

The description that Brazel gave [in the newspaper article in which he was interviewed] that everything would weigh about five pounds when it was all together, is more than you would have gotten from a single balloon.

Q: You indicated that the balsa wood was coated with some sort of glue such as Elmer's glue.

A: That's my memory. It wasn't completely coated. Some of it was and some of it wasn't.

Q: Some of the balsa wood is fairly dense, as far as being durable, and one of the descriptions concerning this "wood-like" material was that you couldn't dent it with your fingernail. So if you have a fairly dense balsa wood coated with a glue, it may be quite possible that a person would not be able to put their fingernail in it.

A: That's correct. It's my memory that the reflective material was more aluminum foil than here. These are second or third generation targets, as evidenced by this picture, wherever that picture is down in here of the 1948 flight. It certainly looks more aluminum foil-like.

Q: Would anyone at Roswell Army Air Field have known about your activities, what your purpose was?

A: Not at all. In fact, we went over and tried to get into the weather station at Roswell and because of the atomic bomb security of the 509th, as I remember, we couldn't even get on the base. We drove up in a weapons carrier to the Roswell Army Air Field, and tried to get on the base because we wanted to go to the weather station, wanted to see if we could put a radiosonde receiver there. As I remember we got turned away.

Q: What about then Colonel Blanchard and General Ramey? Do you think they may have had any knowledge of what your ultimate purpose was?

A: I think not. . . .
    On the morning of this famous [Roswell] press release, July 8th, in *The Roswell Daily Record,* there is a statement about a flying disc being identified, and Col. J. D. Ryan who is in on the staff of the 8th Air Force said that the Air Force was now using radar targets to measure winds aloft in some stations.
    I find that of interest because apparently in reading some of the various things that happened in General Ramey's office, apparently someone that afternoon did think this was a radar target

that had been brought in. But the Roswell morning paper clearly showed that there was a knowledgeable person in Fort Worth.

Q: Is that in the article, the July 8th article, that Ryan made the statement?

A: Yes. Maybe not the article you're talking about.

Q: Is this the one that Walter Haut . . .

A: (interrupting) *No,* this is that morning, not the afternoon. . . .
    Here's the morning paper, "Report of flying disc found." Down here is about Col. J. D. Ryan, and he mentioned the existence of radar wind measuring equipment in the Air Force. . . .

Q: Then there's, subsequently, no mention of the radar targets until General Ramey discusses it on the 9th, talking about the material being a balloon.

A: On the afternoon of the 8th. It may have been published on the 9th, but . . .

Q: You're right. Evening of the 8th. Examination by the Army revealed last night, a high altitude weather balloon. General Ramey, Commander, 8th Air Forces, cleared up the mystery.
    (Later in the interview.) That would be the reason why there would be no one there in the area who could explain this debris that was brought in. There were no experts there who dealt with this particular type of material or radar reflector.

A: There was really no contact, at that time, as far as I know, between Peoples and Roswell, and there's no way Roswell, other than my memory of getting turned away by the MPs at the gate, there's no way that the people at Roswell would have known what was going on over at Alamogordo. When we sent people to Roswell, [Murray] Hackman [a radiosonde operator] worked out of a motel to receive [the radio transmissions from the Mogul flights].

Q: Can you think of, just in general, any other explanation for what became to so-called Roswell incident, other than what we've discussed here as far as potentially your balloon project, which at that time was a very secretive project. Is there any other explanation you can think of?

A: No, and the particulars of this case are sufficiently nearly unique, that I think no one else had anything that could have fit into providing these results. No, we were doing something that was unorthodox, using targets that, as far as I know, had not been flown before in New Mexico. There's no way that the rancher could have ever seen one. And there's no way that either Major Marcel nor General Ramey or General Ramey's people could have come up with providing a radar [reflector] to substitute for the real debris. I think there's a very high likelihood that the unusual things we were doing provided this debris.

Q: These are the pictures taken in General Ramey's office, 8th Air Force Headquarters by a news photographer of the Fort Worth *Star Telegram.* It's four pictures that show various people with some equipment, and I'd just like to know what you believe that equipment to be.

A: (Looking at photos.) . . . [T]here's no question that's a target. The only question is that there are people who allege this is a target that's been substituted for the real debris, and there are also stories where Marcel said the picture in which he appears are the real stuff, etc. That looks very much like our radar targets. And you'll notice that this does look more aluminum foilish than what I have here [in my office]. It's my memory that there was good, bright, aluminum metal foil, not painted stuff on the targets we were using. That looks like more than one target to me in the various pictures. That looks like the stuff we were flying.[30]

These remarks by Prof. Charles Moore are extremely significant with regard to the Roswell incident. Indeed, Moore's detailed description of a Project Mogul balloon device fits the Roswell "UFO" debris accounts to such a perfect degree that it cannot be dismissed. A Project Mogul device, unlike that of an alleged extraterrestrial spacecraft, as Moore's testimony makes obvious, would be comprised of aluminum foil with backing, balsa wood sticks, balloons, and tape with flowers on it. By comparison, it is reasonable to assume that a bona fide extraterrestrial spacecraft would not be constructed with such flimsy materials.

In addition to the damaging testimony of Professor Moore, Dr. Athelstan F. Spilhaus, who was the Director of Project Mogul and the NYU Balloon Project, had this to say in a personal, sworn affidavit signed on June 3, 1994 (the affidavit is contained in Air Force files):

I was the Director of the NYU Balloon Project and also involved with many other sensitive activities. Until these discussions, I had no indication of what the "Roswell incident" was.

I was involved in numerous unusual activities such as reconstruction of captured German rockets, development of drone planes and the like—such as long range balloons. The Army Air Force had seen what the Japanese had done with long range balloons, although not effective as weapons, they did initiate the long-range balloon research which led to use of balloons for the detection and collection of debris from atomic explosions.

Although I was involved in sensitive classified programs, I completed secrecy agreements for various projects, and I understand that this activity (Mogul, etc.) is now declassified and I did enforce "need to know." In part, I left NYU because the administration wanted to know too much about the various projects I was involved in. . . . Even though the war was over, the Cold War had just started and certain things were sensitive.

I recall that it was Colonel Duffy who brought me from the reserves to active duty. . . .

On the December 1947 balloon project reports the "service flights" probably refer to the then Top Secret project AFOAT (related to Project Mogul) which was to produce a report to the President when the Russians exploded an atomic device and were ready to produce a droppable atomic bomb. We coordinated all the listening posts to determine what stage the Russians were at. . . .

. . . I don't recall any specifics. Nor do I recall whether we had reward tags on all the balloons. I went many times to Alamogordo AAF and White Sands—not necessarily for balloon flights. I worked on naval activities such as the thermal affects on Sonar.

Concerning the actual balloon construction, Winzen of St. Paul, Minnesota, in association with General Mills, did most of the balloons. General Mills also did some balloon projects. . . .

. . . The polyethylene material was very durable—it was designed not to burst—you could push a sharp thing through it but it would be difficult to tear it with your hands. There was also debris collection on sticky paper.

Most of the balloon projects were not concerned with weather—that's why there weren't radiosondes on all the balloons. . . .

The balloons were made of sections and had tape reinforcements but I don't recall any specifics on the tape material. Mylar was not called that originally—it may have originated as polyethylene.

All the polyethylene we used was of a translucent material. Neoprene was used during the war, generally for meteorological and artillery firing balloons. The artillery radar tracked the balloons with corner reflectors—this gave the winds aloft [information] to assist the gunners. The radar reflectors were sheets of reflective material and they changed over time but I don't recall the details of the changes.

On reviewing Charlie Moore's letter, the acoustic detection* relates with the atomic debris collection. The reflectors were for tracking and was [*sic*] made up of metalized paper on fabric. Charlie explains the flowers—I'd heard about the flowers before, don't remember where—we used whatever we had in the experimental realm.

The targets were throw-aways—we didn't put a tag on them, maybe a radiosonde, but not a target. Such a [balloon] train would make gouges (shallow) as it was dragging the ground. We used meteorology as a cover story—it was a natural. . . .

Ramey's press conference—the Air Force position makes sense for the mistake that the PIO [Walter Haut] made in his statements. (All the NYU personnel had left Alamogordo when the "material" was brought in—someone stated that it may have been Colonel Duffy's and therefore sent it to him at Wright-Patterson—not because it was extraterrestrial). It is a logical reason to send it (the debris from the desert) there—not because it was special—Colonel Duffy was a fine officer and I'm sure he'd recognize it.

I was not aware of any association between our balloon projects and the alleged "Roswell incident" until this interview. I am not part of any conspiracy to withhold information from either the U.S. government or the American public. There is no classified information that I am withholding related to this inquiry and I have never been threatened by U.S. government persons concerning not talking about this situation.[31]

---

*The rate at which sound waves would be affected or altered due to the presence of a large explosion and the subsequent atmospheric changes.

Spilhaus's comments are most revealing, because they easily explain another aspect of the Roswell incident that pro-UFO advocates make use of, namely, the claim by General DuBose that the debris was secretly flown to Wright-Patterson Air Force base for subsequent examination. Unfortunately, the pro-UFO crowd seizes upon this fact to buttress their argument that the debris was extra-terrestrial in nature.

At the press conference General Ramey held in his office, after announcing that the Roswell material was from a weather balloon, which we *now know was a cover story,* Ramey stated to the press that the flight to Wright Field "has been cancelled."[32] However, according to General DuBose's own words, in his interviews with UFO researcher Jamie Shandera, this is not what happened.

> JHS: What happened to the material [which was photographed] in Ramey's office?
>
> GTD: Well, General [Clements] McMullen in Washington, he was under Vandenburg, but the actual head of SAC [Strategic Air Command] as designated by General Kinney, he ordered me by telephone to take that debris in Roger's [Ramey's] office and put it in a container, lock it, and send it to him in Washington by courier.
>
> JHS: Let me get this straight—General McMullen ordered you personally to take the debris in General Ramey's office and lock it in a container and send it to him by courier?
>
> GTD: That's exactly right, and he said "choose a courier you trust." So I selected [Col.] Al Clark who was the Base Commander at Carswell [Fort Worth]. I put the debris in a heavy mail pouch, sealed it and locked it. I then sealed it to the wrist of Al Clark and escorted him to a B-25 out on the runway and sent him to General McMullen in Washington.

DuBose's testimony now establishes that there were at least two flights, none of which had been "cancelled," one to Washington, D.C., and the other to Wright-Patterson Air Force Base in Ohio. It was perfectly natural for the Air Force to send the debris to Wright-Patterson for scientific examination, whether or not the material had actually come from a flying saucer, because that's where the Air Technical Intelligence Center is located and they would have the necessary labs to examine the material.

THE TESTIMONY OF COL. ALBERT TRAKOWSKI

Col. Albert Trakowski was the project officer for Mogul; in other words, he coordinated activities for the project. His predecessor had been Colonel Duffy, who had received some of the material recovered at Roswell when it arrived at his office at Wright-Patterson. In a personal, sworn affidavit dated June 29, 1994, included among the Air Force records, Trakowski related the following:

> I was the project officer [for Mogul] succeeding Colonel Duffy in approximately November 1946. My primary purpose was nuclear weapons and guided missiles detection programs. Previously, I was appointed as the laboratory chief of the Signal Corp as an Air Force officer in charge of the Spherics program and later for the development of weather radar. Since my background was in physics, I took over Project Mogul. It was the only Top Secret project at Watson Labs and I was the Top Secret Control Officer, so I knew the impacts with security associated with the project.
>
> We moved from Watson Labs to Cambridge which combined became the Air Force Cambridge Research Center, and I later became the Director of the Air Force Geophysics Lab (and remained so until 1949). Through 1949, I was director of . . . Mogul. As the Mogul director, I went to Alamogordo Army Air Field in early July 1947, to observe the New York University balloon group. The "Roswell Incident" occurred after we had returned to Red Bank[, New Jersey] (Watson Lab). I became aware of this only after Colonel Duffy called me from Wright Field from his home. This was just an informal call, he just wanted to let me know that someone had come to him with some debris from New Mexico and he said, "this sure looked like some of the stuff that you launched from Alamogordo."
>
> Duffy was very familiar with the various apparatus and materials for the project, so if he said that it was debris from the project, I'm sure that's what it was. He was not concerned with a breach of security for the project.

. . . I never observed any of the balloon "trains" but I did see some of the early reflectors. Some of the reflectors were procured from sources out[side] of normal channels. Some of the contractors lined up were not quite in concert with typical Signal Corps practices and procedures.

Jack Peterson was very energetic and could make procurement actions take place. Ed Itsvan, who I believe actually arranged for production for some of the reflectors, actually went to a toy manufacturer in New York city to get some. It was kind of a standing joke.

I remember that some of the prototype and pre-production targets had this pink or purplish tape holding the material to the balsa beam. This tape had flowers and other designs on it.

The reflectors were probably made starting in late 1944 but I do not recall how long the production run was. I do not recall any other specific attributes but they were geometrically and structurally simple.

I am not part of any conspiracy to withhold information from either the U.S. government or American public. There is no classified information that I am withholding related to this inquiry and I have never been threatened by U.S. government persons concerning refraining from talking about this situation.[33]

OTHER MOGUL FACTORS

Other factors to consider when trying to link a project Mogul balloon train with the debris recovered near Roswell at the Foster ranch have to do with the direction that the debris was oriented and the overall amount of the material allegedly collected.

Regarding the orientation of the debris, Kevin Randle has gone on record as claiming he has "disproved" the Mogul explanation by using the winds aloft information for the area. This includes information pertaining to high altitude winds, and it is a factor all airborne objects (especially those without any means of propulsion) must contend with. However, because Randle has no expertise in this field, his "explanation" is demonstrably false has come back to haunt him.

In his book *Roswell UFO Crash Update,* a good portion of which tries in vain to refute the Mogul explanation, Randle in a section called "Winds Aloft and Project Mogul: Late Breaking Facts" stated: "The winds aloft data, however, tend to eliminate the Mogul balloons. Couple that to eyewitness testimony, the lack of documentation supporting any other theory, and the conclusions become evident. The Project Mogul balloons were not responsible for the debris found by Mac Brazel and therefore, do nothing to explain the events."[34]

Randle's "reasoning" is that

> The national Climactic Data center in Asheville, [North Carolina,] has microfilmed copies of the winds aloft charts for 1947. While these charts cannot prove that what fell on the Brazel ranch was a project Mogul balloon, they can exclude it. If the winds were blowing in the wrong direction, then it is clear that the balloons would have travelled away from the ranch. If, however, they were blowing in the right direction, the winds aloft data can only show it was possible for a Mogul balloon to have fallen on the ranch.
>
> Four [weather-tracking] stations are of relevance to us. These are the stations at Tucson, Arizona; El Paso, Texas; and Albuquerque and Roswell, New Mexico. No winds data are available from Alamogordo, the launching site of the Mogul balloons. . . .
>
> The relevant charts are those made at 8:30 P.M., MST on July 3, and at 2:30 A.M. on July 4. The only data for the 20,000 foot level on July 3 (8:30 P.M.) is from Albuquerque showing the wind was blowing to the west at 15 knots. At 16,000 feet the wind was blowing at Albuquerque to the northwest at 15 knots.
>
> At 2:30 the following morning, seven hours after the launch, the winds at Roswell at 20,000 feet are blowing to the northwest at 20 knots. At 16,000 feet, the wind at Roswell is blowing at 15 knots, and the wind at Albuquerque is blowing to the northeast at 25 knots. Of course, if the balloon had reached Albuquerque, the wind blowing in that direction would push it farther to the north, away from the Brazel ranch.
>
> Between Albuquerque and the Brazel ranch is the northern end of the San Andreas Mountains with peaks above 9,000 feet. If the balloon stayed aloft long enough to reach Albuquerque, the winds there would have pushed it back into the mountains. It would not have drifted to the Brazel ranch.[35]

While this might be true in Kevin Randle's mind, it does not necessarily mean that it is reality.

When Prof. Charles Moore used the Weather Service data and NYU altitude information to simulate the likely trajectories of the Mogul flights he launched with recorded ground trackings, his results showed conclusively that Randle is wrong, and that a Mogul balloon could easily have fallen on the Foster ranch. Moore is qualified to read and calculate winds aloft and other atmospheric data, whereas Randle is primarily a writer; he has not been trained to make such calculations.

As Moore provided information that was later documented by physicist Dave Thomas,

> [Moore] used the wind data for June 4, 1947, and assumed the flight reached altitudes comparable to those of the subsequent two flights (which were made of very similar balloon trains).
>
> Moore's analysis indicates that after Flight 4 lifted off from Alamogordo, it probably ascended while traveling northeast (toward Arabela), then turned toward the northwest during its passage through the stratosphere, and then descended back to earth in a general northeast direction. Moore's calculated balloon path is quite consistent with a landing at the Foster ranch, approximately 85 miles northeast of the Alamogordo launch site and 60 miles northwest of Roswell. Furthermore, the debris was strewn along the ground at a southwest-to-northwest angle (as reported by Maj. Jesse Marcel); this angle is entirely consistent with Moore's analysis.[36]

The second area of contention against the Project Mogul explanation, specifically that it was Charles Moore's Flight Number 4, is the amount of debris that was supposedly recovered.

Because the witnesses do not agree on this point (Marcel says it filled "half a B-29 full" [most likely yet another exaggeration on his part] and Cavitt said "roughly 20 feet") there's no way to objectively determine how much wreckage landed on the Foster property and was later recovered. However, contrary to what the pro-UFO Roswell authors would have us believe, a Project Mogul balloon is certainly large enough to have filled at least half of a large airplane. As the following figure shows, a Project Mogul ballon train is taller than the Washington Monument, which stands 555 feet tall, but is only about two-thirds as tall as Paris's Eiffel Tower. In fact, Flight Number 4 was more than 600 feet in length.[37]

In the book *The Roswell Incident,* Professor Charles Moore was interviewed by Bill Moore and is on record as stating that a balloon in his opinion could not have accounted for the wreckage recovered at the Foster ranch. "Based on the information you [Bill Moore] gave me, I think it could not have been our balloon."[38]

While Professor Moore has been derided by the pro-UFO community for now changing his mind, the allegation is unfounded because Moore has done no such thing. When Professor Moore was being interviewed by Bill Moore, he was answering questions about *gouges* in the earth, and was asked whether or not a balloon could have made a 500-foot gouge as has been claimed by some Roswell witnesses. If Bill Moore had asked Professor Moore about Mogul, or had shown him J. Bond Johnson's photographs taken in Ramey's office, the whole Roswell myth might have been stopped right there.

Instead, two of the photos showing Mogul wreckage in Ramey's office appear in *The Roswell Incident,* with one of them "identified" by Maj. Jesse Marcel as the "real" saucer debris, and the other, some of the "substituted" wreckage. In other words, by Marcel's *own* admission, he was photographed before the "switch" was made. However, since we now know that no substitution ever took place, because the photos showing *both* Marcel and Ramey and DuBose clearly depict the *same debris* (see figures 2–6) the Roswell object turns out *not* to have been a weather balloon as originally explained by the Air Force, but a formerly classified device that was used to spy on the Soviet Union.

Finally, in a revealing interview with Prof. Charles Moore on February 6, 1997, Moore revealed several details which proved extremely interesting.

When I asked him if he was satisfied that the device recovered by Mac Brazel was a Project Mogul balloon array, he was adamant that yes, he was in the "upper 90 percentile" that this was the case. However, Moore preferred to call the object a New York University balloon rather than a Mogul object because in 1947, due to extreme security compartmentalization, the term "Mogul" was never used.

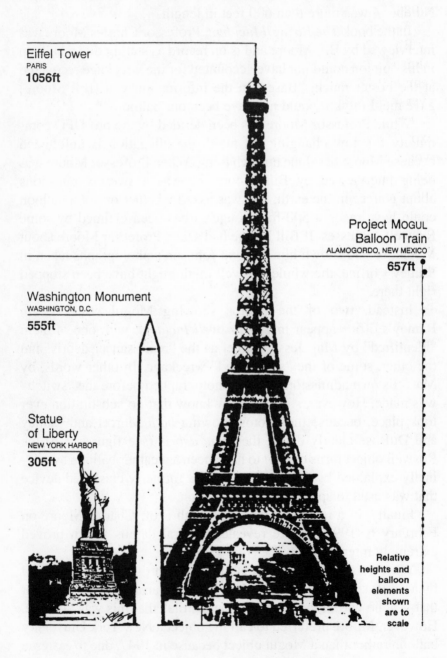

Eiffel Tower
PARIS
1056ft

Project MOGUL
Balloon Train
ALAMOGORDO, NEW MEXICO
657ft

Washington Monument
WASHINGTON, D.C.
555ft

Statue
of Liberty
NEW YORK HARBOR
305ft

Relative
heights and
balloon
elements
shown
are to
scale

It was simply known as the New York University balloon project. The U.S. military is the one that had come up with the name of Mogul.

When I recounted the descriptions of the material as described by Bill Brazel Jr. to Moore, he felt that the claims were an embellishment probably due to the passage of time. Professor Moore then reminded me of one very important point: The only description ever given by Mac Brazel, which appeared on page one of the July 9, 1947, issue of the *Roswell Daily Record,* never described such exotic materials! Indeed, according to the elder Brazel's own words, the material he found was simply "tinfoil, paper, tape, and sticks." Brazel also said that the balloon material was "smoky gray rubber" and that the whole collection weighed perhaps five pounds!

When I asked if UFO researcher Stanton Friedman had ever contacted or interviewed Professor Moore about Roswell, Moore told me that in the early 1990s Friedman had placed a newspaper ad in the local paper soliciting witnesses to Roswell. Moore then told me that he wrote to Friedman, and later met him and Don Berliner at a hotel in Socorro.

When I inquired as to how their discussion went, Moore told me bluntly that Friedman and Berliner did not want to hear his side of the story and then *accused him* and his group as being part of the "flying saucer cover-up"!

It is curious that *nowhere* in Friedman and Berliner's *Crash at Corona* is this meeting ever mentioned, nor has Friedman ever noted it in his published writings, nor has he ever refuted the overwhelming and convincing evidence that the whole Roswell "UFO" hysteria was caused by people who didn't know what the material was at the time; the discovery of which just happened to take place during that unique period of time in mid-1947 when the flying saucer craze was first sweeping America.

Yes, Virginia, there was a "cover-up," but it did not involve the remains of an extraterrestrial flying saucer!

NOTES

1. Kevin D. Randle and Donald R. Schmitt, *UFO Crash at Roswell* (New York: Avon Books, 1991), pp. 75–76.

2. Jamie H. Shandera, "New Revelations about the Roswell Wreckage: A General Speaks Up," *Focus* 5 (December 31, 1990): 9, 11.

3. Kevin D. Randle and Donald R. Schmitt, *The Truth about the UFO Crash at Roswell* (New York: Avon Books, 1994), p. 205.

4. Charles Berlitz and William L. Moore, *The Roswell Incident* (New York: Berkeley Books, 1988), p. 31.

5. Ibid., pp. 74–75.

6. George M. Eberhart, ed. *The Roswell Report: A Historical Perspective* (Chicago: Center for UFO Studies, 1991), p. 60.

7. Randle and Schmitt, *The Truth about the UFO Crash at Roswell*, p. 48.

8. Ibid., pp. 48–49.

9. Irving Newton, sworn affidavit, July 21, 1994, available from U.S. Air Force.

10. Berlitz and Moore, *The Roswell Incident*, p. 36.

11. Randle and Schmitt, *The Truth about the UFO Crash at Roswell*, p. 50.

12. Berlitz and Moore, *The Roswell Incident*, pp. 36–38.

13. Ibid., p. 33.

14. Ibid.

15. Ibid.

16. Shandera, "New Revelations about the Roswell Wreckage," p. 12.

17. Ibid., p. 9.

18. Ibid.

19. Ibid., p. 14.

20. Ibid., p. 12.

21. Newton, sworn affidavit, July 21, 1994.

22. Randle and Schmitt, *UFO Crash at Roswell,* p. 74.

23. Randle and Schmitt, *The Truth about the UFO Crash at Roswell,* p. 50.

24. Ibid., p. 279.

25. Col. Sheridan Cavitt (Ret.), sworn affidavit, May 24, 1994, available from U.S. Air Force.

26. Capt. James McAndrew, USAF, personal interview with Prof. Charles B. Moore, Socorro, New Mexico, June 8, 1994.

27. Prof. Charles B. Moore, sworn affidavit, June 8, 1994, available from U.S. Air Force.

28. Ibid.

29. Bessie Brazel Schreiber, sworn affidavit, September 22, 1993, available from the Fund for UFO Research, Mt. Ranier, Maryland.

30. McAndrew/Moore interview.

31. Dr. Athelstan F. Spilhaus, sworn affidavit, June 3, 1994, available from U.S. Air Force.

32. Berlitz and Moore, *The Roswell Incident,* p. 33.

33. Col. Albert Trakowski, sworn affidavit, June 29, 1994, available from U.S. Air Force.

34. Kevin D. Randle, *Roswell UFO Crash Update: Exposing the Military Cover-Up of the Century* (New York: Global Communications, 1995), p. 190.

35. Ibid., pp. 188–89.

36. Gillian Sender, "Roswell's Legacy: Flying Saucers and Military Cover-ups," *Skeptical Inquirer* Internet Web posting on <http://www.Rosskep.com.html>, pp. 3–4.

37. McAndrew/Moore interview.

38. Berlitz and Moore, *The Roswell Incident,* p. 41.

6

Roswell: Setting the Record Straight

If I had to rely on what's in the public record, I'd throw up. The [Roswell] evidence is not strong and it's not compelling.[1]

Since 1981, I have fielded hundreds of questions at numerous lectures concerning the alleged Roswell UFO crash of 1947. While the answers to almost all of these inquiries have been presented throughout this book, some could not be fitted within the general framework of this discussion. Therefore, this section has been included to specifically address these miscellaneous issues and questions.

QUESTION #1

Is the Showtime® movie Roswell *an accurate portrayal of the event?*

As mentioned previously, Showtime's movie is based upon a loose adaptation of Randle and Schmitt's first book, *UFO Crash at Roswell.* While it is bad enough that Randle and Schmitt's treatise contains substantial errors, some of which were later admitted by the authors,*

---

*The admission of error can be found in the authors' statement on p. xiii of Randle and Schmitt's *The Truth about the UFO Crash at Roswell.*

162

unfortunately the producers of *Roswell* decided to take additional liberties with the supposed "facts."

For example, Maj. Jesse Marcel is presented in the television movie as a hero who champions the cause to "break" the UFO-related secret surrounding Roswell. According to the movie, Marcel did this during a reunion of officers from the 509th Bomb Group. This is simply untrue, and is blatant Hollywood fiction. As noted earlier in chapter 2, if it were not for the meeting between Stanton Friedman and Maj. Jesse Marcel in 1978, it is very possible that we might never have known about Roswell today!

Another piece of fiction in the Showtime production is the ludicrous "telepathic communication" scene between the military and one of the captured, injured aliens. A photo from this scene adorns the cover of Randle and Schmitt's 1991 printing of *UFO Crash at Roswell.*

In the Showtime production, the alien "communicates" with the military brass via telepathy, informing them that while they are benevolent, there are other extraterrestrials out there who are not. The alien's message is intended to be a warning for humanity.

This scene, like several others, is pure Hollywood fantasy. Nowhere in either of the Randle and Schmitt books is this wild claim ever made. For a complete understanding of all the embellishments contained in the television movie *Roswell,* compare the contents of this book to the Showtime production, the video of which can be rented at any number of stores.

QUESTION #2

If the Roswell incident did not involve a real crashed UFO, then why did Colonel Blanchard abruptly go "on leave" and was suddenly "unavailable" after the initial press release by Walter Haut?

The myth that Colonel Blanchard "suddenly" or "conveniently" went on leave after the recovery of the "flying disc" at the Foster ranch was first started by Berlitz and Moore in their book *The Roswell Incident.*[2] The implication is that because of the alleged extraterrestrial nature of the debris found by Mac Brazel, Colonel Blanchard's "leave" was some sort of cover story to mask the true nature of what really happened: the secret recovery of a flying saucer.

In *The Truth about the UFO Crash at Roswell,* Randle and Schmitt take the Blanchard "cover story" a step further by claiming: "Blanchard's leave was a screen. It was his duty to go to the site [at the Foster ranch] and make a determination."[3] Randle and Schmitt also add that Blanchard, "along with a few members of his staff," drove out to the debris field himself.[4]

Randle reiterated this charge in 1994, by writing in an article in the July/August issue of *International UFO Reporter,* an official publication of the Center for UFO Studies, that Blanchard's leave was a cover story for "activities revolving around the [flying saucer] crash." In his article, Randle speculated that the whole diversion was created in order to allow Blanchard "to respond to the situation as necessary without having to worry about awkward questions from reporters." Finally, Randle also reasoned in his *IUR* piece that Blanchard "would not want to be off the base and out of town when the biggest event of the twentieth century took place, unless his leave was part of the cover-up."[5]

Unfortunately, there is no credible evidence that the true nature of Colonel Blanchard's leave was anything out of the ordinary. There is also no firsthand information that proves beyond a doubt that Blanchard was ever present at the Foster ranch, a claim also made by Randle and Schmitt.[6] Indeed, Blanchard's supposed "mysterious" whereabouts are easily accounted for and can be documented by anyone willing to do a proper investigation.

UFO researcher Robert Todd has studied the issue of Blanchard's leave extensively, far more than any other individual. Todd easily found a conventional explanation for Blanchard's whereabouts, and it had nothing to do with the alleged recovery of a flying saucer near Roswell.

In a rather extensive documentation package sent to me on September 2, 1996, Robert Todd was kind enough to share with me the results of his research into the issue of Blanchard's leave. The following are excerpts from what Todd discovered:

Randle's [*International UFO Reporter*] article referred to several documents [as proof], including one incorrectly cited as Headquarters, 509th Bomb Group, "Special Order" No. 9, dated July 8, 1947, which said that Lt. Col. Payne Jennings (Blanchard's second-in-command) assumed command at RAAF [Roswell Army Air Field] effective July 8th. In actuality, the document was General Orders (GO) No. 9. In Randle's . . . world, GO No. 9 is proof that Blanchard went on leave on July 8th and not on July 9th.

Why is this proof? Because, Randle claims, "Eighth Air Force would not want to create a situation whereby two commanders were on station at the same time." Yet, using that . . . "logic" peculiar to Randle, he also proclaims that "Surely Blanchard would not want to be off the base and out of town when the biggest event of the twentieth century took place," and claims that the non-leave leave freed Blanchard "to respond to the situation as necessary," clearly implying that Blanchard was in charge.

. . . The fact is that nothing prevented Blanchard from being on the base after Jennings assumed command. Jennings would have been making the decisions and giving the orders, rather than Blanchard. Only one of the men would have been in charge, even if both men were present on the base. Randle seems to be suggesting that, whenever Blanchard went on leave, he had to leave the base immediately in order to avoid upsetting the Eighth Air Force, who, Randle claims, wouldn't want two commanders "on station" at the same time! Clearly this claim is absurd on its face, and demonstrates how desperate Randle is to mislead the public into believing that every event that occurred at RAAF around the time of the Roswell incident had something to do with the Roswell incident, as if all other government business simply ceased due to the "biggest event of the twentieth century." . . .

Consequently, Randle's contention that Jennings's assumption of command on the 8th *proves* Blanchard's non-leave leave began on July 8th is *utter nonsense!* The fact that such an absurd claim originates with a former military man [Randle] who presumably should know better, makes it inexcusable. It's just another in a long list of attempts Randle has made to "explain" away uncomfortable facts that tend to show his claims about Roswell are little more than exotic fantasies.

Although Randle's article mentions the July 9th Morning Report that documents Blanchard's leave as beginning on the 9th, the article made no mention of the Morning Report for Monday, July 28th, which documents Blanchard's return to duty from his leave, effective Saturday, July 26th. Blanchard's leave was documented in two Morning Reports, and not just one. . . .

Contrary to the proclamations of the General Accounting

Office (GAO) and Congressman Schiff [D-New Mexico], not all RAAF outgoing messages from that critical time period were destroyed.* Back in 1991, I located one outgoing message, dated July 9, 1947, from the Commanding Officer, RAAF, to the Commanding General, Army Air Forces (AAF), Washington, D.C., among the incoming messages to AAF headquarters. Although the message makes no mention of the "Roswell incident," it is relevant to the case, thanks to Randle's fiction writing. The full text of the message reads:

REGARDING TWX [teletype message] AFDOI ONE FIVE ZERO DATED SEVEN JULY COLONEL WILLIAM H BLANCHARD AND MR OLIVER LAFARGE HAVE APPOINTMENT WITH GOVENOR [sic] MABRY FOR NINE JULY TO REQUEST HIS PROCLAIMING OF AIR FORCE DAY PD [period]

The message appears to have been transmitted at 1502Z (Greenwich Mean Time), or about 8:00 A.M. (MST) in New Mexico. So, at about eight o'clock on the morning of July 9th, somebody at RAAF (probably Lt. Col. Jennings, who had assumed command of the base sometime the day before) was telling AAF headquarters that Blanchard had an appointment with Governor Mabry for that very day, to request that the governor make an Air Force Day proclamation.

The designation "AFDOI" apparently stood for the "Air Force Director of Information." Unfortunately, the July 7th AFDOI message did not surface as a result of my request, but we may reasonably assume that the DOI was coordinating all activities associated with the nationwide celebration of Air Force Day, and that the July 7th message asked Blanchard about arrangements he was making.

In his book, *Roswell in Perspective,* Karl Pflock reported that he had located an Associated Press (AP) item published in the July 10, 1947, edition of the *Albuquerque Journal,* concerning Blanchard's leave. Datelined Roswell, NM, July 9, the AP item said that "William Blanchard, commanding officer of the Roswell Army Air Field, left here today [July 9th] for a three weeks vacation in Santa Fe and Colorado." Presumably, Blanchard drove to Santa Fe by automobile.

---

*Messages from approximately October 1946 through mid-1949 were destroyed because of their age and "lack of usefulness."

According to the July 9th edition of the *Albuquerque Journal,* in a story datelined July 8th, Governor and Mrs. Mabry were scheduled to leave on July 9th "on a week's automobile trip to Salt Lake City," to attend the governors' conference scheduled to begin on July 13th. Presumably Governor Mabry met with Blanchard and LaFarge before departing on this trip.

Further evidence that Blanchard did indeed go on leave and was "off the base and out of town when the biggest event of the twentieth century [supposedly] took place" can be found on page one of the July 18, 1947, edition of the RAAF base newspaper, *The Atomic Blast,* produced by then-First Lt. Walter Haut's public information office. It prints the text of a "recent" telegram Blanchard sent to the 509th congratulating them for winning first place in the Eighth Air Force Group Competition. According to the *History of Headquarters Eighth Air Force* for July 1947, scoring for the competition was completed on July 11th. As a result, Blanchard's telegram had to have been sent sometime between July 10th and July 18th.* That he sent a telegram clearly shows he was "off the base and out of town."

Additional evidence which establishes conclusively that Blanchard was "off the base and out of town" can be found in the July 15th edition of the *Albuquerque Journal,* which reported that "Acting Governor Joseph M. Montoya today [July 14th] proclaimed Aug. 1 as Air Force Day in commemoration of the Army Air Force's 40th anniversary, and the week of July 21 to 27 as New Mexico Aviation Week." The story went on to say:

"Col. William H. Blanchard, commanding officer of the Roswell Army Air Field, and Oliver LaFarge, Santa Fe author who was with the Army Transport Command during the last war and who now represents the Air Force Association, a national organization of ex-air force men which is trying to organize a 'wing' in New Mexico, were present."

In fact, page one of the July 25, 1947, edition of *The Atomic Blast* carried a photograph of Acting Governor Montoya seated at his desk in the Santa Fe State House, signing the Air Force Day proclamation, with LaFarge and Blanchard witnessing the event. *The Atomic Blast* identified LaFarge as "one of New Mexico's 'best selling' authors and a Lt. Col. in the Air Force Reserve."

---

*The 509th was so far ahead of the competitors, their victory was assured as early as July 10, 1947.

So, it appears that Blanchard was in Santa Fe from at least July 9th, when he and LaFarge were scheduled to meet with Governor Mabry to request the Air Force Day proclamation, to at least July 14th, when Acting Governor Montoya actually signed the proclamation while Governor Mabry was out of town attending the governor's conference in Salt Lake City, and while the "biggest event of the twentieth century" supposedly was being covered up at Blanchard's base, from which numerous airlifts of debris from one or more alien spacecraft supposedly were being made—while Blanchard was off attending to the far more important matter of arranging for the Air Force Day proclamation. . . .

. . . Presumably Blanchard drove on to Colorado for the remainder of his leave. Sometime between July 10th and July 18th, Blanchard sent a telegram to the 509th to congratulate them for winning first place in the Eighth Air Force Group Competition, a contest Blanchard missed because he was on leave.

QUESTION #3

If the Roswell incident did not involve a real crashed UFO, then why did Lt. Gen. Nathan F. Twining suddenly alter his schedule and head for New Mexico and abruptly cancel his planned tour at the Boeing Airplane Company in Seattle?

The belief that Lt. Gen. Nathan Twining suddenly altered his plans because of the recovery of a flying saucer in New Mexico was first championed by UFO researcher Stanton Friedman. Unfortunately, there is no credible evidence to support this contention.

In *Crash at Corona,* Friedman and Berliner write that

Twining, according to his and his pilot's flight logs, had flown to Alamogordo Army Air Field, New Mexico, on July 7, 1947, remaining in the state (with a side trip to Kirtland Air Force Base, Albuquerque) until July 11 before returning to Wright Field. In a July 17 letter to an executive of the Boeing Airplane Co. Twining wrote: "With deepest regrets we had to cancel our trip to the Boeing factory due to a very important and sudden matter that developed here." Could [Twining] have been in New Mexico in connection with the crash?[7]

While Friedman's basic premise is correct, that the recovery of an actual extraterrestrial spacecraft would probably abruptly affect the schedules of such high-powered military brass as Lt. Gen. Nathan F. Twining, unfortunately, this is not what happened.

According to a now-declassified document dated *June 5, 1947,* from Army Air Force Headquarters in Washington, D.C., and written to the commanding general, Air Materiel Command; a request was made that *confidential orders be issued* that would place Lt. Gen. Twining and others on three-days temporary duty status at Sandia Base, in Albuquerque, New Mexico. The purpose of this request was so that Twining could attend the "Bomb Commanders Course," which was scheduled to begin on July 8. The document also reveals that other high-powered brass such as Maj. Gen. Benjamin W. Chidlaw, Brig. Gen. Samuel C. Brentnall, and Brig. Gen. Arthur Thomas were also signed up to attend the same course.[8]

Visitors' logs and secretaries' calendars prove *undisputedly* that Generals Twining, Chidlaw, Brentnall, and Thomas all took the three-day course, which lasted through July 11—*the very same time window* that the pro-UFO Roswell authors would have us believe that an extraterrestrial spacecraft was being recovered! According to Air Force documents, there were also three other generals present, including George C. Kenney, the commanding general of the Strategic Air Command (SAC).[9]

It stands to reason that if an actual alien ship and its crew had been recovered near Roswell, one would expect that the schedules of at least one of these generals, especially that of Nathan Twining, would have been affected. Instead, the generals proceeded with their scheduled training and commanders course because in reality *no flying saucer had been recovered!*

The reason that Twining had to "abruptly cancel" his long-planned trip to Boeing was because the general did not receive positive confirmation of his clearance to attend the commanders course until July 3, just a few days before the event began.[10] Because of this late confirmation, Twining's subsequent travel plans had to be altered, and the trip to Boeing was canceled as a result.

QUESTION #4

What are the MJ-12 documents?

The MJ-12 documents, as they are collectively known, are a series of papers that have surfaced over the years that purportedly originate from a "supersecret group of extremely important people from the scientific, military, and intelligence fields who were/are charged with the awesome responsibility of learning everything about what crashed in New Mexico in 1947."[11]

The MJ-12 documents first surfaced on December 11, 1984, when a "mysterious" envelope was delivered to the home of Los Angeles movie producer Jamie Shandera. Shandera is a colleague of William L. Moore and together, the two of them have been researching, writing, and publishing articles about Roswell for a number of years.

The envelope contained no return address, and supposedly bore only an Albuquerque, New Mexico, postmark. Inside was an undeveloped roll of black-and-white film which, when processed, showed a purportedly classified document that claims to be a debriefing report prepared for president-elect Dwight Eisenhower. The document is dated November 18, 1952. The other item on the roll of film was a letter supposedly written by former President Harry S. Truman to Secretary of Defense James Forrestal, dated September 24, 1947.

The MJ-12 documents, if genuine, prove that the United States government has in its possession not only the remains of two crashed UFOs and their occupants, but that a super-secret committee (called MJ-12) is empowered to oversee issues regarding these subjects.

After sitting quietly on the material for over a year, Bill Moore and Stanton Friedman finally went public with their discovery after conducting some preliminary research. The two would go on to author several papers regarding the documents.

QUESTION #5

Hasn't UFO researcher Stanton T. Friedman proven that the MJ-12 documents are authentic?

No, Friedman has not, despite spending some $16,000 in research grant money attempting to do so![12]

At best, Friedman's research has uncovered only *circumstantial* evidence that indicates the MJ-12 documents *might* be authentic. However, it is important to remember that circumstantial evidence is *not* scientific or even forensic evidence. Whereas circumstantial evidence is based on *speculation,* scientific and forensic evidence is based on fact.

Friedman's investigation was hampered by the fact that there were and are *no original documents* with which to work. This is a frustrating limitation *everyone* has had to endure who has tried to examine the MJ-12 material with regard to its authenticity.

To make matters worse, Friedman was *not even provided* with the actual roll of film to study that Shandera claims he received anonymously in the mail! Instead, all Friedman had to work with were *photographs* of the documents.[13]

Without the pristine, actual documents to analyze forensically, the paper, ink, and age of the MJ-12 papers (which would prove beyond dispute their authenticity) cannot be determined. Thus, until the originals surface so that they can be properly tested, any proclamations that the MJ-12 papers are "authentic" is an exercise in faith, not fact. The MJ-12 documents, because of their dubious provenance, would not even be admissible as evidence in an American court of law.

QUESTION #6

Is it true that the late Dr. Donald H. Menzel, the famous UFO skeptic, was a member of the secret MJ-12 team?

The only "proof" that Harvard astronomer Dr. Menzel was a supposed member of MJ-12 comes from the contents of the *MJ-12 papers themselves,* whose authenticity is not only unproven, but is highly suspect.*[14] One must remember that there is no irrefutable evidence that MJ-12 ever existed, or exists presently. This aside, there is also no indisputable evidence that the late Dr. Donald Menzel was a "secret member" of the alleged MJ-12 committee.

While some UFO researchers like Stanton Friedman cite the fact that Menzel held numerous security clearances and directed classified projects as "proof" that he might have led a secret life as a member of the as-yet-to-be-proven MJ-12 committee,[15] the fact remains that such "evidence" is purely speculation, and nothing more.

In order to research this issue further, I personally viewed all of the late Dr. Donald Menzel's security files while designing and writing the software code for the Department of Defense, U.S. Pentagon, and Department of Energy's Classified Viewgraph Tracking System in November and December of 1988 while working at Lawrence Livermore National Laboratory.[16]

Dr. Menzel's extensive security files consisted of three folders, each of which listed in chronological order the projects he worked on, the security clearances he held, and most importantly, every committee and professional analysis group of which he was a part. *Nowhere in any of the three files* was there any indication that either MJ-12 existed, or that Menzel was a member of such a committee!

MJ-12 advocates will undoubtedly claim that because MJ-12 is so highly classified, references to Menzel's membership on such a committee in his files would obviously be omitted. However, this is not true.

In order to write the computer master code reference index and software "browser" for the Classified Viewgraph Tracking System project, I was given *unlimited* access to all key project codes, group names, organizations, and relevant files. After all, this was the

---

*One of the many problems with the MJ-12 documents is the fact that the signature of former President Harry S. Truman that appears on one of the papers is *identical* to another signature on a letter Truman wrote to Dr. Vannevar Bush on October 1, 1947. While supporters of the MJ-12 documents cite this fact as "evidence" that the papers are genuine, they have their "logic" backwards, since no one signs his name *exactly the same way twice!* This is a long-established, accepted fact in the scientific discipline of document forensics. (See Albert S. Osborn, *Questioned Documents,* 2d ed. [Montclair, N.J.: Patterson Smith, 1978], pp. 136–38.)

master index for these agencies to use and I was transforming their database into their first ever computerized implementation. Previously, the earlier indexes in use were manually kept, and it was a scathing audit by U.S. Pentagon officials that ordered the change to computerization.

Furthermore, to "debug" the specific software search routine that I had implemented, I used Menzel's name and files as a control to test the search engine in my software code. This allowed me to peruse Menzel's file and I was granted a temporary "Q" or Top Secret security clearance with a *need to know* basis for the assignment. My "need to know" classification meant that I was allowed to view any and *all* complete and relevant information. When it came to accessing Menzel's files, I was allowed to view *everything* uncensored.

In addition to conducting specific checks on three individuals besides Menzel, another search I undertook involved any still-classified air disasters or secret government air vehicle or project tests on and around the date of the Roswell "UFO" crash in New Mexico. Nothing showed up that could possibly account for the debris that Mac Brazel discovered. However, there was a reference to Project Mogul in the *declassified* listings!

Because I continued to work at Lawrence Livermore National Laboratory for a few more years, resigning my position in January 1991 during the final days of the Persian Gulf War and Operation Desert Storm, I have never mentioned anything about this incident and my knowledge of Dr. Menzel's background until this writing. Before this book went to press, Lawrence Livermore National laboratory finally gave me official clearance and permission to talk about this event.

As a final attempt to learn more about the claim that Dr. Menzel was part of MJ-12, I also conducted an interview with the late Dr. Menzel's wife, Florence, and his daughter, Elizabeth Davis. While they were well aware of the allegations concerning Menzel, both of them were emphatic that the charges were "ridiculous." Furthermore, Menzel's daughter specifically stated that "I tried to tell [Stanton] Friedman this but he would not listen."[17]

In their revealing interview, both Mrs. Menzel and her daughter reiterated something that was noted in Menzel's security files: that it had become known to the United States government that Menzel had told his family for whom he was working, but not specifically on what projects, on several occasions. In other words, when Dr. Menzel did work for the CIA, he let his wife know. However, honoring his security oath, he would not tell his wife or anyone else what he was *doing* for the CIA, according to surviving members of his family.

In their interview with me, both Mrs. Menzel and her daughter made it very clear that they consider the allegation that Dr. Menzel was a secret member of MJ-12 to be "preposterous." Furthermore, they do not believe that MJ-12 exists, and labeled it "a myth."[18]

While the security files on the late Donald Menzel do *validate* Friedman's claims that Menzel worked on classified projects, this does *not* prove that Menzel was a member of MJ-12, or that MJ-12 exists. The security files chronicle Menzel's work from the very beginning, and noted that he began his fascination with cryptography while he was a young boy and an Eagle scout, a fact confirmed by Menzel's widow and daughter in their discussions with me.

Finally, in the original manuscript for their book *Beyond Roswell*, Michael Hesemann and Philip Mantle mention the fact that Menzel wrote two letters to President-elect John F. Kennedy in 1960 and tried ingratiate himself, hoping to obtain a position in the new administration. Hesemann and Mantle use the facts that Menzel mentioned his work in intelligence dating back to 1930 and his occasional stints at the CIA to Kennedy to buttress their argument that this "made Menzel an ideal member of the secret [MJ-12] team!"[19]

Unfortunately for Hesemann and Mantle, the truth is not quite as sinister as they make it sound.

Both John F. Kennedy and Dr. Menzel attended Harvard University. They served together on a couple of committees at Harvard and knew each other personally. When Kennedy later became President of the United States, it was quite logical for Dr. Menzel to approach the newly-elected president and offer his services because they were friends.[20]

It stands to reason that if the late Dr. Menzel were truly a member of the super secret MJ-12 committee, he would hardly have needed to approach JFK for a job! Instead, Menzel would probably have participated in some sort of briefing for Kennedy to educate him on the issue of UFOs, especially since they knew each other.

The fact that Menzel approached Kennedy in search of a job, as numerous others whom JFK knew did after he became president, is yet another piece of evidence which argues *against* Menzel being a "secret member" of the MJ-12 team. Since the MJ-12 documents list Donald Menzel as such a member, this casts further suspicion on their authenticity.

QUESTION #7

In a now-declassified memo, former FBI Director J. Edgar Hoover wrote "I would do it but before agreeing to it [helping the Air Force investigate UFO reports] we must insist upon full access to discs recovered. For instance in the Sw. case the army grabbed it and would not let us have it for cursory examination." Doesn't this notation by J. Edgar Hoover refer to Roswell and doesn't it prove that the government has in its possession the remains of a crashed UFO?

Unfortunately, the memo does not prove that the U.S. government has in its possession a crashed UFO, and it has nothing to do with Roswell.

The notation written by Hoover was done so in his own handwriting and is somewhat difficult to read. While some pro-Roswell authors believe that Hoover wrote "Sw" (meaning "southwest,")[21] what the former FBI Director actually penned were the letters "La." This has been conclusively identified by people familiar with Hoover's handwriting.[22]

The "La." notation made by Hoover does not refer to Roswell, and in all likelihood is a reference to the Shreveport, Louisiana hoax of 1947 in which a man-made "UFO" consisting of a sixteen-inch aluminum disc and some old discarded radio parts was found.[23]

QUESTION #8

Is original Roswell UFO researcher William L. Moore really a U.S. government "disinformation" agent as he has ciaimed? If so, hasn't he discredited himself?

The only person who can definitively answer this question is Bill Moore himself. However, let us review the known facts and statements that Moore has made in regard to this matter.

On July 1, 1989, at the Mutual UFO Network's Annual Symposium in Las Vegas, William L. Moore shocked the UFO community by claiming that he had actively participated in what he described was a U.S. government-sponsored "disinformation" campaign, designed (in part) to hurt the UFO field.[24]

Specifically, Moore confessed to researchers (myself included) that he not only helped "spread disinformation" among the UFO community, but that he had in fact "spied" on certain UFOlogists, reporting on their activities back to his contacts at the Air Force Office of Special Intelligence (AFOSI).[25]

In trying to rationalize both his behavior and stunning public admission, Moore claimed that "There was no way I was going to allow the opportunity [to work for the government] to pass me by without learning at least something about what was going on. I would play the disinformation game, get my hands dirty just often enough to lead those directing the process into believing that I was doing exactly what they wanted me to do, and all the while continue to burrow my way into the matrix so as to learn as much as possible about who was directing it and why."[26]

UFO researcher Jerome Clark has written a rather extensive article in volume one of his *UFO Encyclopedia* series documenting Bill Moore's purported disinformation/espionage activities and the campaign he says he was "under orders" to launch against certain UFO researchers.

While Bill Moore first made his startling "confession" in 1989 before the crowd at the MUFON convention, I have known about Moore's alleged clandestine "double agent" activities since *1982*, some *seven years earlier!* Since it was Bill Moore *himself* who told me what he was "up to," I am in the very unique position to not only comment on what Moore told me, but now share information that has *never been released publicly* until now on this entire affair. Let us start by setting the record straight before disclosing this information.

Bill Moore claims that he was directed by members of the AFOSI to actively "spy" on six UFO researchers "who were the subject of intelligence community interest between 1980 and 1984."[27] The six UFOlogists Moore mentioned were as follows:

1. The late Len Stringfield—A researcher who specialized in the collection of "crashed UFO" stories.
2. The late Pete Mazzola—Founder of the Scientific Bureau of Investigation (SBI) in New York.
3. Peter Gersten—An attorney who served as the chief legal counsel (along with Brad Sparks) for the Citizens against UFO Secrecy (CAUS). CAUS has filed several lawsuits against the U.S. government in a never-ending battle to pry loose formerly classified UFO documents.
4. Larry Fawcett—A top official in CAUS.
5. The late Jim and Coral Lorenzen—The directors of the now-defunct Aerial Phenomena Research Organization in Tucson, Arizona.
6. Larry W. Bryant—A researcher who has also sued the U.S. government in order to try and secure formerly-classified UFO-related documents.

In his *UFO Encyclopedia,* Jerome Clark mentions me, Kal Korff, in connection with Pete Mazzola and Moore's attempts to spy on him. On page 106, Clark writes:

> The late Pete Mazzola, whose knowledge of film footage from a never-publicized Florida UFO case was of great interest to counterintelligence types. Moore was directed to urge Mazzola to send the footage to ufologist Kal Korff (who knew nothing of the scheme) for analysis; then Moore would make a copy and pass it on to [AFOSI member Sergeant Richard] Doty. But Mazzola never got the film, despite promises, and the incident came to nothing.

While Jerome Clark's account is, for the most part, basically accurate, it is incomplete because he does not know the entire story.

The fact is *I was most definitely aware* of Moore's "scheme," (as Clark puts it) and I disclose here the full details about it now for the first time. The following account is based on notes I made within hours of this incident.

Bill Moore's Disinformation "Secret"

In February 1982, Bill Moore telephoned my residence in Union City, California, and said that it was "urgent that we meet." I had gotten to know Moore through our collaborative efforts in exposing the infamous Eduard "Billy" Meier hoax,* and at the time considered him a friend. Moore had been instrumental in getting my first book, *The Meier Incident,* published in May 1981.

When I asked Moore what was so urgent, he was vague and refused to discuss the matter further. He then asked if he could drive up from his house in southern California, more than four hundred miles away, and visit. Of course I agreed.

When Moore arrived and we were in my living room, he offended my girlfriend, Roma, by asking her to leave! This was, after all, her house and mine, so to diffuse the situation Moore and I decided to "go for a walk" outside. This put me in an awkward situation because, if nothing else, Roma would naturally be curious as to what was supposedly so secret. Whatever it was that Moore had to tell me, it had better be worth it.

The night was very foggy, and Moore was acting very "James Bond" like. He began our conversation by stressing to me that there was a concerted effort by the U.S. government to withhold the truth about the Roswell UFO crash. Moore emphasized, in a very melodramatic fashion, that through his extensive research efforts he had

---

*For those who wish to read a thorough exposé of the infamous Eduard "Billy" Meier hoax, please see my previous book *Spaceships of the Pleiades: The Billy Meier Story* (Amherst, N.Y.: Prometheus Books, 1995). *Spaceships* documents my undercover investigation, which included several clandestine trips to Billy Meier's cult compound in Switzerland. *Spaceships* is one of the few books endorsed by both UFO believers and skeptics alike. *Spaceships* contains more than 116 photos, most of which have never been published before, and exposes the false claims made by author Gary Kinder in his bestselling book on the Meier case, *Light Years* (New York: Atlantic Monthly Press, 1987).

managed to "get closer than ever" to blowing the lid off of the government's cover-up of the crashed UFO information it possesses.

Moore then stated that through the "contacts" he had managed to acquire since the publication of his *Roswell Incident* book, he was "let inside" the inner workings of an ultra-secret group which possessed the classified information regarding alien bodies and crashed UFOs.

As I listened to Moore, I was intrigued, especially when he disclosed the shocking information that "in exchange for doing them certain favors, I get privy to some of this information which I can then work on and release to the public."

In other words, Moore was telling me that in order to get his "inside scoops," he had to do the bidding of the intelligence community! "This is the reason," Moore stated, "that I have come up here to see you."

Admittedly, I was baffled at this point. Moore mistook my confused hesitation for skepticism and continued to try and convince me.

"Does Stanton Friedman know about this?" I asked Moore.

"No, he does not, and you must promise me that you will never tell anyone. It could prove dangerous to you," Moore shot back.

I was surprised to hear this, because Moore and Friedman were, at the time, close friends. However, I was more focused on Moore's "warning" to me. Admittedly, Moore now had my full attention, and I wanted to know further details. "What do you mean I am in some sort of danger?" I asked him.

"I need to know *everything* you're working on before I can tell you," Moore emphasized. "Tell me everything, I mean *everything* you are into right now, UFO-wise."

After thinking over Moore's request, I decided to tell him. Usually, I keep my UFO research projects to myself until a logical disclosure point is reached, but I decided to tell him nonetheless.

"No, that's not it," Moore responded, obviously unsatisfied. "Are you sure you've told me everything?" he inquired.

"As far as I know, Bill," was my reply.

Moore hesitated, then asked me what my "dealings" were with Pete Mazzola of the Scientific Bureau of Investigation.

"Not much," I remember telling Moore. "Mazzola has promised to publish some articles of mine, but that's about it. He's also made me a member of his SBI group and he sends me free copies of his magazine."

"Is that all?" Moore inquired.

"Well, he also has told me that he admires the column I write and how I analyze UFO photos using computers."

"Is that all?" Moore asked again.

"Yes," I replied.

Still not satisfied, Moore finally cut to the chase and disclosed the real purpose of his visit.

"I have been told by the operatives that I work for that you are about to come into possession of a UFO motion picture film that was taken near Cape Kennedy in Florida. The film shows a UFO near the space shuttle launching pad and Mazzola is about to send it to you for analysis," Moore stated.

Shocked, I replied, "Really?"

"It is extremely important that when you get this film that you immediately turn it over to me," Moore emphasized. "The people I work for in intelligence don't want this thing out. You are not supposed to see it. I have been sent here to try and retrieve it, and turn it back over to them. Now, has Mazzola ever said anything about this to you?"

"No," was all I could tell Moore. In my numerous conversations with Mazzola he had never mentioned this.

"Are you absolutely sure?" Moore kept asking me. "Because I have information that Mazzola is going to send it to you. It's important that you give the film to me when you get it. Are you sure Mazzola hasn't talked with you about it at all?" Moore asked again.

"No," I replied.

"Now think, is there anything you can remember?"

"Wait a minute!" I suddenly snapped to Moore. "He did say something. But it was about another film. Mazzola told me that he was due to receive a UFO film taken by some guy while driving on vacation in the mountains. He told me if he ever received it, and he seemed doubtful, that he would send it to me for analysis."

"He didn't mention anything about Florida or the space shuttle?" Moore inquired.

"No, just some guy in the mountains, somewhere up near New

York or up north, something like that. It might have been Maine or New Hampshire," I told Moore.

"Doesn't sound like it's the same thing I'm after," Moore lamented.

"Will you call Mazzola first thing tomorrow and try to learn more, without telling him anything?" Moore asked me.

"Yes," I replied.

Now that we had gotten past the Mazzola thing, I asked Moore to elaborate on his earlier remark when he said that I might be in some sort of "danger."

"You see," Moore continued, "this whole UFO thing is very complex. We are not ready for it. When the truth comes out, it will affect everything, including religion. The aliens have been intermingling with our culture and evolution for thousands of years. Two thousand years ago they did things which people now attribute to Jesus Christ."

Not knowing what to think of this, I asked Moore once again if Stanton Friedman knew anything about what he was telling me, specifically about him working for the government.

"Friedman doesn't know a thing," Moore responded. "And furthermore, he's looking in the wrong places. To keep him busy, we send him on wild goose chases. Here, I'll show you."

Bill Moore then reached into his pocket and pulled out a photocopy of a computer teletype purporting to be from the AFOSI instructing them not to cooperate with Friedman should he inquire about the subject of UFOs. Moore then assured me that "There's a Friedman memo like this on file with virtually every appropriate government agency."

I then asked Moore if I could have a copy of the memo, and he told me "No, I can't give it to you. Pretend you didn't see it."

"Wow," I commented to Moore. "Imagine if Friedman knew."

"He doesn't," Moore shot back. "Here, take a look at this."

Moore then removed from his pocket a second document which he claimed had *my* name written on it. The memo contained his instructions about the alleged UFO movie film that was shot in Florida, and how he was supposed to retrieve it.

Naturally, I examined the document very carefully, but could not see my name printed anywhere. I mentioned this to Moore and he said "Trust me, it's there. It's under this blacked out part."

Of course, I couldn't tell if Moore was being truthful, for I could not see whose name was under the parts that had been conveniently obscured.

"I would like you to call Mazzola as soon as you can and ask him about the film. Try and encourage him to send it to you as soon as possible. When you receive it, call me, and I'll come pick it up, even if I have to drive up here again from Los Angeles," Moore assured me.

"What did you say could happen to me if I don't turn over this film?" I asked Moore.

"You could be killed," was his unequivocal response.

"Oh," was all I could think to say.

As Moore and I started heading back up the hill toward my house, he hinted that depending on how this matter turned out, that he might let me "in" on some of his contacts and "get me in on the inside."

"It's the only way to handle this, Kal," Moore assured me. "The UFO researchers out there don't have a clue as to what's really going on. They might as well get out of the business. They're worthless. In order to move things forward, I've got to play both sides," were Moore's final remarks as we approached my house.

"Call Mazzola tomorrow. I'll be in town for another day or so and I'll call you to find out."

Bill Moore and I then parted company. He got into his car and drove away into the fog. The whole bizarre incident would have made a beautiful scene worthy of the fictional television series the "X-Files." Only this was real. But had Bill Moore told me the truth? Was he really a disinformation agent on assignment to do the government "occasional favors" in exchange for access to selective crashed UFO secrets?

I was bothered by what Moore had said, and rightly so.

"So, what did you and Bill talk about that was so damned important that I get asked to leave my own house?" were Roma's first words as I returned.

I hesitated, and refused to tell her at first.

That night, after we had gone to bed, I held Roma in my arms and simply said that I was due to receive some UFO material and that once I had it in my possession, I was to turn it over to Bill Moore.

"Why?" she asked me, curious of course.

"Because it turns out that Bill does work for the government. They want me to give him the film," I told her.

"And what happens if you don't turn it over to him?" Roma asked me.

"Then Bill says they'll kill me."

For the rest of the night, Roma and I did not say a word to each other. Instead, we went to sleep, but I could tell that she was troubled by the whole affair, as was I.

The next morning, I promptly called Pete Mazzola in New York and asked him about the UFO film "from that guy in the mountains" that I was supposed to receive several weeks ago.

Mazzola replied that he hadn't received the film, and didn't know if he ever would. I then took the opportunity to ask Mazzola about the space shuttle angle Moore had mentioned.

"Are you sure that this film doesn't show a UFO near the space shuttle instead of the mountains?" I inquired of Mazzola.

"No, some guy took it while he was on vacation," Mazzola replied.

"Have you ever heard of any film footage taken near Cape Canaveral which shows a UFO near the space shuttle on its launching pad?" I asked Mazzola.

"No, that's a new one on me," he replied.

"Well, if you hear any rumors about this, please let me know," I told him.

"When you receive this film from the guy who was up in the mountains, please send it to me, I'll be more than happy to analyze it for you," I reminded Mazzola. He reiterated that he would do so.

In the early afternoon, Bill Moore telephoned my house like he said he would and asked if I had talked with Mazzola.

"Yes I have," I told Moore. "He doesn't know anything about it."

Moore was silent for a few moments, then remarked, "Well, if you hear anything further, give me a call."

While I promised Moore that I would do so, in reality I had no intention of turning over any such film to him if I were ever to come into possession of it. I found Moore's behavior that night to be personally insulting and an affront to our friendship.

If Moore was telling the truth, and he really was working in a

U.S. government-sanctioned "disinformation" campaign, then the *last thing* I wanted to do was cooperate at the expense of the truth. Unless I had verifiable, legitimate reasons that were conveyed to me at a much higher and outright official level that the national security interests of the United States government were truly at stake in this affair, I felt that whatever this film purported to show should be made *public*.

On the other hand, if Moore was lying to me, (after all, I did *not* see my name on the memo he showed me, contrary to his assurance that it was there), then I wanted nothing to do with him any further.

The incident with Moore, especially his hints that I might someday be invited to "join" the inner circle of his alleged "ultra-secret intelligence group" bothered me so greatly that I violated Moore's confidence and called up my friend Brad Sparks to discuss the matter with him.

Brad Sparks is a veteran UFO researcher of more than twenty-five years, and is one of the foremost experts on UFO-related U.S. government documents. Brad and I had become good friends, and I decided to confide in him to get some sort of "reality check" concerning Moore's startling claims.

After I told Sparks the details, Brad started laughing, and after we compared notes, we both felt that whatever Moore was "up" to, that I should at least be careful in my future dealings with him, but not take things too seriously. After all, Sparks reminded me, Moore was known to be cavorting with former AFOSI Sergeant Richard Doty. Sparks reasoned at the time that it was probably Doty who "put Moore up to it," and eventually, Brad Sparks was proven right; Moore later confirmed this to me.[28]

Richard Doty is certainly *not* a member of any government-sponsored "ultra-secret UFO group." Indeed, it is up to those who claim he is to provide evidence that would prove their case. What Doty has done, however, is play games with UFO researchers by doling out photocopies of various alleged "secret" government memos and making tall tales only to renounce them later when asked to go on official record or before a camera.[29]

Is Bill Moore *really* a bona fide, officially sanctioned government "disinformation" agent like he has claimed? While the evidence is dubious at best, only Bill Moore knows the *real* answer to this question. However, as the above-mentioned incident between Moore and me establishes, if this is the "best" that this supposedly "ultra-secret group" can do, then the U.S. intelligence community is in severe trouble and the supposed UFO "cover-up" is a sick joke at best.

QUESTION #9

How many other UFO "crash" cases have as much evidence as Roswell?

The answer is simple: none! However, one must remember that the so-called evidence for the Roswell UFO "crash" of 1947 is not scientifically credible. In fact, it is only "believable" if one accepts purely at face value, with absolutely no critical thinking or cross examination, the numerous (and contradictory) claims made by the Roswell advocates and alleged "witnesses."

Unfortunately, as of this writing, there is no known, scientifically verifiable evidence that *any* UFO has ever crashed at any location on this planet. If indeed such an occurrence has ever taken place, then the hard evidence that proves it has so far remained elusive.

QUESTION #10

Isn't it true that the U.S. government is involved in an official UFO cover-up and that its agencies are withholding UFO-related documents that they refuse to release?

Yes, it is true that the U.S. government has refused to release certain "UFO-related" files. However, while the subject of UFOs are mentioned in these documents, according to affidavits submitted for independent review by the courts, disclosure of this information would jeopardize national security and reveal intelligence-gathering methods or the presence of intelligence-gathering capabilities.

This explanation, which has been given under oath and reviewed on camera by Federal Judge Richard Gazell in 1981, has been often exploited by pro-UFO researchers who complain that there is a cover-up.

Since *we do not know* what is in these still-classified documents, one cannot use them to *support* the argument that the government is "covering-up" UFO information one way or another. Until the contents of such documents are declassified, speculation about what they contain is folly.

QUESTION #11

Isn't the now-declassified General Bolender memo proof that at least the USAF is covering up the subject of UFOs?

No, it is not. This is yet another myth that is often touted by some of the Roswell authors.

In Randle and Schmitt's *The Truth about the Roswell UFO Crash,* the authors state:

> In 1969, when Brig. Gen. C. H. Bolender wrote, "Moreover, reports of unidentified flying objects which could affect national security are made in accordance with JANAP 146 or Air Force Manual 55-11, and are not part of the Blue Book* system," he knew the truth, as outlined by air force regulations. Real responsibility for UFO reports was located in Virginia and not Ohio [where Project Blue Book was officially located]. Project Blue Book was nothing more than a public relations outfit designed to identify objects and convince the public that something was being done.[30]

As "proof" that there's a "secret" government group charged with specifically investigating UFO reports, Stanton Friedman has also cited the Bolender memo.[31] However, unlike Randle and Schmitt, Friedman's interpretation has been more on the conservative side. Nonetheless, in order to fully understand the complexities of what Brig. Gen. Carroll H. Bolender wrote in his now-famous "memo," I consulted with UFO researcher Robert Todd.

Todd is, undisputably, the world's foremost expert on the

---

*Project Blue Book was the name of the USAF's official investigation into the subject of UFOS. JANAP 146 was an official military regulation that outlined reporting procedures for UFO reports.

Bolender document. He has more experience than any UFO researcher in filing Freedom of Information Act requests for UFO-related documents and has received more material than anyone from various government agencies. Todd was the *first person* to ever obtain a copy of the Bolender memo, and he did so directly from the Air Force through one of his numerous Freedom of Information Act requests. Todd's account of what the Bolender memo is, and more importantly what it really says, is as follows:

> In December 1978, the Air Force Freedom of Information Act (FOIA) office in the Pentagon furnished a batch of records in response to my request submitted earlier that month. Among the documents was a three-page "Department of the Air Force Air Staff Summary Sheet," dated 20 October 1969, and signed by C. H. Bolender, Deputy Director of Development, Deputy Chief of Staff, Research and Development. This Summary Sheet has come to be called the "Bolender memo."
>
> Two sentences of text of the Summary Sheet have given rise to wildly exaggerated claims by self-styled "experts" with tabloid mentalities. These fanatical UFO hobbyists invariably present these two sentences out of context, and cynically exploit their own ignorance of the subject by filling the vast voids in their knowledge with their completely undocumented, paranoid ravings. This has led to the idea that the "Bolender memo" is "proof" that the "good" UFO reports never went to Project Blue Book, and that Blue Book was little more than a public relations ploy intended to divert attention away from the "real" UFO investigation carried out by the Air Force in complete secrecy.
>
> Paragraph four of the Summary Sheet states: "Moreover, reports of unidentified flying objects which could affect national security are made in accordance with JANAP 146 or Air Force Manual 55-11, and are not part of the Blue Book system." Paragraph six observes that the termination of Blue Book would leave no official office to receive UFO reports, and states: "However, as already stated, reports of UFOs which could affect national security would continue to be handled through the standard Air Force procedures designed for this purpose."
>
> Taken alone and out of context, and with a sinister spin applied in the right direction, these appear to be fairly damning statements suggesting that Blue Book was a fraud and the UFO

cases which could affect national security never made it to Blue Book. So let's put these two sentences back in context and see if that makes any difference.

Omitting the references to the corresponding attachment numbers, paragraph four reads as follows:

"As early as 1953, the Robertson Panel concluded 'that the evidence presented on Unidentified Flying Objects shows no indication that these phenomena constitute a direct physical threat to national security.' In spite of this finding, the Air Force continued to maintain a *special reporting system* [emphasis added]. There is still, however, no evidence that Project Blue Book reports have served any intelligence function. Moreover, reports of unidentified flying objects which could affect national security are made in accordance with JANAP 146 or Air Force Manual 55-11, and are not part of the Blue Book system. The Air Force experience therefore confirms the impression of . . . researchers 'that the defense function could be performed within the framework established for intelligence and surveillance operations without the continuance of a special unit such as Project Blue Book.' "

The "special reporting system" was the system established by the Air Force in 1948 requiring the reporting of UFOs in support of Project Sign, Blue Book's predecessor.

. . . UFO "experts" have interpreted Bolender's remarks to mean that UFO reports made under JANAP 146 and Air Force Manual (AFM) 55-11 never went to Blue Book, that these "good" cases went somewhere else for investigation.

JANAP 146, "Communications Instructions for Reporting Military Intelligence Sightings (CIRMIS)," was first published in July 1948, and was based on similar publication that first appeared during World War II. The 1948 edition made no mention of UFOs, and imposed no requirement that UFOs be reported. UFOs were not included in JANAP 146 until September 1950, with the publication of JANAP 146(A). The title of the publication was changed to "Communications Instructions for Reporting Vital Intelligence Sightings from Aircraft (CIRVIS)," and the reports generated under this publication thereafter were referred to as "CIRVIS reports."

Based on Air Force Intelligence records located at the National Archives, and historical reports for the Air Force's Directorate of Intelligence, it seems clear that, once UFO reports were required under JANAP 146, a conflict arose between the two reporting systems. The Air Defense Command (ADC) was experiencing difficulty in getting follow-up reports from Air Force Intelligence. These follow-up reports apparently were going to the UFO investigators at Wright-Patterson AFB, but ADC was left hanging, which made their air defense mission suffer.

One result of this confusion was that the Air Force published Air Force Regulation (AFR) 200-3, "Reporting Vital Intelligence Sightings from Aircraft," on 2 July 1952, in order "to put 'teeth' into the CIRVIS reporting program." Prior to publication of AFR 200-3, the Air Force also revised Directorate of Intelligence Office Memorandum No. 200-23, dated 22 April 1952, entitled "Responsibilities and Processing 'CIRVIS' Messages," which prescribed the Standard Operating Procedure (SOP) for handling CIRVIS reports within the Directorate of Intelligence. This office memo furnished a lot of details on how CIRVIS reports were handled.

According to Office Memo 200-23, "JANAP . . . is worldwide instructions for the reporting of incidents observed while airborne which, in the opinion of the pilot, requires prompt defensive and/or investigative action by the Armed Forces." It further states that "CIRVIS is designed in large measure to prevent a second Pearl Harbor and provides for the most rapid and uninterrupted passing of raw information from an observer to the three agencies having the greatest interest." The three agencies were identified as:

1. Air Defense Command (ADC), "for positive air action if required";

2. Secretary of Defense, "for appropriate action by the three services"; and

3. Nearest Military Command, "for local evaluation and defense."

Paragraph 4g of Office Memo 200-23 specifically assigned AFOIN-2B (the Evaluations Division of the Directorate of Intelligence) with responsibility for *"Keeping ATIC informed of such reports as are pertinent to Project Bluebook"* [emphasis added].

In October 1959, the reporting requirements under AFR 200-3 were shifted to AFR 55-88, entitled "Communications Instructions for Reporting Vital Intelligence Sightings (CIRVIS) from Aircraft." With the May 1966 edition of AFR 55-88, copies of CIRVIS reports were being addressed directly to the Foreign

Technology Division (FTD), the successor to the Aerospace Technical Intelligence Center (ATIC), and the home of Project Blue Book.

AFR 55-88 was superseded by Air Force Manual 55-11, "Air Force Operational Reporting System," published on 20 May 1968. AFM 55-11 appears to have been a consolidation of *all* reporting requirements imposed on the Air Force. These requirements involved a multitude of subjects, the vast majority of which had nothing whatever to do with UFOs. That portion of the manual dealing with UFOs was merely an abbreviated version of JANAP 146, knowledge of which has been available to the UFO field since at least 1965 when Donald Keyhoe's book, *The Flying Saucer Conspiracy,* was published.

The obvious point is that the available documentation clearly shows that the Air Force instituted procedures to be sure Blue Book was informed of CIRVIS reports of UFOs, even if the documentation proving this is difficult to find and not known to those "experts" who eagerly substitute their own peculiar ideas and speculations in place of the facts.

But why did two separate reporting systems exist? The single best explanation I have seen is found in the September 1959 "Staff Study" located among the Project Blue Book files at the National Archives. Paragraph four of the study says:

"The methods by which UFO reports are forwarded is by TWX [teletype] or telephone from military installations and by letter or phone from civil organizations or private citizens. This, when compared to the reaction time necessary for survival in event of an attack using modern weapons, is ridiculous. The ATIC interest in these objects, in view of the foregoing, can only be its intelligence or scientific and/or technical significance after successful defense action has been accomplished by another agency."

It should be emphasized again that the vast majority of CIRVIS reports undoubtedly had little or nothing whatever to do with UFOs. "UFO" reports (which, for ADC, included reports of Soviet aircraft which had not yet been identified as such) apparently were going to Air Force Intelligence in the Pentagon and to Blue Book at Wright-Patterson, with inadequate follow-up reports being sent to ADC, which was trying to fulfill the defense function. One might hope that even the most ardent UFO hobbyists would agree that the defense mission should take precedence over the more leisurely investigation of UFOs carried out by

ATIC, and that the special reporting system that supported Blue Book was not adequate when it came to the timely reporting of *possible* threats to national security.

The "Bolender memo" did not state that CIRVIS reports of UFOs which could affect national security did not go to Blue Book. It merely acknowledged the existence of two separate reporting systems, intended to serve two entirely different purposes. . . . Given the Air Force mission to defend the sovereign airspace of the United States, there is no way they can divest themselves fully of the UFO subject. And the termination of Blue Book was never intended to get the Air Force out of the UFO business completely. The record has *always* been clear on this point. Despite the availability of this record, so-called UFO experts continue to feign surprise when they learn that a particular "UFO" event has been documented in government files, suggesting some level of government interest in the subject.

But the government, and the Air Force in particular, is not blameless. They have [inadvertently] helped cultivate the idea that a cover-up exists by repeatedly pronouncing that they got out of the UFO business when Project Blue Book was terminated in 1969. And every time new UFO-related records surface, the UFO "experts" point to the documents and say "See, they're still conducting investigations in secret." These apparent contradictions lend credence to the idea that a cover-up exists, especially when exploited by supposed UFO "experts" just for that purpose. This, in turn, creates an atmosphere that invites all manner of wild, unsupported claims by certain UFO "visionaries" whose objective seems to be to establish themselves more firmly as "authorities" on the "UFO cover-up," which doesn't necessarily mean these paranoid individuals don't honestly believe their own hype.

While there undoubtedly are a number of factors that explain the pronouncements claiming official disinterest in UFOs, the most compelling probably is that it's the simplest, easiest response to make, and one that discourages further inquiry by bluntly closing the door on the subject. Most likely contributing to the problem is a lack of personnel who really understand what was supposed to happen when Project Blue Book ended. . . . Air Force personnel responsible for answering UFO-related queries simply are [usually] not knowledgeable enough to distinguish between what was *supposed* to happen when Blue Book ended, and what they *think* happened.

Another problem is one of semantics. The term "UFO" has two completely different meanings within the Air Force and within the UFO community. For the Air Force, a "UFO" could be an unidentified commercial aircraft that strayed from its flight plan, or a Russian aircraft testing U.S. defense systems. For the UFO community, the term "UFO" has come to mean spacecraft of extraterrestrial origin. No doubt when UFO buffs communicate with Air Force personnel, the assumption is that the UFO buff is referring to spacecraft of extraterrestrial origin.

This is not to say that "UFOs"—however one defines the term—do not come to the attention of Air Force agencies from time to time. If any given "UFO" exhibits indications of being a *possible* threat, no doubt efforts are undertaken to "investigate" (another term that requires definition) the sighting, at least to the point where officials are satisfied that the "UFO"—be it a Russian aircraft or some aerial phenomenon that remains unidentified—poses no threat to national security. The transitory nature of all such "sightings" allows for little more. . . .

The boring reality is that the Air Force's interest in UFOs is as transitory as the phenomenon itself, although certain elements within the UFO field would have us believe otherwise. When certain of these self-appointed "experts" cannot find the facts, they have the annoying habit of inventing new "facts" to take their place, from which they construct elaborate scenarios that are the envy of the best fiction writers. While this practice might be enormously convenient, it rarely (if ever) results in an accurate picture, especially when these new "facts" are more than ignorance-based fantasies. This fantasy-driven game of "connecting the dots" always results in a picture consistent with the belief that the government is engaged in a "Cosmic Watergate," which in turn is consistent with the belief that the Earth is being visited by one or more alien races. These supposed "experts" are so immersed in the subject and believe so strongly in the reality of ET visitations that they cannot accept the idea that the government doesn't share their beliefs and concerns. Their inability to accept this idea leads them to conclude that the government must be lying about their level of interest in the subject. And if they're willing to lie about it, well, the subject must be very important indeed. This circular reasoning has their fantasies feeding off of themselves.

The "Bolender Memo" is *not* proof that the cases never went to Blue Book, notwithstanding . . . proclamations to the contrary.[32]

It is ironic that Stanton Friedman, in particular, chooses to use the Bolender memo to buttress his UFO conspiracy theories. Friedman was first notified about the Bolender document *by Robert Todd,* and obviously, something has been lost in its interpretation.[33]

When it comes to assessing the Bolender memo and putting it in its proper perspective, it appears that Todd's explanation makes much more sense and is more accurate.

QUESTION #12

Wasn't Project Moon Dust formed because of the Roswell UFO Crash?

Project Moon Dust was a program begun in the late 1950s to retrieve objects which are either unknown, or foreign made, that fall to Earth from the atmosphere. While some UFO proponents have seized upon the charter of Project Moon Dust to mean that it is empowered specifically to recover UFOs, or that this must be the name of the government's "secret" UFO recovery project, this is simply not true. There is no credible evidence that Project Moon Dust was created because of the alleged "flying saucer" recovered near Roswell, New Mexico, in 1947.

It is reasonable to argue that should a bona fide extraterrestrial spacecraft ever crash to Earth, that the United States government would use whatever means it felt were logical and practical to handle such an occurrence. It would not automatically defer such an issue to Project Moon Dust personnel since this is not their specific charter, nor has it ever been.

Finally, in a letter to UFO researcher Robert Todd, dated July 1, 1987, Col. Phillip E. Thompson, deputy chief of staff in intelligence, stated that the name Project Moon Dust "has been replaced by another name that is not releasable."

While some in the pro-UFO community will cry "foul," and accuse the U.S. government of "covering-up" the "secret UFO recovery project's name," the truth of the matter is that Project Moon Dust, or whatever its current name might be, was never empowered nor created for the specific, sole reason of recovering crashed flying saucers.

QUESTION #13

If the Roswell UFO Crash of 1947 did not really happen, then why has the city of Roswell declared July 2, 1947, as the official anniversary date of the event?

There are two words that answer this question: *tourism dollars!*

According to current (i.e., 1996) Roswell Mayor Tom Jennings, who majored in marketing in college, the need arose to identify the town of Roswell with some sort of "event" that would help put it on the map. Jennings reasoned that UFOs were "another industry that could be developed."[34]

After the military closed the base at Roswell in the 1960s, the town purchased the land and managed to convert it into an industrial park. However, other than possessing the world's largest mozzarella cheese factory, the small town of Roswell lacked a publicly marketable image of its own, and lost its unique identity. Jennings reasoned, and rightly so from a purely commercial, profit exploitation standpoint, that UFOs were the next market.

Jennings's commercial and tourist exploitation of the UFO "crash" at Roswell has been so financially successful that he has even been featured in *Forbes* magazine! According to Mayor Jennings' office, "the Roswell UFO myth pumps an additional five million dollars a year into our local economy. That's why we embrace it."[35] *Forbes* has also noted this $5 million figure, as well as the fact that "Civic leaders are absolutely giddy about prospects for [the upcoming] 50th anniversary."[36]

"We get those UFO calls. Seems like that's all we get 'round here nowadays. Other than that, things are pretty slow," remarked Mayor Jennings's secretary.[37]

QUESTION #14

Doesn't a UFO museum in Hakui, Japan, have on display some actual metal fragments from the Roswell·flying saucer crash of 1947?

No. In fact, as of this writing, there is not even a UFO-related museum in the *entire town* of Hakui! However, the story behind this popular myth is an interesting one, the spreading of which I personally observed in part.

On November 17, 1995, while I was in the audience and on the Seattle, Washington-based popular television show, Ken Schram's "Town Meeting," UFO researcher Robert Dean boldly announced that a UFO museum was going to open in Japan in 1996 and that it was being funded with over $50 million. Dean, being his usual melodramatic self, then made the startling proclamation that pieces of an actual flying saucer would be on display there!

During the next several months Dean repeated these claims, but in all fairness to him he was not the only one to do so. Other individuals such as British UFO researcher Colin Andrews, who specializes in the study of so-called crop circles, also chimed in.[38]

With rumors of the much-touted UFO museum in Japan scheduled to open in early July 1996, the flying-saucer-faithful eagerly waited with baited breath. The UFO community, and in particular the Internet, were abuzz over the much anticipated event.

Raising everyone's expectations even further was a company called Teleport USA, a Los Angeles-based supplier of banking and promotional services between the city of Hakui and the United States. Teleport USA offered a tourist package called "Cosmo Isle Hakui Museum" which included not only a trip to Hakui and the museum, but featured various UFOlogists as speakers for a planned convention.[39]

On June 12, 1996, the sad reality of the "UFO Museum" came crashing down to Earth. The following announcement was made by Teleport USA:

To whom it may concern:

Re: Cosmo Isle Hakui Museum

We regret to inform you that the Cosmo Isle Hakui Museum Symposium scheduled for July 19–21 and the Tour that was set for July 16–23 has been canceled. At this late stage in time, it is very unfortunate that for political and bureaucratic reasons this symposium has been canceled.

There is opposition and controversy regarding the usage of the word UFO and some of the material that was set to be displayed. Museum officials have decided that now is not the appro-

priate time to hold this symposium. Museum officials are looking
to reschedule the symposium at a later date.

Since no official statement has been made about the Grand
Opening, it is anticipated that [the museum] will open July 1.
Please be aware that the Opening Ceremony is by invitation only.

Thank you for your understanding.

Sincerely,
Teleport USA.

With this brief and sudden declaration, the much-hyped "UFO
museum" disappeared on a whimper. It turned out to be the biggest
non-UFO related event of 1996. While the museum did open, it was
not about UFOs, nor was it ever supposed to have been. The
museum was dedicated to space and space exploration.

However, when the UFO community received word of Teleport
USA's disappointing announcement, several researchers cried
"conspiracy" and wondered *what political issues* or concerns had
led to the sudden termination of their beloved "UFO" museum.

Mr. Tetsu Matsuo, a spokesman for Teleport USA, fielded most
of the questions from UFO researchers, and made vague statements
about "election year concerns" by officials in Hakui. Matsuo also
assured those who inquired, but only when pressed, that the alleged
UFO convention might be rescheduled, "when more of the desired
speakers become available."[40]

In response to the sudden fizzling out of the UFO museum, con-
spiracy buffs in the UFO community began to speculate that the
United States government had pressured Japan to "back off" on its
UFO display plans—especially the exhibition of allegedly real
metallic debris from the supposed flying saucer crash at Roswell.
According to one of these researchers, the "inducement" offered to
Japan by the U.S. government, was the recently signed trade agree-
ment between the two countries![41]

This "reasoning" illustrates just how *absurd and desperate*
some of the "logic" can be by UFO conspiracy nuts whose standards of "critical thinking" are almost nonexistent. Since the recently ratified trade agreement between the United States and
Japan, signed by President William Clinton in 1996, was *tougher
on Japan* than any previous trade agreement had ever been (it put

an end to many of Japan's import quotas against American goods), it could hardly have served as a "bribe" in exchange for withholding UFO data as claimed.

Finally, when I asked Matsuo to comment on allegations and rumors that pressure from U.S. officials had forced the museum to cancel its UFO-related exhibits, he denied it.[42]

With the much-hyped UFO museum turning out not to be about UFOs after all, the question still remains how, where, and why did such a rumor get started?

Part of the blame rests squarely on Colin Andrews and Bob Dean's shoulders. These two researchers enthusiastically and naively helped fan the fires about what admittedly would have been an Earth-shattering event, if it had been true. But like all rumors, it had to start somewhere and have a place of origin. While Dean and Andrews certainly didn't start the UFO museum myth, they championed it, and have now been embarrassed by it, especially because of their hyperbole in promoting it via their dogmatic proclamations.

As it turns out, the source of the unfortunate UFO museum rumors has been found: it originates in Japan and has been traced to a man named Joshen Takano.

In August 1995, Japan's foremost and senior UFO researcher, Mr. Jun-Ichi Takanashi, chairman of the Japan UFO Science Society, wrote an exposé of the affair. Excerpts from his report follow:

> The much publicized "UFO Museum" in Hakui City, Japan, has opened on July 1, 1996, as scheduled, but it turned out to be an ordinary space museum. It has never been called UFO museum in the district [of Hakui]. Only Mr. Joshen Takano, an officer in charge of land planning in the Hakui City municipal office, called it so abroad. It has always been called "Space Museum" in the city, and it was changed to "Cosmo Isle Hakui" at the end of 1994. This "UFO Museum" was publicized as "the beginning of a very important government program following adoption of a new policy to educate the Japanese people about the UFO phenomenon within the next three years" [which appeared] in the fall 1993 issue of the *Circle Phenomenon Research International Newsletter,* as the result of a conversation between Mr. Johsen Tokano and [British crop circle researcher] Colin Andrews. It caused a worldwide uproar of doubts and comments from all

serious UFO researchers. But, it was a total laughing stock for all
Japanese UFO researchers. We have never known our government's interest in the UFO subject—there was absolutely no
inkling of such interest on the part of our government in the past.
Perhaps Mr. Tokano expressed his own interest and Colin
Andrews was deceived, and by his naive or deliberate propagation of this false news, the world was deceived. Ever since, the
world has been awaiting the opening of the "UFO Museum," but
that proved to have been a dream.[43]

Takanashi also mentioned in his report that the UFO angle on
the museum was the brainchild of a small group of Hakui city officials, who decided to exploit the subject in the hopes of bringing in
additional tourists, much like the town of Roswell capitalizes today
on its famous UFO "crash" of 1947.

"This was not the government's plan," Takanashi noted, "but
the city's [Hakui's] own plan, and it now appears that they have
failed in such [an] endeavor miserably. And it appears that the town
has already given up the policy to utilize the UFO subject as the
special attraction to lure visitors to this remote community."[44]

QUESTION #15

*Some people have called you, Kal Korff, a CIA operative or a dis-
information expert who is out to debunk the Roswell case and the
issue of UFOs in general.*

I first answered this question and dealt with this ridiculous charge
in my previous book *Spaceships of the Pleiades: The Billy Meier
Story.** For the last time (since I have no intention of dignifying
such an absurd allegation in my future written works), I am *not* a
CIA operative or any sort of "disinformation expert" or agent.

As I mentioned in my previous book, as UFO researcher Russ
Estes has said, "If you have half a brain in this field, you're automatically labeled 'CIA.' "

It is true that for several years I worked at Lawrence Livermore
National Laboratory. I was one of some 10,000 people who worked

_____

*See pages 408–409 of that book.

there at the time. While I did both unclassified and classified work, I am not a CIA "disinformation" agent nor do I work for any other branch of the government. In fact, I have worked for various federal agencies as either a consultant or a contractor in the fields of computer systems analysis and design, computer programming and multimedia, computer teaching, weapons design, weapons tracking systems, and antiterrorist and intelligence analysis only when my country has asked me to. I officially terminated my work for the United States government in January 1991, during the final days of the Persian Gulf War and Operation Desert Storm.

Although I will still be occasionally consulted for my opinions about certain issues, especially by law enforcement, I have never served in the military and have always been a *civilian* contractor, having worked for various police agencies and branches of the United States government as a *consultant* whenever my services and expertise are requested.*

The claim that I am a "disinformation agent" is equally absurd. *I am a UFO researcher pure and simple.* While I do not belong to any UFO groups or organizations, because I wish to avoid potential conflict of interest concerns, I advocate the *serious, objective, and scientific study* of UFO cases. If I were out to "debunk" the issue of UFOs, I would hardly promote this position in my writings, public lectures, and numerous media appearances.

Despite this fact, I am amazed that I still occasionally get labeled a "disinformation" agent or specialist by pro-UFO zealots and other paranoid types. UFO researcher and publisher Michael Hesemann, for example, has called me nothing less than "a debunker who spreads lies."†[45]

---

*Recent examples of how my analytical expertise has been requested by various agencies include a 1994–95 request to help consult the federal government on nuclear weapons technology acquisitions by terrorist groups. I also served for a very short time as a consultant to the prosecution in the famous O. J. Simpson double-murder case. However, after observing how the prosecution was, in my opinion, mishandling things, I resigned.

†Michael Hesemann, who is one of Billy Meier's staunchest supporters and is the European publisher of a book about the Meier case in Germany, has been extremely upset with me ever since *Spaceships of the Pleiades* was published. *Spaceships* conclusively proves that the Meier case is a monstrous fraud, and

Those who claim "Kal's with the government" are *ignorant* of the facts (to put it politely) and do not want to admit that both the Roswell and Billy Meier cases aren't credible evidence for the existence of visitations to Earth by extraterrestrials.

Whenever I study a purported UFO case, I am after the *truth*. I do not care what that "truth" ultimately turns out to be, I just want the truth if it is at all possible to determine. I believe that each UFO case must be considered on its own individual merits and analyzed according to the standards of scientific evidence.

NOTES

1. Kevin D. Randle, interview with reporter Arthur S. Levine, October 13, 1996. See also, Art Levine, *The Roswell Incident: Truth or Fiction?* MSNBC Internet Web Site, p. 3, posted on <http://www.msnbc.com/news>.

2. Charles Berlitz and William L. Moore, *The Roswell Incident* (New York: Berkeley Books, 1988), p. 46.

3. Kevin D. Randle and Donald R. Schmitt, *The Truth about the UFO Crash at Roswell* (New York: Avon Books, 1994), pp. 77–78.

4. Ibid., p. 205.

5. Kevin D. Randle, *International UFO Reporter* (July/August 1994): 3.

6. Kevin D. Randle and Donald R. Schmitt, *UFO Crash at Roswell* (New York: Avon Books, 1991), pp. 65–66.

7. Stanton T. Friedman and Don Berliner, *Crash at Corona: The U.S. Military Retrieval and Cover-Up of a UFO* (New York: Paragon House, 1992), p. 65.

8. Lt. Col. Thomas Badger Jr. by Command of Gen. Carl A. Spaatz, Issuance of Orders, June 5, 1947.

9. Robert Todd, "Blunder Alert: Roswell Record Found," *The Cowflop Quarterly: Reporting on UFOlogical Frauds and Fantasies,* no. 4 (March 8, 1996): 2.

10. Ibid.

11. Friedman and Berliner, *Crash at Corona,* p. 55.

12. Ibid., pp. 59, 69–70.

13. Ibid., p. 59.

14. Joe Nickell and John F. Fischer, "The Crashed-Saucer Forgeries," *International UFO Reporter* 15, no. 2 (March/April 1990).

---

although Hesemann has threatened to "expose me and my research," he has never done so.

Now that *this book refutes* most of what Hesemann and Philip Mantle have written in their upcoming treatise, *Beyond Roswell,* it appears that I shall continue to remain one of Hesemann's least favorite UFO researchers.

15. Stanton T. Friedman, "The Secret Life of Donald H. Menzel," *International UFO Reporter* 13, no. 1 (January/February 1988): 20–24.

16. Kal K. Korff, *Spaceships of the Pleiades: The Billy Meier Story* (Amherst, N.Y.: Prometheus Books, 1995), p. 340.

17. Kal K. Korff, personal interviews with Mrs. Florence Menzel and Elizabeth Davis, September 4, 1996.

18. Ibid.

19. Michael Hesemann and Philip Mantle, *Beyond Roswell: The Alien Autopsy Film, Area 51, and the U.S. Government Coverup of UFO's* (New York: Marlow & Co., 1997), p. 12.

20. Korff interviews with Mrs. Florence Menzel and Elizabeth Davis, September 4, 1996.

21. Berlitz and Moore, *The Roswell Incident*, pp. 150–51.

22. Kal K. Korff, interview with Brad Sparks, Irvine, California, May 30, 1992. Sparks interviewed several of Hoover's assistants regarding this matter and has numerous samples of Hoover's handwriting.

23. Ibid.

24. William L. Moore, lecture at the MUFON Annual Symposium, July 1, 1989, Las Vegas, Nevada.

25. William L. Moore, private discussion with Kal K. Korff, February 1982, Union City, California.

26. Jerome Clark, *The UFO Encyclopedia*, Vol. I. *UFOs in the 1980s* (Detroit: Apogee Books, 1990), p. 105.

27. Ibid., p. 106. Also William L. Moore, private discussion with Korff, February 1982, Union City, California.

28. Jerome Clark, *The UFO Encyclopedia*, Vol. I, p. 106.

29. Timothy Good, *Alien Contact: Top-Secret UFO Files Revealed* (New York: William Morrow and Company, 1993), pp. 114–17, 122, 126–27, 132–35. See also Jerome Clark, *The UFO Encyclopedia*, Vol. I, pp. 104–107.

30. Randle and Schmitt, *The Truth about the UFO Crash at Roswell*, p. 115.

31. Stanton T. Friedman, personal interviews with Kal K. Korff, November 12, 1979; April 5, 1980; and others.

32. Robert G. Todd, "Bolender Memo Reality Check," *The Cowflop Quarterly: Reporting on UFOlogical Frauds and Fantasies* 1, no. 2 (September 1, 1996): 1–2.

33. Robert G. Todd, personal letter to Kal K. Korff, dated September 2, 1996.

34. William F. Barrett, "Unidentified Flying Dollars," *Forbes* (July 15, 1996): 52.

35. Kal K. Korff, personal conversation with Mayor Tom Jennings's office, Roswell, New Mexico, September 27, 1996.

36. Barrett, "Unidentified Flying Dollars," pp. 49–52.

37. Korff conversation with Mayor Tom Jennings's office, Roswell, New Mexico, September 27, 1996.

38. Colin Andrews, *CPR Newsletter,* Fall 1993, p. 1.

39. Kal K. Korff, personal phone conversation with Tetsu Matsuo, spokesman for Teleport USA, Los Angeles, California, June 14, 1996.

40. Ibid.

41. Joyce L. Murphy, comments cited in Jorgen West's WUFOC, the free UFO-alternative on the Internet, "Japanese UFO Museum, part 2," issue no. 3, posted on <http://www.wufoc.com>.

42. Korff phone conversation with Tetsu Matsuo, June 13, 1996.

43. Jun-Ichi Takanashi, *The So-Called "UFO Museum,"* Japan UFO Science Society, August 1995.

44. Ibid.

45. Arthur S. Levine, "Alien Autopsy Film Gets Dissected," MSNBC Website, October 21, 1996, p. 5.

7

The Alien Autopsy Film

Why have you not submitted the original film, and not just film with leader, to Kodak for analysis?

Kal Korff

Film with image and not leader tape has been given . . . to the English broadcasters, the French broadcasters. It has been submitted to Kodak by the broadcasters.

Ray Santilli[1]

Extensive checking has revealed that no broadcaster, either French, English, or any other nationality, or the Eastman Kodak Company, has ever been given a single frame 'with image' of the alleged alien autopsy footage.

Kent Jeffrey[2]

In January 1995 the most bizarre and recent chapter in the Roswell legend began to unfold on another continent and would originate from a surprising source, a rock 'n' roll star! Reg Presley, the former lead singer of the British rock group The Troggs,* was being interviewed on the British Broadcasting Corporation's

---

*The Troggs are probably best known for their late 1960s hit single "Wild Thing."

morning talk show "Good Morning with Anne and Nick" when he made a startling announcement. Presley, who has a passionate interest in the subject of UFOs and so-called crop circles, claimed that he had just recently viewed motion picture footage of an actual autopsy being conducted on one of the aliens from the 1947 Roswell flying saucer crash![3]

Shortly thereafter, a British video producer named Ray Santilli stepped forward and announced that he had purchased actual autopsy and debris footage from an elderly cameraman who had filmed it all.

During the next several months, Santilli (with considerable help from British UFO researcher Philip Mantle) began to tease the media and hype the film. His purpose was to build up an eager audience for an upcoming "preview" that was scheduled to take place on May 5, 1995, at the London Museum. Santilli's objective was to screen the film for the media and certain UFO researchers, and then launch a bidding war to sell broadcast rights to the highest bidder in as many countries as possible. Admittedly, if the footage proved to be genuine, it would constitute the most sensational discovery of the millennium.

THE ROBERT KIVIAT FACTOR

Over 100 journalists, producers, and several UFOlogists traveled from all over the globe to attend the screening of Santilli's film. One of those individuals present was Robert Kiviat, a former television producer for NBC's "Unsolved Mysteries" and the Fox network's popular "Encounters" program.

Kiviat, like many of the people who attended the showing, has a passionate interest in the subject of UFOs and the paranormal. Kiviat had also recently left Fox television and was looking to branch out and start his own production company. He was scouting for material, and the purported "alien autopsy" footage that Santilli had boasted about just might fit the bill.

After the screening, Kiviat was intrigued enough by what he saw to meet with Ray Santilli in private. After their discussion, they reached an agreement in principle. Santilli would give Bob Kiviat

and his new production company, Kiviat-Greene Productions,*
exclusive first broadcast rights to the film. In exchange for doing
so, Santilli was eventually paid a sum of $125,000.

After returning to the United States, both Kiviat and Santilli
worked quickly. A broadcast video tape master was made from the
footage by Santilli and Kiviat soon reached an agreement with the
Fox television network to air a one-hour special about what promised to be a potentially historic event.

Ray Santilli, in the interim, was busy working things on his end
as well. Not content to stop with just a television broadcast, Santilli
decided he would market a videocassette called "Roswell: The
Footage." The entire venture would be marketed under the name of
"Roswell Limited." For the tidy sum of $59, plus shipping and han-
dling, one could order the videotape that contained the controversial alien autopsy footage.

The Fox Alien Autopsy Special

I had first gotten to know and work with Bob Kiviat when he was a
producer for the show "Encounters." Kiviat had been following the
Eduard "Billy" Meier case of Switzerland for a number of years and
wanted to make it the subject of an episode for the show. Since my
book *Spaceships of the Pleiades* definitively exposed that case as a
hoax, and Bob thought that a debate over the merits of the Meier
evidence would make for good television, I agreed to participate.

After the production ended, Kiviat and I stayed in touch with
one another. I was impressed with both his detailed knowledge of
the subject of UFOs and his sincere journalistic desire to investigate many of the same cases that I had felt also needed studying. As
it turned out, Kiviat and I had several things in common, and we
were both independently studying many of the same cases.

After learning that he had acquired the rights to the alleged
alien autopsy footage, I volunteered my services to Kiviat and

---

*Kiviat-Greene Productions ceased to exist in early 1996. Robert Kiviat
now owns and runs his own television production company known as Kiviat Productions, which has produced several paranormal-related specials for the Fox
network.

made sure that TotalResearch, a think tank dedicated to investigating various phenomena which I headed, and its resources would be available. Kiviat agreed, and asked that I start putting together an analytical gameplan in order to try and authenticate the alien autopsy footage. We joked about the fact that I was going to be the "Forensic UFOlogist" in the affair and I felt honored that of all the UFO researchers with whom Kiviat was well acquainted he gave me the nod.

At first Bob started asking for old documents that might be used as visual brain candy (filler) for his special. At his request, I forwarded to him copies of USAF reports on UFOs and newspaper clippings from 1947 from my own and TotalResearch's libraries. I also sent Kiviat an assortment of UFO graphs and statistics charts which were generated based on computer studies and modeling of data.

The original idea that Kiviat pitched to me was one that would have made any UFOlogist worth his salt more than happy. His original plan called for a live, one-hour simultaneous broadcast in both the United States and Great Britain, with a variety of medical and film experts, who would collectively analyze the material. By the end of the show, everyone would know what the verdict was. As Bob and I discussed the project, it was similar to Geraldo Rivera's opening of Al Capone's vault. This would be live television, only this time there would be no empty vault.*

However, shortly after I had sent Kiviat the material he requested, things began to change. The production in which I was eagerly looking forward to participating began to evaporate.

Almost immediately, I received several telephone calls from mutual acquaintances in the UFO field that had been in touch with Kiviat. The scope of the production was changing, and because certain forensic and analytical issues which could have definitively settled the authenticity issue of the alien autopsy footage once and for all were now being bypassed, I began to see that there would be no role for either TotalResearch or myself. The team I had assembled were also disappointed, since they were just as eager to get to

---

*In the Rivera special, after the opening of Capone's newly discovered vault was built up during almost the entire show, the catacomb turned out to be empty! What had been planned to be an exciting climax to Rivera's special ended up as a disappointment.

the truth of the matter as I was. However, Kiviat's hands were being shrewdly tied by Ray Santilli, in part because he would not provide any original film with images of the alien on it for proper scientific testing and age dating.

Unfortunately, the alien autopsy footage became an artificial and deliberate manmade "mystery"; one entirely avoidable if Santilli had just produced a single frame of film with the image of an alien for proper testing. However, he refused to do so.

Meanwhile in the United States, the subject of the alleged Roswell alien autopsy footage reached new frenzied heights. UFO believers were hopeful, UFO skeptics puzzled. Did such footage actually exist? While no one knew as yet with absolute certainty, the subject was on everyone in the UFO community's mind and lips and soon took center stage over all other cases.

In late August 1995, Fox's "Alien Autopsy: Fact or Fiction?" aired to television audiences. After viewing it, I was struck by the fact that not much of anything had been resolved with regard to the authenticity of the film, and this concerned me.

After the broadcast, I telephoned Bob Kiviat and congratulated him on his film. I wanted to know what would happen next, what the fallout from the special would be. Although I had decided at that point to try and write a book on Roswell, I knew that because of all the issues that had been left unresolved that I would have to add the alien autopsy circus to my list of things to study.

In discussing the situation with Kiviat, I learned that his production had been a ratings blockbuster. Millions of people were intrigued by the gruesome footage of the alien being sliced and diced on the autopsy table.

Because of the success of the show, Fox ordered another airing, and Kiviat added some material.

By this point in time I was busy on a book tour and was doing lectures and media appearances in southern California, right in Bob Kiviat's backyard. I called Kiviat from my hotel after a book signing and pressed him for a one-on-one meeting. I felt that this was a test of our professional, collaborative friendship. If Kiviat refused to meet with me or not deal with me "straight up," then I would have nothing further to do with him.

After talking with Kiviat on the phone, he agreed to meet. Not only was he his usual, friendly self, but I was able to observe things firsthand at his office (he was in the middle of producing an alien autopsy update for Fox). It became obvious to me how Ray Santilli was feeding him a line.

When the subject of the film came up, I asked Kiviat if I could examine as much of it as possible. I wanted to absorb as many facts about the case as I could. Bob quickly agreed, and in one of his conference meeting rooms I began to view the alien autopsy footage one frame at a time.

Over the course of the next several hours, I pointed out to Kiviat numerous problems in the Santilli film which made me believe that it was a hoax. Bob eagerly listened, and then asked me if I might be able to go on camera and conduct some quick computer enhancements to air these issues. He put me up in a nearby hotel and I stayed up all night working on it.

Per his instructions, I called early in the morning and told him that I was ready. However, because of production problems and the fact that "Star Trek's" Jonathan Frakes (who narrated the special) was being filmed that morning, there was simply no time to film another presenter. Because the production had to be turned over to Fox within forty-eight hours, there was no way my analytical opinions could be included.

As I left to fly home, I was satisfied with what had happened between Kiviat and myself. I saw firsthand that he really tried, but the reality was my last minute, impromptu visit had been too late. I promised Kiviat I would stay in touch, and report to him whatever I found as I continued my study.

THE ALIEN AUTOPSY FILM ANALYSIS

The first problem with the alien autopsy footage that indicates it is a hoax has to do with the type of movie camera that Santilli has claimed was used, a Bell and Howell Filmo 70 model.

The Bell and Howell Filmo 70 is a spring-loaded, manually wound camera. Unlike today's cameras which have electrically driven motors to advance the film frames, the Filmo 70 does not. Because of this, when a person films something with this particular model and then stops and starts again, the first few frames are over-exposed while the spring loaded mechanism gets going. As a result, a white "hot flash" area will saturate the first few frames and this effect is visible both to the naked eye and certainly through frame-by-frame examination.

Despite this unavoidable fact, it is interesting to note that Santilli's alien autopsy film displays *no such hot flashes!* In other words, where it is obvious that the camera had to be stopped and started again (such as when angles change), the resulting hot flash which should be present is not. This is very incriminating evidence that contrary to what Santilli claims, the camera used to film the autopsy footage was not a Bell and Howell Filmo 70 model, but rather a more modern one.*

While advocates of the authenticity of the alien autopsy footage will argue that hot flashes do indeed appear in the Santilli Roswell video that he directly markets, (which was released *after* the Fox special originally aired), this is not true. Indeed, a careful examina-tion of these purported "hot flashes" in Santilli's video reveals that they are digitally created, and are not real! This can be easily proven by the fact that the light moves from left to right in every "hot flash" instance, a sure sign that a special effects filter was used! By comparison, real hot flashes generated by spring coiled mechanisms produce much more random lighting spots and vary widely.

In addition to this, a frame-by-frame examination shows more than twenty-two instances of "jump" cutting, sequences which sud-denly start and stop. Because none of these have hot flashes either, the film has been either edited or a more modern camera than the Filmo 70 was used. This means that the integrity of the film is sus-pect, since it has obviously been manipulated by either Santilli or someone else.

---

*Autopsies are normally filmed with a stationary camera positioned above the workspace to provide a full view of the body and filming from this angle is continuous. In addition, a still photographer is often used to provide detailed close-up images. Yet, despite the fact that this was the autopsy of the millennium, no still photos were ever taken, nor was there a stationary camera positioned to show the body at all times. This is further evidence that the alien autopsy film is not credible.

Because Ray Santilli has conveniently refused to submit even *one frame* showing the alien for proper scientific dating and testing, not much additional commentary can be rendered as to the forensics or physical characteristics of the footage. Since a video master made directly from what Santilli had supplied Kiviat is all I had to work with, my examination was limited accordingly. Thus, in order to further try and determine the issue of the film's credibility, we must turn to what the footage itself shows since there is no original film to examine. (This is an important point, because Mantle and Hesemann and other supporters of the footage never address this. They endorse the film, yet without original stock to examine they are in no position to credibly do this.)

Supporters of the Santilli autopsy film have often made the claim that Kodak has authenticated the age of the footage because of the markings on the edges of the frames which indicate their year of manufacture. This is not true.

When Ray Santilli supplied a strip of film for examination that he claimed was from the autopsy footage, he furnished only *blank leader film,* the transparent plastic portion that one feeds into a projector when threading the reel. While this blank leader film did contain the appropriate edge codes, since there was no image on it, the claim that it is from one of the autopsy reels cannot be proven.

On November 10, 1995, I was in the studio audience of the popular show "Town Meeting" on ABC's Seattle-based station KOMO. Ray Santilli was one of the featured guests via satellite hook-up to England. Because Santilli could not see me, and had only an earpiece to rely on, I took advantage of the fact that I could see *him* and decided to test his honesty. I was already aware of the numerous times Santilli had made false claims about Kodak having "authenticated" his footage, as well as the misleading information he gave the media regarding the edge code dating.

As Santilli was fielding questions, I asked him why he had never bothered sending any film with image to Kodak for authentication. Santilli replied to me that he had indeed supplied such material and that "the broadcasters" had done so as well.

However, when I checked with Kodak I found out that this wasn't true. While Santilli initially contacted them to *pick their brains* about what *would* be the proper edge code markings for

1947-vintage film, he has never supplied a single image for examination! Indeed, as of this writing, Kodak has a *standing offer* to examine Santilli's film for *free,* but he refuses to send it. This is inexcusable, since according to Kodak, all they need to do is punch a small hole in a single frame to properly date the film!

There is another problem with the alien autopsy film: Ray Santilli has posted on the Internet copies of some of the labels from film canisters that supposedly contain the autopsy footage. These labels, which Santilli claims were written by the cameraman, bear the Department of Defense seal—which did not exist in June or July 1947!

Another problem with the film canister labels that Santilli has posted as his "proof," is the fact that they indicate that an "85 filter" was used. Unfortunately, an 85 filter is used when shooting *color* film only, not black and white, yet the alien autopsy footage is black and white, and Santilli claims it was shot in black and white. This also doesn't make sense.

Ray Santilli has also stated that in footage he has yet to release, former President Harry S. Truman can be seen. This would indicate that Truman was either in New Mexico where the "UFO" was supposedly recovered, or in Texas where, we are told, the autopsy was performed.

However, a check with the Truman Library established that President Truman was *not* in either New Mexico or Texas during the entire months of June through August 1947!

Curiously, since late 1995, when Santilli originally made this statement, he has since changed his story. He now claims that the reel of film showing President Truman could not be salvaged due to its age.

THE "MYSTERIOUS" CAMERAMAN

Now that we have established that many of Ray Santilli's claims are false, and that the optical characteristics of the footage and the physics of the camera are equally bogus, what about the individual who supposedly took the film, the alleged cameraman?

Shortly after Ray Santilli came forward and started granting press interviews, he wrote a personal account of how he acquired the footage and posted it in the public domain and officially on record for all to see. His official statement is as follows:

> As a result of research into film material for a music documentary, I was in Cleveland, Ohio, . . . in the summer of 1993. Whilst there I had identified some old film material taken by Universal News in the summer of 1955. As Universal News no longer existed and I needed the film . . . [I] was able to determine that the film was shot by then a local freelance cameraman. He had been employed by Universal News because of a Film union strike in the summer of 1955.
>
> The cameraman was located, following which a very straight-forward negotiation took place for his small piece of film, i.e., cash for three minutes of film. Upon completion of this the cameraman asked if I would be interested in purchasing outright very valuable footage taken during his time in the forces. He explained that the footage in question came from the Roswell crash [and] that it included debris and recovery footage, and of most importance, autopsy footage.
>
> At this time I had no knowledge whatsoever of the Roswell event but when someone tells you they have real footage of an alien autopsy of course it's of interest.
>
> The cameraman was in his eighties [and] seemed a genuine enough person. He explained that from 1942 to 1952 he worked as a cameraman for the Army Air Force and special forces, that during this time he was sent to many places and filmed many events including the tests that were part of the Manhattan Project (Atomic bomb testing White Sands).
>
> He explained that on June 2nd 1947 he received an order directly from General [Clements] McMullen stating there had been a crash and to go immediately to White Sands and film everything he could. . . .
>
> After hearing the story I was taken to the cameraman's house and viewed the footage. . . .
>
> The footage was and is quite incredible, from his house I telephoned Kodak to ask their advice in checking the film. I was given the codes which corresponded with the codes on the film.
>
> I quickly confirmed a cash offer subject to further checks and the cameraman accepted. I said I would require a few days and a small sample of the film to take back. The cameraman gave me

around two feet of leader from the film itself which I brought back to the UK.

Unfortunately raising the money needed became a problem and a few days turned into a few weeks, then a few months. This was made all the more difficult because the cameraman needed money for a family wedding. By now the cameraman was becoming very nervous and refused to take my calls. Each time I called, his wife would simply take a message.

The story stops there until November of 1994 when with the money in hand I flew over without warning and tried; this time I succeeded.

My impression of the cameraman is that he is totally genuine, he is an ordinary person who never really made a great deal of money in his life, has been married to the same woman for over 50 years and seems as stable as you could wish. I had the opportunity of going through his many old photo albums, his film collection, and personal papers. I am certain that the cameraman was everything he claims.

I came away with 22 reels of film, 21 safety prints and one negative.[4]

While Santilli's story is interesting, like so much of what he has said in this affair, it is demonstrably false. The archive footage that Santilli claims he was looking for that led him to travel to Cleveland, Ohio, was some motion picture film of rock 'n' roll legend Elvis Presley taken on July 20, 1955. This is the earliest known film ever shot of Elvis, and it featured him performing in two concerts, at a high school and in an auditorium later that evening.

As Santilli's statement makes it very clear, he eventually met the cameraman who shot the Elvis footage, and after purchasing the film was shown alien autopsy movie for the first time, which was taken by the cameraman while he was "in the Forces" (i.e., the military), to use Ray Santilli's own words. Santilli has since gone on record as stating that the cameraman's name was Jack Barnett.

Unfortunately, for Santilli's credibility, while Jack Barnett was indeed a cameraman, he was *never in the military and died in 1967!* It is therefore impossible for Ray Santilli to have met with him in 1993, let alone negotiate a fee and buy some film footage.

Since there is no denying the fact that Santilli did indeed

acquire the rare concert films of Elvis Presley, the question now becomes where did he get the film?

According to officials at Polygram records, which purchased the Elvis movies, Ray Santilli acquired the Elvis films from Bill Randle in Cleveland, Ohio. However, the date of this transaction is not what Santilli represented it to be. According to Randle, he met with Santilli on July 4, 1992—nearly a *whole year* before Ray claimed he met and purchased film from his imaginary cameraman.

To make matters worse for Santilli, Bill Randle had hired Jack Barnett back in 1955 to film the young Elvis Presley! This explains where Ray Santilli "appropriated" Barnett's name from.

Despite this, Ray Santilli still insists his cameraman exists. He has conceded that he made up several names, (Jack Barrett and Jack Snow among them), but says that he did so in order to protect the cameraman's privacy and prevent retaliation from the U.S. government.

This notion is absurd, since it is obvious that if the cameraman was the only person to ever be chosen to film the alien autopsies, the moment the film was aired it would have been obvious to the government who this individual was, especially if the highly organized, super-secret, and ominous government UFO cover-up that the pro-Roswell authors claim exists.

As this book goes to press, the latest bizarre chapter in the saga of Santilli's cameraman has unfolded. Fuji TV in Japan has aired a videotape of the purported cameraman answering a series of questions that, ironically, Bob Kiviat prepared and gave to Ray Santilli.

Does the formerly dead now alive cameraman really exist? Only time will tell. Now that we have seen his face (see figure 24), maybe someone will come forward and identify him. He is either the real cameraman, or an actor hired to portray him in yet another Ray Santilli scam.

THE ALIEN AUTOPSY BLUNDERS

There is an abundance of evidence to indicate that the autopsy procedure shown is not being carried out by real doctors, but by actors.

The first obvious point has to do with the way the scissors are being held by the alleged pathologist. In real autopsies, the scissors are held in one's hand with the thumb and middle finger. The index finger is used to steady the scissors. However, as fig. 21 shows, in the alien autopsy film, the "pathologist" is holding the scissors the wrong way—as if he's cutting a piece of paper, using the thumb and index finger to hold them. This is laughable.

Another problem with the autopsy procedure is that according to the clock on the wall, which the "cameraman" makes a point to repeatedly show, the entire dissection of the alien took roughly two and a half hours! This is a remarkably short period of time considering the fact that we're supposedly dealing with an extraterrestrial here. One would assume that a real autopsy of an alien would take weeks, if not months. It would be a one-time historic opportunity, one that would not be rushed or hurried.

In a real autopsy, the body is always placed on a small block that arches the back and extends the chest upward. This is done to provide easier access to the chest cavity and to make any cuts that are needed. However, in the alien autopsy film, the alien lies flat on the table, with no block placed under it. Imagine this, the most important autopsy ever conducted, and the "specialists" don't follow even the most basic of procedures: They can't hold their instruments correctly and they don't elevate their corpse!

There are problems regarding the body itself. For example, the creature exhibits a strong, stocky, muscular physique. Yet when the "doctors" cut it open, its internal organs are just sitting in the body as if they are dumplings floating in a bowl of chicken soup! In addition, once the doctors remove the aliens' internal organs, they place the organs into metal pans. In reality, to avoid potential contamination, internal organs are always placed in glass jars. This is a fact that any first year medical student would know.

Another problem occurs when the "pathologist" cuts open the alien. The camera is perfectly in focus (whereas in every other portion of the autopsy where minute details might be seen the camera is conveniently out of focus) and the "creature" bleeds easily. This is highly unlikely. When living things that have blood in them die, gravity takes over and causes all fluids to sink to the lowest point in the body. This is basic physics. However, in the alien autopsy film, the creature "bleeds" as if it were still alive. Yet according to the "cameraman," the alien had been dead for many days!

There are other problems, only one more of which will be discussed here. In the scene where the brain is removed, one of the doctors holds the head of the alien still while this procedure is taking place. After removal, the head snaps back, just like one would expect a latex or special effects dummy to do!

CONCLUSION

The "alien autopsy" footage has *zero credibility*. The preponderance of evidence indicates that it is a hoax, and not a very good one at that; although the special effects are certainly commendable. Those pro-UFO Roswell authors and alien autopsy supporters such as Philip Mantle and Michael Hesemann simply ignore the bounty of evidence which discredits the Santilli film.

NOTES

1. Kal K. Korff, personal interview question to Ray Santilli, "Town Meeting," KOMO TV, November 10, 1995.

2. Kent Jeffrey, "Santilli's Controversial Autopsy Movie," (SCAM), Internet posting, <http:// www. Roswell.org>, p. 5.

3. Reg Presley, "Good Morning with Anne and Nick," British Broadcasting Corporation, January 13, 1995.

4. Posted on CompuServe, Sightings Forum, and <http://www.Roswell Center.com>.

8

The Roswell UFO Crash:
Whatever Happened to the Truth?

Scientific credibility has high standards indeed. Why should this
burden be placed upon UFOlogy?
M. S. LaMoreaux, *MUFON Journal,* May 1994

Prior to the publication of this book, the so-called Roswell UFO
crash of 1947 appeared to be an invincible case, the "Holy Grail"
of all UFO incidents that UFOlogists had been hoping for to prove
once and for all that we are indeed being visited by extraterrestrials
and, more ominously, that the United States government has lied
and covered up this fact for nearly fifty years.

Now that we have examined, and unfortunately refuted, the
bulk of what has been touted for years as "hard evidence" in the
Roswell case, we know better.

But where does this leave us? What are the lessons to learn as
we now sift through the rubble among the ruins of what was Roswell? As we shall see, while the lessons we need to learn are relatively simple, applying them is not.

The Roswell "UFO crash" of 1947 is not the only case in UFO
history to be blown out of proportion, nor is it going to be the last.
Unfortunately, the UFO field is overloaded with so-called investigators who simply aren't capable of doing a very thorough, and

more importantly, competent job. As if this weren't bad enough, the UFO field is comprised of people who are willing to take advantage of the gullibility of others, especially the paying public. Let's not pull punches here: The Roswell UFO myth has been very good business for UFO groups, publishers, for Hollywood, the town of Roswell, the media, and UFOlogy.

While I define "UFOlogy" as "the scientific study of UFO reports," I admit I'm being a bit idealistic because that's what UFOlogy *should* be. Instead, the number of researchers who employ science and its disciplined methodologies is appallingly small. While I shall decline to list any names, let me just say that out of the hundreds of UFOlogists with whom I have corresponded during my twenty-three years in this field, the number of researchers who truly apply the rigors of science can be counted on the fingers of my two hands!

Although most of these people do not correctly apply the methods of science, at least a few employ critical thinking. But like the scientific practitioners, the critical thinkers also constitute a small tribe. If critical thinking were applied by more UFO researchers as well as the general public, then the blatant lies spouted by such Roswell "heroes" as Maj. Jesse Marcel would have been identified and exposed for what they truly were back in 1978 or 1979 at the latest. Instead, the UFO community and the media *embraced* the tales of Marcel eagerly and whole-heartedly, blindly repeating them without thinking objectively.

It was Stanton Friedman's responsibility, *more than anyone else's,* to double check and verify Major Marcel's claims about *both* his background and the supposed Roswell "UFO events" of 1947. After all, it was Friedman who unleashed Jesse Marcel on the world, and we are worse off today for it.

While Friedman eagerly and very doggedly pursued the *UFO aspect* of Marcel's stories, for which he should be commended because he *thought* Marcel was telling the truth, he appears to have done no significant checking on Marcel's claimed background. If Friedman had done so, he would have discovered what researcher Bob Todd and I did.

In their book *Crash at Corona,* Berliner and Friedman write: "Jesse Marcel was exactly who he claimed to be, and as such was an important cog in a machine whose bare outline was just starting to take form. He had indeed been in the right place at the right time to become aware of the crash and the wreckage and the return of the mysterious material to Roswell Army Air Field. The one-time intelligence officer of an elite Army Air Forces unit was exactly the sort of firsthand witness who could propel the story of the crash into the history books."[1]

While Friedman was certainly right in one aspect, Marcel indeed, with Friedman's considerable help, put Roswell into the history books—but it was for entirely the *wrong* set of reasons! Major Marcel was hardly, to use Friedman's and Berliner's words, "exactly who he claimed to be."

While Friedman continues to endorse Maj. Jesse Marcel as a credible witness,[2] his failures in this arena are inexcusable nonetheless.

To further compound this unfortunate situation, Friedman has championed, ironically, *exposing* frauds in the UFO field in the past. He has also published papers exposing the false background claims of UFO researcher Bill Spaulding. In fact, for the 1995 Mutual UFO Network (MUFON) Annual Symposium, Friedman was preparing to present a paper called "Deceit in UFOlogy," which exposed the tall tales and false backgrounds of other popular UFO luminaries such as Milton William Cooper, the aforementioned Spaulding, Guy Kirkwood, and Frank Stranges. In this same paper, Friedman also planned to expose the *dozens* of false claims by Roswell researcher Kevin Randle regarding his investigation and the two books he has co-authored on the subject.[3] Unfortunately, Friedman's paper never saw the light of day because MUFON requested instead that he do a Roswell update treatise, which he did.[4]

The point here is not to pick on or single out Stanton Friedman. Friedman works hard and diligently in his tireless efforts to blow open what he calls the "Cosmic Watergate"—the U.S. government's alleged all-encompassing, sweeping, purported cover-up of the UFO phenomenon. However, as we have seen, much of the evidence Friedman and others use to buttress their arguments is fatally flawed. In short, their "case" is weak, and they have no smoking guns.

When Robert Todd wrote a short summary of Major Marcel's exaggerated background claims in Jim Moseley's popular *Saucer*

*Smear,** Friedman's response was a lame reply which never refuted Todd's charges against Marcel.

Whatever happened to the truth?

As of this writing, the whole Roswell affair has become an embarrassing circus of "eyewitness" bandwagon jumpers and profit exploitation hyperbole. As Roswell Mayor Tom Jennings proudly boasts, "New Mexico is a tourism state. Roswell did not have a tourist attraction in the past, now the cash registers are ringing."[5]

Part of the problem with regard to the UFO community's almost blind acceptance of the Roswell myth is a fundamental *lack of understanding* of the true nature of the so-called UFO evidence. For example, a significant number of my colleagues tell me that UFOs are unquestionably real (and among my associates are all of the well-known names in this field). Since the term "UFO" stands for unidentified flying object, I have no quarrel with this. As long as there are people on this planet there will always be sightings of objects which are unidentified. So, from this standpoint, UFOs cannot be anything else *but* "real." However, when some of these same colleagues point to the mounds of "scientific evidence" as a means of justifying their beliefs I feel compelled to ask them (quite seriously) to which evidence do they refer? I certainly know of none. And in theory, I should, having been a UFOlogist for more than twenty-three years now and having investigated thousands of cases.

More often than not I'll get a reply like: "Well, you know, Kal, the millions of sightings, all of those photographs, the landings, the abductions, the government memos we now have; all these people can't be lying." While I certainly agree, such a statement conveys once again, in my opinion, a fundamental lack of understanding as to the true nature of the UFO "evidence."

All UFO cases can be broken down into four fundamental categories, the first of which is a sighting, when a person sees a UFO. UFO photos and films are also included in this category since they, too, are supposed to depict what the witness(es) allegedly saw.

The second category includes the radar-visual cases, instances where a UFO is seen and tracked on radar.

The third category covers the landing-trace cases, incidents

---

*Located on the Internet at <http://www.mcs.com/~kvg/Smearv42>.

where a UFO hovers above or near the ground or lands and produces some sort of physical evidence to show that it has been there. Examples of such physical evidence are landing-gear impressions, radioactivity, burnt circular rings, flattened grass, and so on.

The fourth and final category of UFO data covers the alien being/occupant or abduction cases: instances in which the actual alien pilots are seen in or about their craft, or have forcibly taken on board their ship one or more human beings. Usually, these people claim they are subjected to some sort of interrogation or physical examination (sometimes with a sexual component) and are then released.

Surely the existence of millions of reports worldwide proves *something,* doesn't it? Of course it does, but unlike a good deal of my colleagues, *I don't profess to have the answer(s)* as to what it might prove. The reason for my cautious stand rests with the very nature of this so-called evidence. Unfortunately, most of it is *scientifically worthless!*

Consider if you will the first category of UFO data: sightings. In truth, a sighting is nothing more than a story. You can't prove it actually happened. Unless glaring evidence of a hoax is detected, all you can do is accept the person's *word* that what he or she is telling you is the truth. After you've gotten this far, and made this leap of faith (not science), you have another problem: How can you prove that the incident actually occurred precisely the way the witness(es) describes? Practically and scientifically speaking, you cannot.

What about the second category of UFO reports: radar-visual cases? Once again we're left with the same problem in that you cannot prove that the object(s) in question is an extraterrestrial spacecraft.

The landing-trace or landing-track cases offer theoretically the largest potential for scientific pay dirt. But while there are more than 4,500 such reports on record, a truly unexplainable physical trace or irrefutably extraterrestrial artifact has yet to be uncovered, even in the Roswell case!

The "creature" and abduction reports bring us full circle to the same, fundamental problem once again: They are nothing more than stories, perhaps genuine, perhaps not.

So, where's the plethora of "scientific evidence" to which many of my fellow UFO colleagues often refer? Well, it's located entirely throughout the four categories of data just reviewed. At least that's what a good many appear to believe. However, as we have shown above and for the reasons described, things unfortunately aren't always that simple. Again, this is due to a lack of critical thinking.

Whatever happened to the truth?

To put it bluntly, if critical thinking were applied by more UFO researchers and especially the general public overall, then the Roswell promoters, and especially the purported "eyewitnesses," would find it difficult to continue their activities. Instead, they are thriving!

For example, I am sure that most people remember a series of books written by Erich von Däniken. He is the Swiss hotelier who wrote *Chariots of the Gods?*, *Gods from Outer Space,* and *Gold of the Gods,** among other titles. To date, von Däniken's numerous books have managed to generate worldwide sales of over *42 million copies!* [6]

Undoubtedly, the enormous success of von Däniken's books can in part be attributed to widespread fascination in the possibility that benevolent beings from outer space once visited us as "gods" who later helped humanity build the world's greatest ancient monuments. But I would submit that the underlying reason why von Däniken's books have been so successful is a distinct absence of critical thinking.

As much as some may hate to admit it, the public is gullible. We have a penchant for believing a good deal of what we read and see on television. If you disagree with this point then ask yourself the following question: Which has a larger reading audience: *Time* or the *National Enquirer*? If you picked *Time,* you're wrong. Next to *TV Guide, National Enquirer* is the most widely read magazine in the United States! Now if this doesn't say something about the reading habits of the populace, I don't know what else does.

The public accepts what it reads as being for the most part true. And when you have such books as Kevin Randle and Donald Schmitt's mistitled *The Truth about the Roswell UFO Crash* being marketed and cleverly crafted as a work of "nonfiction," then the truth is even more difficult to distinguish unless the unsuspecting reader decides to independently check the data presented in such works.

---

*New York: G. P. Putnam's Sons, 1970, 1971, and 1973, respectively.

The public accepts the tabloids' stories of Hollywood's affairs and scandals, stories of werewolves and vampires and other gobbledygook such as President Clinton's alleged consultations with ETs, just like they accepted von Däniken's ancient astronaut stories. But the public is not alone, for some of the "experts" (UFOlogists in this case) have fallen victim to subjectivity as well. Their lack of a fundamental understanding of the unfortunately unscientific nature of the so-called UFO evidence as mentioned earlier is the main problem.

On the other side of the coin, getting back to the issue of the general public and the question of whatever happened to the truth: How many of you remember a book by the title of *Guardians of the Universe?* by Ronald Story? How about *The Space Gods Revealed,* by the same author?* These two books conclusively prove that Erich von Däniken does not have a case, and that von Däniken even *manufactured* some of his "evidence," particularly the material cited in his bestselling book *Gold of the Gods.* If neither of these two titles strikes a chord of familiarity, I am not the least bit surprised. Unlike the books of von Däniken, they were never runaway bestsellers. The masses didn't flock to the bookstores by the millions to read the true story that these works told. Their minds were made up: von Däniken is right, let reality be damned. Again, lack of critical thinking.

Whatever happened to the truth?

People seem to *want* UFOs, ancient astronauts, crashed saucers, and pickled aliens to be real. They seem to want to believe in ESP, ghosts, and reincarnation. Historically, these phenomena have seemingly always held a special place in the minds and many cultures of humankind.

As our species rapidly approaches the end of this century, uncritical acceptance of paranormal phenomena, as well as a rise in the membership of cults, is bound to increase severalfold. Historically, the end of every century has brought forth scores of false prophets and self-proclaimed "Messiahs" who preach gloom and doom and the impending end of our world, or the formation of some sort of "new world order."

Guardians of the Universe? (London: New English Library, 1979); *The Space Gods Revealed* (New York: Harper and Row, 1976).

The year 2000 is considered by many people to be a "special time." Depending on whom you ask, we're either approaching the End Times, with God soon to render judgment on us all; or we're headed toward World War III; or perhaps even the Age of Aquarius and brotherly bliss! Regardless of what the future ultimately holds, it is prudent to exercise caution when studying paranormal claims and other such purported events. This is especially true today, where our latest bout with Millennial Madness has resulted in an all-time high of almost blind, uncritical acceptance of all things "paranormal." As we march toward the year 2000, it should be a time of reexamination, a time of reflection, about who and what we are and, more importantly, where we are going! Now, perhaps more than ever, we especially need more critical thinking as our world and the major powers that be struggle to redefine themselves.

As we look back on this century, we have gone from the horse-drawn carriage to the automobile, through two world wars and the atomic age to men on the moon and to personal computing and nanotechnology. This century has seen more changes and quantum leaps in paradigm shifts than any other in our history.

As we go forth into the twenty-first century, we cannot afford to repeat the mistakes that have plagued us in the twentieth century. If we do, the twenty-first century may very well turn out to be our last one, and if this should come to pass than it will be no one's fault but our own. There's no need or excuse for this. What we need is clear, concise, critical thinking now more than ever.

The topic of UFO phenomena, which are composed of numerous and diverse claims, is an area certainly worthy of scientific study. However, professing to know just *what* UFOs are, and claiming that there is "hard, quantifiable, scientific evidence" for their existence, is another matter entirely. While a priori belief in paranormal phenomena, or any other subject for that matter, is everyone's universal, individual right, one should exercise caution against those who mislead and misinform.

Remember, con-men and pseudoscientific puffery exist in just about *every* field of study and are *not* unique to the world of UFOlogy and the paranormal. Will you become their next victim?

If the Roswell "UFO crash" is supposed to represent both the "truth" and the "best" UFO case that UFOlogy has to offer, then the

UFO field is in deep trouble. As long as UFO researchers and the groups they belong to continue to blindly spout the Roswell "gospel" as if it were proven fact, then the study of UFO reports will never gain acceptance or credibility by mainstream science, nor should it.

The time has come for the UFO community to take an *honest* look at itself in the mirror concerning Roswell. If and when they ever decide to do this, they will see for the first time that they have two black eyes and a huge hole in their head—all of which have been self-inflicted.

✳   ✳   ✳

AUTHOR'S POSTSCRIPT

As this book goes to press, the disposition of the Roswell authors and where they stand on the case is most intriguing. Here's a brief synopsis:

Don Berliner

Although he co-authored *Crash at Corona* with Stanton Friedman and originally endorsed the Plains of San Augustin "crash"/Gerald Anderson tale in the book, Don Berliner has now changed his mind and no longer supports the San Augustin crash story. He has also renounced his support for Gerald Anderson. Berliner still apparently believes that the wreckage of a flying saucer was recovered by Mac Brazel, and refuses to accept Project Mogul as an explanation.[7]

Stanton Friedman

Stanton Friedman still maintains that Roswell involves a crashed UFO and extraterrestrial bodies. However, unlike the conclusion reached in his earlier book, *Crash at Corona,* he no longer appears to endorse the tall tales of Gerald Anderson. It's unfortunate he believed them in the first place!

Friedman still believes that a crash also took place in the plains of San Augustin. He also endorses the MJ-12 documents and, despite irrefutable proof that his star witness, Maj. Jesse Marcel, lied to him repeatedly during their interviews, he still regards Marcel as a credible witness![8]

Michael Hesemann and Philip Mantle

Michael Hesemann and Philip Mantle have written the ultimate *subjective* Roswell treatise, *Beyond Roswell: The Alien Autopsy Film, Area 51, and the U.S. Government Coverup of UFO's.* In this work, the authors endorse virtually every Roswell tale, no matter how far-fetched, as well as the infamous alien autopsy film. While much of Hesemann and Mantle's claims are disproven throughout this book, unfortunately Jesse Marcel Jr. has seen fit to write the foreword for their tome, claiming that, "I am delighted to offer this, my first written public statement, in support of Michael Hesemann and Philip Mantle's book."[9]

Hesemann and Mantle truly go "beyond" the fictional scenarios of Randle and Schmidt in their treatise, and for serious Roswell UFO researchers new all-time low has been reached.

Hesemann and Mantle appear to have also conducted some of their "research" via séance or other "psychic" means. In their original manuscript, for example, the following text appears:

> "I shall have to get [the sheep] over with the truck this afternoon," said Mac Brazel, rather disgustedly to Dee [Loretta Proctor's son], "or they'll die of thirst!" He [Brazel] then picked up a few of the fragments and stuffed them into [the] pockets of his saddle. "I'll show them to your parents," he said, "and see what they say about it." They [Brazel and Dee Proctor] then rode back to the ranch house.[10]

While this paragraph is interesting, it is pure fiction passed off as fact. Since Mac Brazel *died in 1963,* Hesemann and Mantle couldn't possibly quote him since Brazel *never spoke with any UFO investigator* about what he had found!

William L. Moore

William Moore still maintains that a UFO was recovered near Roswell, but has been a virtual recluse from the UFO community ever since his "confession" that he was a government "disinformation" agent. Not much has been heard from Moore in the public UFO arena for nearly ten years.

Karl Pflock

Karl Pflock seems to vacillate in his opinion about the Roswell case. At the July 1995 MUFON Annual Symposium in Seattle, Washington, Pflock told me that *both* a UFO and a Mogul device were involved. I informed Pflock that I agreed with him about the Mogul part.

This conclusion of Pflock's is pretty much on par with what he stated in his treatise *Roswell in Perspective,* where he wrote: "Whatever the exact circumstances, an encounter between some sort of crewed vehicle and one of Charlie Moore's unwieldy monsters brought both down."[11] According to Col. Albert Trakowski, whom Pflock had interviewed for his book, "Karl Pflock apparently wanted to establish the 'incident' of Roswell as a UFO incident."[12]

However, in late October, 1996, Pflock told journalist Arthur S. Levine, for an article Levine was writing for the Website at MSNBC, that he was "sure" *no extraterrestrial device* was involved at Roswell.[13]

Despite Pflock's apparent "change" in opinion, he hedged when the subject of former Roswell mortician Glenn Dennis came up. Pflock still has problems trying to make Glenn Dennis's testimony "fit" into his new (as of October 1996), non-extraterrestrial scenario. In trying to rationalize Dennis's yarn, Pflock told Levine that the "aliens" Dennis was told about and the drawing of the creature he claims his nurse friend showed him, may have been badly mangled human crash victims![14] Apparently, at this late stage in the Roswell circus, it still hasn't occurred to Pflock that Dennis may simply be lying.

Kevin Randle

Kevin Randle has *backpedaled* from almost *all* of his earlier Roswell pronouncements. Incredibly, he now says that, "If I had to rely on the public record [in the Roswell case], I'd throw up. The evidence is not strong and it's not compelling."[15]

This is extremely ironic, to put it mildly, since it is *Kevin Randle and Donald Schmitt's two books* that account for *most* of what is in the public record!

While Randle still believes that Roswell involved a crashed UFO, he has pinned most of his hopes for the case's legitimacy on the tall tales of Frank Kaufmann, the man who claims to have been part of the government's UFO recovery team. Randle has bet what's left of his farm on a set of faxed, photocopied documents from 1947 which Kaufmann claims prove there was a crashed saucer.

Despite the fact that there were neither faxes nor photocopiers in the 1940s, and the incriminating truth is that Kaufmann can't produce any original material for scientific examination, Randle has boldly declared, in an incredible statement to reporter Arthur S. Levine for an Internet Web article on MSNBC, "If Frank Kaufmann goes down, we're in deep trouble."*

Donald Schmitt

Schmitt has disgraced himself within the UFO community by blatantly lying about his background.[16] In his many publications, Schmitt had claimed that he was a medical illustrator. However, it was quickly discovered by James Moseley and published in *Saucer Smear* that Schmitt was a postal clerk who delivers mail, a job he

---

*For a devastating and fairly accurate critique of Randle's confabulations, errors, and omissions regarding his Roswell "research," see Stanton T. Friedman's excellent "Open Letter to Kevin Randle" dated November 10, 1995—now available on many Internet Websites (http://www.kdrfals2.txt at medianet. nbnet.nb.ca is one such example). In this missive, Friedman documents no less than thirty-eight significant mistakes made by Randle, many of which cannot be explained innocently. Friedman has his own Website and is in a position to supply plenty of material regarding his battles with Randle should anyone reading this desire to inquire more deeply.

had for a number of years![17] Randle has distanced himself from Schmitt in a "To whom it may concern" letter dated September 10, 1995, and no longer associates with him, citing flawed research and dishonesty, among other things.[18]

As Robert Todd has astutely observed in an article he wrote called "Randle Dumps—And Dumps On—Schmitt": "Randle now has a convenient scapegoat on whom he can pin every false claim, fact, characterization, or other mistruth that appears not only in their two books, but the countless articles the CUFOS 'investigators' wrote for the *International UFO Reporter* [the official publication of the Center for UFO Studies]."[19]

NOTES

1. Don Berliner and Stanton T. Friedman, *Crash at Corona* (New York: Paragon House, 1992), p. 15.

2. Stanton T. Friedman, *Top Secret/MAJIC* (New York: Marlowe & Company, 1996). See also Stanton Friedman, personal interview with journalist Art Levine, late September 1996. (Interview transcribed by Kal K. Korff.)

3. Stanton T. Friedman, "Open Letter to Kevin Randle," Website Internet posting on <http://www.kdrfals2.txt at medianet.nbet.nb.ca>, November 10, 1995, p. 7.

4. Ibid.

5. Gary Campbell, "Roswell to be Subject of Forbes Magazine Article," *Roswell Daily Record* Website at <http://www.rdr.com.rfa>.

6. Ronald D. Story, *Guardians of the Universe?* (London: New English Library, 1980), p. 9.

7. Don Berliner, personal interview with journalist Art Levine, October 1996. (Interview transcribed by Kal K. Korff.)

8. Friedman, *Top Secret/MAJIC*. See also Levine interview with Friedman, late September 1996.

9. Jesse Marcel Jr., foreword to *Beyond Roswell: The Alien Autopsy Film, Area 51, and the U.S. Government Coverup of UFO's*, by Michael Hesemann and Philip Mantle (New York: Marlowe & Co., 1997).

10. Hesemann and Mantle, *Beyond Roswell*, p. 4.

11. Karl Pflock, *Roswell in Perspective* (Mount Rainier, Md.: Fund for UFO Research, 1994), p. 116.

12. Col. Albert Trakowski, sworn affidavit, June 29, 1994.

13. Art Levine, personal interview with Karl Pflock, October 1996. (Interview transcribed by Kal K. Korff.)

14. Ibid.

15. Pflock, *Roswell in Perspective,* pp. 86–87.

16. George M. Eberhart, ed., *The Roswell Report: A Historical Perspective* (Chicago: Center for UFO Studies, 1991), back cover text.

17. James W. Moseley, *Saucer Smear,* posted on <http://www.mcs.com/~kvg/Smear/v42>.

18. Kevin Randle, "To whom it may concern," September 10, 1995, copy received from Stanton Friedman, who received it directly from Randle.

19. Robert Todd, "Randle Dumps—And Dumps On—Schmitt," *Cowflop Alert* (September 22, 1995): 1–2.

Appendix

The Roswell Incident and the NYU Balloon Project

by James McAndrew, 1st Lt. USAFR
Declassification and Review Officer

Throughout the latter half of the twentieth century the subject of Unidentified Flying Objects (UFOs) has evoked strong opinions and emotions. For some, the belief in or study of UFOs has assumed the dimensions of a religious quest. Others remain nonbelievers or at least skeptical of the existence of alien beings and elusive vehicles which never quite seem to manifest themselves. Regardless of one's conviction, nowhere has the debate about UFOs been more spirited than over the events that unfolded near the small town New Mexico city of Roswell in the summer of 1947. Popularly known as the Roswell Incident, this event has become the most celebrated UFO encounter of all time and has stimulated enthusiasts like none other. Numerous witnesses, including former military personnel and respectable members of the local commu-

---

For a complete copy of Jim McAndrew's report [a brief introductory note to McAndrew's office staff comprises most of what has been omitted] and over 1,000 pages of documentation that proves the Mogul connection to the object recovered near Roswell, see the publication *The Roswell Report: Fact vs. Fiction in the New Mexico Desert,* available from the U.S. Government Printing Office, Superintendent of Documents, Mail Stop: SSOP, Washington D.C., 20402-9328. ISBN 0-16-048023-X. All footnotes in this Appendix are editorial or authorial additions and are not part of the original report.

nity, have come forward with tales of humanoid beings, alien technologies, and government cover-ups that have caused even the
most skeptical observer to pause and take notice. Inevitably these
stories coming from the desert have spawned countless articles,
books, films, and even museums claiming to have proof that visitors had come from outer space.

In February 1994, the Air Force was informed that the General
Accounting Office (GAO), an investigative agency of Congress,
planned a formal audit to ascertain "the facts regarding the reported
crash of an UFO in 1949 [1947] at Roswell, New Mexico."[1] This
task was delegated to numerous agencies, but the focus was on the
U.S. Air Force, the agency most often accused of hiding information and records on Roswell. The Presidential Science Advisor had
also expressed an interest in the investigation. Thereupon, the Secretary of the Air Force directed that a complete records search identify, locate, and examine any and all information available on this
subject. From the outset there was no predisposition to refute or
overlook any information. Moreover, if any of the information discovered was under security classification, it was to be declassified,
and if active or former Air Force officials had been sworn to a
secrecy oath, they were to be *freed* from it. In short, the objective
was to tell the Congress, and the American people, *everything* the
Air Force knew about the Roswell claims.

Subsequently, researchers conducted an extensive search of Air
Force archives, record centers, and scientific facilities. Seeking
information that might help to explain peculiar tales of odd wreckage and alien bodies, the researchers reviewed a monumental number of documents concerning a variety of events, including aircraft
crashes, errant missile tests, and nuclear mishaps.

The researchers reported to the Administrative Assistant to the
Secretary of the Air Force (SAF/AA), the office responsible for
both Air Force records and security policy oversight. Within
SAF/AA, the task fell to the Director of Security and Special Program Oversight and its specialized subunit, the Declassification and
Review team. This team, comprised entirely of Reservists, was well
versed in the Air Force's records system and its complex declassification procedures. Previously, Declassification and Review Team
members demonstrated their expertise and effectiveness by declas-

sifying millions of pages of Southeast Asian War and Prisoner of War–Missing in Action records.

As this study makes abundantly clear, the Declassification and Review Team found no evidence of any extraterrestrial craft or alien flight crew. In fact, what they did find had been declassified for more than twenty years—a shadowy, formerly Top Secret project, code-named Mogul.

[In the 1940s] determining whether the Soviets were testing nuclear devices was of the highest national priority; it demanded the utmost secrecy if the information gained was to be useful. When the Soviets exploded their first atomic device in August 1949, the experimental Project Mogul was not in operation. However, the explosion was detected by a specially equipped Air Force B-29 aircraft. Accordingly, Mogul was conducted under stringent security— secluded laboratories, code words, maximum security clearances, and strictest enforcement of need-to-know rules. Nevertheless, while the nature of the project remained shrouded in secrecy, some of its operations obviously could not. The deployment of giant trains of balloons—over thirty research balloons and experimental sensors strung together and stretching more than 600 feet—could be neither disguised nor hidden from the public. Moreover, the operational necessity required that these balloons be launched during daylight hours. It was therefore not surprising that these balloons were often mistaken for UFOs. In fact, Mogul recovery crews often listened to broadcasts of UFO reports to assist them in their tracking operations. Additionally, the balloons were unsteerable, leading to such amusing events as the one reported by the *New York Times* in which a secret Mogul balloon "floated blithely over the rooftops of Flatbush . . . causing general public excitement . . . before it came to rest on top of a [Brooklyn] tavern."[2] In another episode, Mogul balloon recovery technicians directed a B-17 bomber, which was tracking one of the tests, to buzz and scare off a curious oil rig crew that was about to "capture" a balloon train that had fallen near Roswell. The ruse worked. However, too much activity was going on for the project to remain completely hidden. A Mogul project officer later noted, "It was like having an elephant in your backyard . . . and hoping no one would notice."[3] These occurrences were typical, leading the recovery crews to describe themselves as Balloonatics, due to the predicaments in which the wandering balloons sometimes placed them, but the information the balloons were attempting to obtain was vital.

To attempt to limit unauthorized disclosure, the Air Force employed a security mechanism known as compartmentalization. Compartmentalization controlled access to classified information by dispersing portions of the research among several facilities and institutions. Each participating entity received only enough information necessary to accomplish its assigned tasks. In the case of Mogul, only a small circle of Air Force officers received the intimate details that linked together these unrelated research projects. The use of compartmentalization along with strict enforcement of the need to know enabled Mogul to remain a secret—despite its obvious security difficulties—and to remain unevaluated for many years as the cause of the Roswell Incident.

The issue of compartmentalization was significant because some UFO researchers assert that the persons who recovered the Mogul equipment, members of the 509th Bombardment Group stationed at Roswell Army Air Field, should have been able to recognize the debris collected at the crash site as that of a research balloon. Although members of the 509th possessed high-level clearances, they were not privy to the existence of Mogul; their job was to deliver nuclear weapons, not to detect them. The unusual combination of experimental equipment did not encourage easy identification that undoubtedly left some members of the 509th with unanswered questions to support their flying saucer recovery scenario, while eagerly supplying unfounded explanations of extraterrestrial visitation and cosmic conspiracy. Additionally, many claims of a flying saucer crash at Roswell rest on the description of debris collected at the Foster ranch site. UFO researchers, including those who are said to have known *all about* Mogul, apparently did not compare the descriptions of the suspect debris with that of the components of a Project Mogul balloon train. Mogul reports and documents that contain descriptions, illustrations, and photographs have been publicly available for at least twenty years. Had the researchers completed even a cursory comparison, they would have found that the materials were suspiciously similar; detailed examination would have shown them to be one and the same. In the final analysis, it appears these individuals have pursued the convenient red herring provided by Roswell Army Air Field [i.e., the "flying disc"], while the real explanation lay just over the Sacramento Mountains at the Mogul launch site in Alamogordo.

This report explains the events that transpired in and near Roswell, New Mexico, in the summer of 1947. It is based on written documentation and firsthand accounts of participants, all of which are provided here in their entirety. While these answers are not as titillating as tales of unearthly craft and creatures, it is a fascinating story nonetheless.

On July 7, 1947, W. W. (Mac) Brazel, a rancher from approximately seventy-five miles northeast of Roswell, New Mexico, contacted the local sheriff and reported that some metallic debris had come to rest on the ranch on which he worked near the town of Corona, New Mexico. This was during the "UFO Wave of 1947," and he told the sheriff that he thought this debris may be part of a "flying disc."[4] The sheriff contacted Roswell Army Air Field (AAF), which in turn sent intelligence officer Maj. Jesse Marcel, and two Counterintelligence Corps Agents, Capt. Sheridan Cavitt and M.Sgt. Lewis S. Rickett, to evaluate the debris. The officers collected a portion of the material and brought it back to Roswell AAF on the evening of July 7.[5] The following day, the Public Information Office released a statement saying that the Army Air Forces had recovered a flying disc. This press release was provided to local newspapers who sent it out to wire services. Meanwhile, Brig. Gen. Roger Ramey, Eighth Air Force Commander, ordered that the debris be flown to Eight Air Force Headquarters at Fort Worth AAF, Texas, for his personal inspection. Upon viewing the debris, he and his staff recognized parts which looked similar to a weather balloon. He then summoned the base weather officer, who identified the debris as the remnants of a weather balloon and its attached metallic radar target.[6] General Ramey then invited the local press to view and take photographs of the materials and he declared the episode to be a misunderstanding.

The above summarizes the previously reported information of what happened on July 7 and July 8, 1947. Before now, however, a larger portion of the story was never told. Recent research indicates that the debris recovered from the ranch on July 7, 1947, was a weather balloon—but it was not being used strictly for weather purposes; its real purpose was to carry classified payloads for a Top

Secret U.S. Army Air Force project. The project's classified code name was Mogul.

The current investigation discovered that an experimental balloon project was being conducted at nearby Alamogordo Army Air Field (now Holloman Air Force Base, New Mexico) during the summer of 1947.[7] An examination of unclassified technical and progress reports prepared by the balloon project revealed that a highly classified program, Project Mogul, was the ultimate reason for the balloon experiments. Project Mogul was classified Top Secret and carried a priority level of 1A [the highest possible level].[8] It is Project Mogul that provides the ultimate explanation of the "Roswell Incident."

PROJECT MOGUL

Project Mogul was first conceived by Dr. Maurice Ewing of Columbia University, New York, and Woods Hole Oceanographic Institution, Massachusetts. Dr. Ewing had conducted considerable research for the Navy during World War II, studying, among other things, the "sound channel" in the ocean. He proved that explosions could be heard thousands of miles away with underwater microphones placed at predetermined depth within the sound channel. He theorized that since sound waves generated by explosions could be carried by currents deep within the ocean, they might be similarly transmitted within a sound channel in the upper atmosphere. The military application of this theory was the long-range detection of sound waves generated by Soviet nuclear detonations and the acoustical signatures of ballistic missiles as they traversed the upper atmosphere. He presented his theory to Gen. Carl Spaatz, Chief of Staff of the Army Air Forces, in the fall of 1945.[9] The project was approved, and research was begun by the scientific research agency of the U.S. Army Air Forces (USAAF), the Air Materiel Command (AMC), early in 1946. The project was assigned to HQ AMC, Engineering Division, Electronics Subdivision, Applied Propagation Subdivision, located in Red Bank, New Jersey.

Scope

Project Mogul initially focused on three areas of technology: (1) an expendable microphone, capable of detecting, at long range, low-frequency sound transmissions generated by explosions and missiles; (2) a means of telemetering [transmitting] these sounds to a ground or airborne receiver; and (3) a system from which to suspend the microphone and telemetering device in the upper atmosphere for an extended period of time. To meet these criteria, contracts were awarded by AMC to Columbia University . . . for the acoustical equipment, and to New York University (NYU) for the development of constant level balloons. . . . After the initial contracts were awarded, Project Mogul branched out into many areas related to the geophysical properties of the upper atmosphere, including radiowave propagation, radar propagation, ionospheric physics, solar physics, terrestrial magnetism, meteorological physics, and weather forecasting. Considerable resources were devoted to Project Mogul which included numerous bomber and transport aircraft and two oceangoing vessels. At one point the staff, exclusive of contractors, numbered over 100 persons. To accommodate this sensitive, high-priority project, facilities of the secluded Oakhurst Field Station of Watson Laboratories [in New York state] were used. Balloon operations associated with Project Mogul were conducted at various locations throughout the United States and the Pacific, and later in reference to acoustical detection research associated with the Sandstone atomic tests at Entiwetok Atoll in April and May 1948.[10]

By December 1948, serious concerns had arisen regarding the feasibility of the project as first conceived. Even though the principle on which the project was based was determined to be sound, questions concerning cost, security, and practicality were discussed that ultimately led to the disbandment of the project, and Project Mogul as first conceived was never put into operational use. However, Mogul did serve as the foundation for a comprehensive program in geophysical research from which the USAF and the scientific community have benefitted to the present time. These benefits included constant-level balloon technology, first developed by NYU for Project Mogul.

Watson Laboratories

Over the course of the project, Mogul had three military project officers, or "chiefs": Maj. Robert T. Crane, [who was in charge from] spring 1946 to July 1946; Col. Marcellus Duffy, [who headed the program from] August 1946 to January, 1947; and Capt. Albert C. Trakowski, [who was in charge] from January 1947 to May 1949. Major Crane had been personally recommended by Dr. Ewing, originator of the project, but by June 1947, Mogul had not met the expectations of HQ USAAF, and Colonel Duffy replaced Major Crane.[11] Colonel Duffy was a respected, highly capable career Army Air Forces officer. During World War II, Colonel Duffy had reported directly to Gen. Hap Arnold, Chief of Staff USAAF, as the Army Air Forces Liaison Officer to the U.S. Army Signal Corp, with primary duties for securing meteorological equipment from the Army for use by the USAAF. Colonel Duffy had a reputation for accomplishing difficult assignments by getting the most out of his personnel—exactly what was desired by HQ USAAF to solve the numerous administrative and personnel problems that had arisen in Project Mogul under Major Crane. In a short period, Colonel Duffy was able to make the necessary corrections and was reassigned to become the Assistant Chief, Electronics Plans Section, Electronics Subdivision, HQ AMC, at Wright Field, Ohio. Colonel Duffy also continued to monitor "the upper air research program" (i.e., Project Mogul) in addition to his duties as the Assistant Chief of the Electronics Plans Section.[12] The primary scientist for Mogul was Dr. James Peoples, assisted by Albert P. Crary, the Field Operations Director. Both scientists had previous associations with Dr. Ewing: Dr. Peoples at Columbia, and A. P. Crary at Woods Hole. Both scientists were assigned to Mogul for the entire length of the project.

New York University "Balloon Group"

From September 30, 1946, until December 31, 1950, the Research Division of the College of Engineering of NYU conducted research under contract for the Army Air Forces, in conjunction with Project

Mogul.[13] The NYU "balloon group" was to develop and fly constant-level balloons while simultaneously developing telemetering equipment to transmit data obtained in the upper atmosphere.[14] Group members launched, tracked, and recorded data only in regard to constant-level balloon flight telemetering information. They did not have access to observations and measurements that had military applications. Mogul, in other words, was conducted as a compartmentalized, classified project in which particular participants knew only what they needed to know, and no more. Due to compartmentalization, balloon flights made by NYU were divided into two categories, "research" and "service."[15] Research flights tested balloon controls and telemetering systems and were fully reported in the unclassified NYU reports.[16] A total of 110 research flights were flown during the contract. Service flights were flown at the direction of Watson Laboratory personnel, but the military purpose was Top Secret. These flights carried classified equipment, which could not be fully reported in the unclassified NYU documents. Further evidence of the exclusion of classified information from the reports is the lack of data for balloons flown in association with the Sandstone nuclear tests held in April and May of 1948.[17] In recent interviews with former NYU personnel, Dr. Athelstan F. Spilhaus, NYU Balloon Project Engineer, stated that they were never informed of the classified name, Mogul, nor did they ever have access to the scientific data that was obtained by the USAAF as a result of their efforts. In response to inquiries, professional or casual, project personnel simply said that they were engaged in balloon research.[18]

The first balloon launches associated with Project Mogul were carried out at several locations on the East Coast of the United States.[19] However, unfavorable winds, conflicts with commercial air traffic, and the need to gather data on the V-2 flights currently being conducted at White Sands Proving Ground, New Mexico,* led the NYU group to conduct further tests from Alamogordo AAF.[20] The NYU group would make three "field trips" during the

---

*V-2 rockets were captured by the Allies during World War II. They were then reverse-engineered and launched in New Mexico in what was the beginning of the American rocket and missile development program.

summer of 1947 for the test and evaluation, labeling them Alamogordo I, II, and III. The majority of the balloon flights over the next four years originated from Alamogordo AAF.

New York University, in accordance with contractual requirements, produced monthly progress reports, technical reports, and final reports detailing the various aspects of the balloon and telemetering research. In addition, Crary maintained a detailed journal of his work throughout his professional career to include the summer of 1947. The following discussion is based on these . . . documents and interviews with [Charles] Moore, who was present on all three of the Alamogordo field trips, and, with Trakowski, who was present at the Alamogordo II and III field trips.

Note: Technical Report No. 1, Table VII, "Summary of NYU Constant-Level Balloon Flights," and Technical Report No. 93.02, Constant Level Balloons, Section 3, "Summary of Flights," do not fully account for all balloons flown during the initial stages of the contract to include the Alamogordo I field trip. Absent from the reports are service flights numbers 2, 3, and 4. Flight number 2 was flown April 18, 1947, at Bethlehem, Pennsylvania, in an attempt to obtain acoustical data from the explosion of 5,000 tons of TNT by the British on the German island of Helgoland.[21] NYU flight number 3 was flown on May 29, followed by NYU flight number 4 on June 4. Both launched from Alamogordo AAF.

ALAMOGORDO I (MAY 28, 1947–JUNE 7, 1947)

The first NYU "field trip" departed Olmstead Field, Middletown, Pennsylvania, by C-47 for Alamogordo AAF on May 31, 1947, arriving on June 1, 1947.[22] Present on this flight were C. B. Moore, NYU Project Engineer, Charles S. Schneider, NYU Project Director, and other supporting staff members from both NYU and Watson Laboratories. A. P. Crary, along with other personnel from Watson Laboratory, were already present in Alamogordo, but they did not conduct any balloon operations. During this time, Crary and several technicians detonated ground explosives, or "shots," for sound-wave generation purposes, on the nearby White Sands Proving Ground. These detonations were monitored by ground-based GR3 and GR8 sound ranging equipment at locations in New Mexico and west Texas.[23] On May 28, the advance party of the balloon group arrived by B-17.[24] On May 29, the advance team made the first launch for Project Mogul from Alamogordo (NYU flight number 3). The equipment carried on this flight was identified as essentially the same as that carried on NYU flight number 2.[25] NYU flight number 4 was launched on June 4, with a configuration the same as on flight numbers 2 and 3. Crary's diary indicated that flight number 4 consisted of a "cluster of (meteorological) balloons" and a "regular sonobuoy."[26] Presumably, flight number 3 was configured the same.

The objective of this trip, so far as the NYU was concerned, was to perfect handling of large flight trains of meteorological balloons and to evaluate the operations of altitude-controlling and telemetering devices.[27] Already established before the trip to Alamogordo was that the use of the standard, 350-gram meteorological balloons, constructed of neoprene, was, at best, a "stop gap" [temporary] method of achieving constant-level flight.[28] Balloons most suitable for this type of work were made of polyethylene, a very thin, translucent plastic. These balloons, however, had just been developed, and, although the NYU group had contracted for some of them, the balloons had not been received until after the group departed for Alamogordo.[29] For Watson Laboratory scientists Peoples and Crary, the purpose of the trip was to experiment with different types of equipment to collect and transmit sound waves in the upper atmosphere. Therefore, just as the "balloon group" was using meteorological balloons as a stopgap method in attaining constant-level flight, the Watson Laboratory scientists utilized an AN/CRT-1A Sonobuoy while awaiting the delivery of acoustical equipment specifically designed for Project Mogul.[30] The NYU personnel developing the telemetering equipment experimented with components of the sonobuoy, which was cylindrical, nearly three feet long and four and three-fourths inches wide, and weighing thirteen pounds. The sonobuoy contained both the acoustical pickups, known as hydrophones, and the means of telemetering the sounds by use of an FM transmitter, the T-1B/CRT-1.

Soon after arriving at Alamogordo AAF, a problem developed. Dr. Peoples, Project Scientist, decided not to bring the radiosonde recorder (an AN/FMQ1 weighing approximately 500 pounds), due to the weight and space limitations of the B-17 aircraft originally scheduled to transport the equipment from Olmstead Field. Radiosondes, a widely used and accurate method of tracking weather balloons consisting of a transmitter, which was carried aloft with aircraft, were to be the primary method to track the Project Mogul balloons.[31] Dr. Peoples, however, believed that the radar currently in place at Alamogordo for tracking V-2 firings would be sufficient for tracking the balloon trains. However, this radar did not work well and often lost contact with the balloon while it was still within visual range. Accordingly, Moore, the project engineer, experimented with an "unorthodox" method, in the absence of a radiosonde recorder. He tried to track the balloons using multiple radar targets.[32] A radar target was a multisided object, which, in appearance, resembled a box kite constructed of balsa wood and metallicized paper. Moore and his technicians conducted test flights, attempting to obtain a better radar return by attaching additional targets. They received satisfactory results when the number of targets was increased to between three and five.[33] Interestingly, during July 1948, a similar test would be made at Alamogordo AAF by another organization.[34] This test confirmed Moore's theory that when targets were increased to at least three, satisfactory returns were received by the radar. This procedure, according to Moore, was employed on flight numbers 3 and 4, but it was only marginally successful. This prompted Moore and his associates to configure the two remaining flights of Alamogordo I, flights number 5 and 6, with radiosonde transmitters.

For these two final flights, Moore devised a method of manually determining azimuth [angle] and elevation, in the absence of a radiosonde recorder, by counting clicks as pressure-sensitive contacts [from the sensors] closed. NYU Technical Report No. 1 shows two "interpretations" of the data which confirm that manual calculations were used. In regard to flight number 5, it appears there was a typographical error in Technical Report No. 1, Table VII, for the time of launch which is erroneously listed as 1517 MST, contrary to figures 32 and 33 in Technical Report No. 1 and Crary's diary. The correct time of launch for flight number 5 appears to be 0516 MST. With the launching of flight number 6 at approximately 0530 on June 7, the NYU group departed Alamogordo via B-17 for Newark AAF, New Jersey.

ALAMOGORDO II (JUNE 27, 1947–JULY 8, 1947)

On the morning of June 28, 1947, personnel from NYU and Watson Laboratories arrived at Alamogordo AAF to resume balloon flights. Present during this field trip were Dr. Peoples, A. P. Crary, Captain Trakowski, C. B. Moore, and Charles Schneider. The objective during this trip was to experiment with the newly developed polyethylene balloons which replaced the neoprene meteorological balloons used on the previous field trip. Also tested was an improved aluminum ballast reservoir that had been developed to replace the plastic tubes used during the June field trip.[35] Another improvement that resulted from the experiences in June was the presence of a radiosonde receiver/recorder for improved balloon tracking and plotting. This eliminated the need for radar "corner reflectors" on the balloon train since radar was not to be used as a primary method of tracking the flights. This is confirmed by Technical Report No. 1, Table VII, "Radiosonde Reception %," which indicates the use of the radiosonde recorder on all flights except for no. 7. Flight no. 7 was not recorded by radiosonde because the equipment was not operable.[36] Also, figures 36, 39, 42, and 44 in Technical Report No. 1, corresponding to the July flights, do not depict corner reflectors. All numbered flights (except for number 9) flown during the July field trip were summarized in NYU Technical Report No 1, Table VII. Flight no. 9 appeared to have been launched on July 3.[37] On July 8, their work completed, twenty-three members of the combined NYU and Watson Laboratory group boarded a C-54 aircraft at 10:30 A.M. and returned to the East Coast.[38]

Based on the above, it appeared likely that the debris found by the rancher [Mac Brazel] and was subsequently identified as a "flying disc" by personnel from Roswell AAF was, with a great degree of certainty, Mogul flight number 4, launched on June 4, 1947. This conclusion is based on the following:

1. Descriptions of the debris provided by Brazel, Cavitt, Crary's diary, and the photos of the material displayed in General Ramey's office. These materials were consistent with components of a Mogul service flight, with neoprene balloons, parchment para-

THE ROSWELL UFO CRASH

chutes, plastic ballast tubes, corner reflectors, a sonobuoy, and a black electronics box that housed the pressure cutoff switch.

2. According to Brazel's July 8 statement [published in the *Roswell Daily Record,* July 9, 1947], the debris was recovered on June 14, obviously eliminating any balloons launched in July.

3. Only two flights launched in June were unaccounted for, i.e., flights nos. 3 and 4. Flight no. 3 most likely would not have had the "unorthodox" configuration of corner reflectors devised by Moore, who did not arrive until June 1, three days after flight no. 3 was launched.

On July 7, as the NYU group members were winding down their work preparing to return to New York City, a train of events began to unfold at Roswell AAF, sixty miles away. Roswell AAF was home of the 509th Bomb Group of the Strategic Air Command's Eighth Air Force, the only unit in the world capable of delivering nuclear weapons. It now appears that the debris from Mogul flight number 4 had come to earth on the plains east of the Sacramento Mountains, about seventy miles from the launch point at Alamogordo AAF. The fact it descended there was not unusual. Over the course of Project Mogul, several balloons had landed and been recovered from that area. In fact, in August 1947, the NYU group had to receive special permission from the Civil Aeronautics Administration to continue to launch balloons from Alamogordo AAF since "balloons have been descending outside the area [White Sands Proving Ground] in the vicinity of Roswell, New Mexico."[39] According to the sole living participant in the recovery, Sheridan Cavitt, he, Maj. Jesse Marcel, and M.Sgt. Lewis Rickett gathered some of the material, which appeared to resemble "bamboo type square sticks, one quarter to one inch square," that was "very light"—reflecting material—and a "black box, like a weather instrument." Cavitt believed this material to be consistent with what he knew to be a weather balloon. This debris would soon become, for a short time, the focus of national and even worldwide attention when it was thought to be a "flying disc."

On July 8, the same day that the NYU/Watson Laboratory group departed Alamogordo, the Public Information Officer of

Roswell AAF [Walter Haut] announced the recovery of a "flying disc" and that it would be flown to Fort Worth AAF for further examination. How could experienced military personnel have confused a weather balloon for a "flying disc"? The answer is that this was not an ordinary "weather balloon." Typical weather balloons employed a single, 350-gram neoprene balloon and a radiosonde for measuring temperature, atmospheric pressure, and humidity, housed in a cardboard box. If it was to be tracked by radar for wind-speed measurement, a single corner reflector was added. The balloon that was found on the Foster ranch consisted of as many as twenty-three 350-gram balloons spaced at twenty-foot intervals, several radar targets (three to five), plastic ballast tubes, parchment parachutes, a black "cutoff" box containing portions of a weather instrument, and a sonobuoy. After striking the ground, the radar reflectors, constructed of very light materials for minimum weight, would tear and break apart, spreading out over a large area when pulled across the ground by balloons that still possessed some buoyancy. It should also be understood that the term "flying disc" was not at this time [in 1947] synonymous with "space ship." It denoted a disc-shaped flying object of unknown (or suspected Soviet) origin.

Before the announcement was made, the "disc" was flown to Fort Worth AAF at the direction of Brigadier General Ramey, Commander, Eighth Air Force. General Ramey personally inspected the "disc," became skeptical, and summoned the base weather officer, Warrant Officer Irving Newton, to make an identification. Newton positively identified the debris as the remnants of a balloon and Rawin target.[40] With this identification, the incident officially closed.

THE "COVER STORY"

From research, it appears that the wreckage displayed on July 8 consisted of unclassified components of a Mogul balloon assembly. Possibly withheld, if it was indeed recovered, was the AN/CRT-1 Sonobuoy, which could have compromised Project Mogul. Although the Sonobuoy was not itself classified, its association with a balloon would have exposed a specific military purpose, an obvious violation of project [Mogul] classification guidelines. A device described in "crashed disc" publications as "a giant thermos jug" was allegedly transported from Fort Worth AAF to Wright Field.[41] This description is consistent with the appearance of an AN/CRT-1 Sonobuoy such as was used on flight number 4. At some point General Ramey decided to forward the material to Wright Field, home of the AMC, the appropriate agency to identify one of its own research devices or a device of unknown origin. If the debris was determined to be from an unknown source, the AMC, T-2 Intelligence or Analysis Division, would conduct scientific and/or intelligence analysis in an attempt to discover its origin. But since the balloons, reflectors, and Sonobuoy were from an AMC research project, the debris was forwarded to the appropriate division or sub-division, in this case the Electronics Subdivision of the Engineering Division. There, it was identified by Colonel Duffy, under whose purview Project Mogul operated. Colonel Duffy, a former project officer of Mogul with specific directions to "continue to monitor upper air programs," was the appropriate headquarters officer to make an identification, which he apparently did. According to Captain (now Colonel) Trakowski, the officer who succeeded Colonel Duffy as project officer on Mogul, after returning from the Alamogordo II field trip, Colonel Duffy contacted him by phone at Watson Laboratories and informed him that the "stuff you've been launching at Alamogordo," had been sent to him for identification. He described the debris to Captain Trakowski, and Trakowski agreed that it was part of his project (Mogul).[42]

Another occurrence sometimes said to "prove" that General Ramey was part of a cover story is that portions of the debris were flown to Andrews AAF, Maryland. Andrews would have been a probable location to send the debris since it had components of weather observation equipment. Andrews AAF was headquarters of the Army Air Forces Weather Service. It is also interesting to note that the commanding general of the Weather Service, Brig. Gen. Donald N. Yates, was quoted in wire service newspaper articles on July 9, providing his opinion of the incident. Additionally, in 1949, General Yates received a full briefing of the projects, including constant-level balloons, that made up Project Mogul.[43] While crashed disc proponents claim that General Ramey ordered a "colonel courier" to transport portions of the debris in a briefcase handcuffed to his wrist for the inspection of his superior, Maj. Gen. Clements McMullen, Deputy Commander of Strategic Air Command, it is more likely that any forwarding of such debris was another attempt to identify the research agency to which it belonged. It if did go to General McMullen, it would not have been difficult for him to have obtained the opinion of the Weather Service, since SAC and the Weather Service were located in the same building (no. 1535) at Andrews AAF.

"HIEROGLYPHICS"

One of the most puzzling aspects of the reports that a "UFO" crashed near Corona in 1947 were the later descriptions of "hieroglyphic-like" characters by seemingly reliable, firsthand witnesses. Research has revealed that the debris found on the ranch and displayed in General Ramey's office probably did have strange characters. These, however, were not hieroglyphics, but figures printed on the pinkish-purple tape used to construct the radar targets used by the NYU group.

The witnesses have recalled small pink/purple "flowers" that appeared to be some sort of writing that couldn't be deciphered. These figures were printed on tape that sealed the seams of the radar target. The radar targets, sometimes called corner reflectors, had been manufactured during or shortly after World War II, and due to shortages, the manufacturer, a toy company, used whatever resources were available. This toy company used plastic tape with pink/purple flowers and geometric designs in the construction of its toys and, in a time of shortage, used it on the government contract for the corner reflectors. A depiction of these figures, as described by Professor C. B. Moore, is shown in [the following] figure. . . .

Allegations have also been made that the debris displayed to the press on July 8 and subsequently photographed was not the original wreckage; i.e., a switch occurred sometime after the debris left Roswell AAF. However, statements made by Moore and Trakowski attested that the corner reflectors they launched during that period

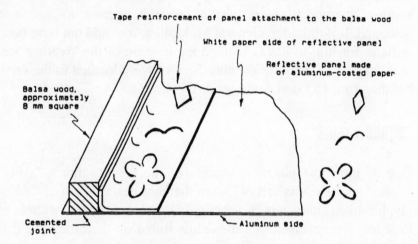

MY RECOLLECTION OF THE REFLECTOR MATERIAL ATTACHMENT TO THE BALSA WOOD PIECES ON THE ML-307/AP PILOT BALLOON RADAR TARGETS IN 1947.

AN APPROXIMATE REPRODUCTION OF THE FIGURES PRINTED ON THE TARGET-REINFORCING TAPE
(This is not authoritative since I last saw one of these targets more than 20 years ago.)

C. B. Moore
C.B. Moore
August 28, 1992

of time had the same flowers and figures that were later reported by Marcel, Cavitt, and Brazel as being on the debris found on the Foster ranch in Corona. In fact, Trakowski distinctly remembered the figures on the tape because, when the targets were first produced, much fanfare was made over the use of a toy manufacturer for production. He related that a fellow USAF officer, John E. Peterson, monitored the procurement of the targets and "thought it was the biggest joke in the world that they had to go to a toy manufacturer" to make the radar targets and an "even bigger joke when . . . the reflecting material on the balsa frames was some kind of a pinkish purple tape with hearts and flowers designs on it."[44] Furthermore, the Fort Worth Army Air Field Weather Officer, Irving Newton, who was called in to identify the wreckage, also remembers the purple/pink marks. Newton stated that when he was called to General Ramey's office he remembers meeting Marcel, who attempted to convince him that the wreckage on the floor of the office was a crashed "flying disc." Newton, having seen many weather balloons and targets, positively identified the debris as a weather device.[45] In short, descriptions of the wreckage found on the ranch near Corona and of the wreckage displayed in General Ramey's office are entirely consistent with each other.

THE REAL COVER STORY

On July 10, 1947, a newspaper article appeared in the *Alamogordo Daily News* displaying for the press the devices, neoprene balloons, and corner reflectors which had been misidentified as the "flying disc" two days earlier at Roswell AAF. The photographs and accompanying article quoted Maj. Wilbur D. Pritchard, a Watson Laboratory Project Officer (not assigned to Mogul) stationed at Alamogordo AAF. This article appeared to have been an attempt to deflect attention from the Top Secret Mogul project by publicly displaying a portion of the equipment and offering misleading information. If there was a "cover story" involved in this incident, it is this article, not the statements of Ramey.

The article in the *Alamogordo Daily News* stated that the balloons and radar targets had been used for the last fifteen months for the training of long-range radar personnel and the gathering of meteorological data. The article lists four officers—Maj. W. D. Pritchard, Lt. S. W. Siegel, Capt. L. H. Dyvad, and Maj. C. W. Mangum—as being involved with the balloon project, which was false. Moore and Trakowski could not recall any of the officers in the photograph [of them], with the exception of Dyvad, whom Moore identified as a pilot who coordinated radar activities.[46] Additionally, some of the details discussed (balloon sightings in Colorado, tracking by B-17s, recovery of equipment, launching balloons at 5–6 A.M., and balloon altitudes of 30,000–40,000 feet) relate directly to the NYU balloon project, indicating that the four officers had detailed knowledge of Mogul.[47] Moore's unorthodox technique of employing several balloons and several radar targets was shown in one of the photographs. Other techniques unique to Moore, including the boiling of balloons before launch (which he personally developed during World War II) and a stepladder used to launch balloons, could not all have coincidentally been used by other organizations.[48]

The details may have been provided to the radar officers by Crary, Project Mogul Field Operations Director, who did not depart by C-54 with the rest of the NYU/Watson Laboratory group on July 8, but who later left by car on July 9, the day the staged launch took place. . . . It was apparent from Crary's diary that he had worked very closely with Major Pritchard and reported to him on occasion (twelve documented meetings from December 1946–April 1947). One instance, on April 7, 1947, Crary gave Pritchard a "progress report for Mogul project to date," indicating that Major Pritchard had access to Mogul information.[49] Another statement which appeared to confirm a cover story appeared in the caption below the balloon picture [in the newspaper article] and described a typewritten tag stapled to the target identifying it as having come from Alamogordo AAF. Moore believed this not to be true because any equipment found was not to be associated with the USAAF, only with NYU; therefore flights carried "return to" tags identifying NYU as the responsible agency.[50]

CONCLUSION

Many of the claims surrounding the events to July 1947 could be neither proved nor disproved. Attempts were not made to investigate every allegation, but rather to start with what was known and work toward the unknown. To complicate the situation, events described here took place nearly fifty years ago and were highly compartmentalized as well. Interviews with individuals and review of documents of organizations revealed that the ultimate objective of the work, or even the name of the project, in many instances was not known. It was unlikely, therefore, that personnel from Roswell AAF, even though they possessed the appropriate clearances, would have known about Project Mogul. In fact, when the NYU/AMC group returned to Alamogordo in September, their first trip since the "incident" occurred, one of the first activities of the project scientists, Peoples and Crary, who were accompanied by Major Pritchard and Captain Dyvad, was to brief the commanding officer of Alamogordo AAF and the 509th Bomb Group Operations Officer, Lt. Col. Joseph Briley, on Mogul.[51]

When the civilians and personnel from Roswell AAF (Marcel, Cavitt, and Rickett) "stumbled" upon the highly classified project and collected the debris, no one at Roswell had a "need to know" about information concerning Mogul. This fact, along with the initial misidentification and subsequent rumors that the "capture" of a "flying disc" had occurred, ultimately left many people with unanswered questions that have endured to this day.

NOTES

1. Memo, Marcia J. Van Note, Department of Defense Investigative Group, for Distribution, subject: General Accounting Office (GAO) letter dated February 9, 1944, February 23, 1994.

2. "Balloon Staggers Down to Brooklyn Tavern, Hooks Itself to Roof and Upsets Decorum," *New York Times,* October 1, 1948.

3. "Wreckage of a 'Spaceship': Of This Earth (and U.S.)," *New York Times,* September 18, 1994.

4 . *Roswell Daily Record,* July 9, 1947, p. 1.

5. Lt. Col. Sheridan Cavitt, USAF (Ret.), personal interview with Col. Richard L. Weaver, May 24, 1994.

6. Irving Newton, personal interview with Lt. Col. Joseph V. Rogan, June 21, 1994.

7. Letter from Lt. Col. Edward A. Doty to Mr. David Bushnell, March 3, 1957.

8. Letter from Brig. Gen. E. O'Donnell, Deputy Chief, Engineering Division, HQ AMC, to Commanding General, USAAF, subject: Change in Classification of Mogul, Item 188-5, July 8, 1946.

9. Report, Maurice Ewing for Gen. Carl Spaatz, "Long Range Sound Transmission in the Atmosphere," n.d.

10. Report, HQ Fitzwilliam Fwd, "Sonic Balloon Test Kwajalein," May 17, 1948 (hereafter "Sonic Balloon Test Kwajalein").

11. Memo, Brig. Gen. Tom C. Rives, Chief Electronic Subdivision, Engineering Division, AMC, to Maj. Gen. Curtis LeMay, subject: Relief of Major Crane as Project Officer Mogul and Torrid, June 18, 1946.

12. Memo, Maj. Gen. Curtis E. Lemay, Deputy Chief of Air Staff for Research and Development, to Maj. Gen. L. C. Craigie, Chief Engineering Division, AMC, April 16, 1947.

13. Research Division, College of Engineering, NYU, Technical Report No. 93.03, *Constant Level Balloons, Final Report,* March 1, 1951 (hereafter NYU, *Final Report*), p. 3.

14. Research Division, College of Engineering, NYU Technical Report 93.02, *Constant Level Balloons, Section 1, General,* November 15, 1949, p. 5.

15. NYU, *Final Report,* p. 13.

16. Research Division, College of Engineering, NYU, Technical Report No. 1, *Constant Level Balloon,* April 1, 1948, Table VII, "Summary of NYU Constant-Level Balloon Flights" (hereafter NYU Technical Report No. 1, Table VII); Technical Report No. 93.02, *Constant Level balloons, Section 3, Summary of Flights.*

17. "Sonic Balloon Test Kwajelein."

18. Athelstan F. Spilhaus, C. S. Schneider, C. B. Moore, "Controlled-Altitude Free Balloons," *Journal of Meteorology* 5 (August 1948): 130-37.

19. NYU, Technical Report No. 1, Table VII.

20. Research Division, College of Engineering, NYU, *Progress Report No. 6, Constant Level Balloon,* Sect. II, June 1947 (hereafter *Progress Report No. 6,* Sect. II), p. 4.

21. Research Division, College of Engineering, NYU, *Special Report No. 1, Constant Level Balloon,* May 1947 (hereafter NYU, Special Report No. 1), p. 27.

22. Personal journal of Albert P. Crary, p. 13.

23. Ibid., pp. 4-16.

24. Ibid., p. 13.

25. NYU, *Progress Report No. 6,* Sect. II, p. 5.

26. Crary journal, p. 12.

27. Research Division, College of Engineering, NYU *Progress Report No. 7, Constant Level Balloon,* Sect. II, July 1947 (hereafter NYU, *Progress Report No. 7,* Sect. II), p. 5.

28. NYU, *Special Report No. 1,* p. 26.

29. NYU, *Progress Report No. 7,* Sect. II, p. 6.

30. Research Division, College of Engineering, NYU, *Progress Report No. 4, Radio Transmitting Receiving and Recording System for Constant Level Balloon,* Sect. I, April 2, 1947, p. 1.

31. Professor Charles B. Moore, personal interview with Col. Jeffrey Butler and First Lt. James McAndrew, June 8, 1994.

32. Ibid.

33. Ibid.

34. Report, Holloman AFB, "Progress Summary Report on USAF Guided Missile Test Activities," vol. 1, August 1, 1948.

35. NYU, *Progress Report No. 7,* Sect. II, p. 5.

36. Crary journal, p. 15.

37. Ibid.

38. Ibid., p. 16.

39. NYU, *Technical Report No. 1,* Table VII, p. 43.

40. Rawin is short for radar wind, a technique in which a single corner reflector is towed aloft by a single neoprene balloon to measure wind speed by radar.

41. Kevin D. Randle and Donald R. Schmitt, *UFO Crash at Roswell* (New York: Avon Books, 1991), p. 103.

42. Col. Albert Trakowski, personal interview with Col. Jeffrey Butler and First Lt. James McAndrew, June 29, 1994.

43. Report, Cambridge Field Station, AMC, "Review of Air Materiel Command Geophysical Activities by Brig. Gen. D. N. Yates, and Staff, of the Air Weather Service," February 10, 1949.

44. Trakowski interview with Butler and McAndrew, June 29, 1994.

45. Irving Newton, personal interview with Lt. Col. Joseph V. Rogan, June 21, 1994, available from U.S. Air Force.

46. Professor Charles B. Moore, personal interview with Col. Jeffrey Butler and First Lt. James McAndrew, June 8, 1994.

47. NYU, *Technical Report No. 1,* Table VII.

48. Moore interview with Butler and McAndrew, June 8, 1994.

49. Crary journal, p. 10.

50. Moore interview with Butler and McAndrew, June 8, 1994. See also Research Division, College of Engineering, NYU, *Technical Report No. 93.02, Constant Level Balloons,* Sect. 2, *Operations,* January 31, 1949, pp. 36–38.

51. *Combined History of the 509th Bomb Group and Roswell Army Air Field,* September 1-30, 1947, p. 79. See also Crary journal, p. 64.

Bibliography

Adamski, George. *Inside the Spaceships.* London and New York: Abelard-Schuman, 1955. Also published in paperback as *Inside the Flying Saucers* (New York: Warner paperback Library, 1967; 1974).

———. *Flying Saucers Farewell.* London and New York: Abelard-Schuman, 1961. Also published in paperback as *Behind the Flying Saucer Mystery* (New York: Warner Paperback Library, 1967; 1974).

Adler, Bill, ed. *Letters to the Air Force on UFOs.* New York: Dell, 1967.

Alberts, Don E., and Allan E. Putnam. *A History of Kirtland Air Force Base 1928-1982.* Albuquerque: 1606th Air Base Wing, 1985.

Allingham, Cedric. *Flying Saucers from Mars.* New York: British Book Centre, 1955.

Arnold, Kenneth, and Ray Palmer. *The Coming of the Saucers.* Amherst, Wis.: Amherst Press, 1952.

Babcock, Edward J., and Timothy G. Beckley. *UFOs around the World.* New York: Global Communications, 1978.

Baker, Raymond D. *Historical Highlights of Andrews AFB 1942–1989.* Andrews AFB, Md.: 1776th Air Base Wing, 1990.

Beckley, Timothy G. *MJ-12 and the Riddle of Hangar 18.* New Brunswick, N.J.: Inner Light Publications, 1989.

Berlitz, Charles, and William L. Moore. *The Roswell Incident.* New York: Berkeley Books, 1988.

Bloecher, Ted. *Report on the UFO Wave of 1947.* Washington, D.C.: Ted Bloecher, 1967.

Blum, Howard. *Out There: The Government's Secret Quest for Extraterrestrials.* New York: Simon and Schuster, 1991.

255

Blum, Ralph, and Judy Blum. *Beyond Earth—Man's Contact with UFOs.* New York: Bantam Books, 1974.

Bowen, Charles, ed. *The Humanoids.* Chicago: Henry Regnery Company, 1974.

Brown, Eunice. *White Sands History.* White Sands, N.M.: Public Affairs Office, 1959.

Cahn, J. P. "Flying Saucer Swindlers." *True* (August 1956).

Cameron, Grant, and T. Scott Crain. *UFOs, MJ-12 and the Government.* Seguin, Tex.: Mutual UFO Network, 1991.

Citizens against UFO Secrecy. "MJ-12: Myth or Reality?" *Just Cause* (December 1985).

———. "The MJ-12 Fiasco." *Just Cause* (September 1987).

———. "MJ-12 Update." *Just Cause* (June 1989).

Clark, Jerome. *UFOs in the 1980s: The UFO Encyclopedia.* Detroit, Mich.: Apogee Books.

Condon, Edward, ed. *Scientific Study of Unidentified Flying Objects.* New York: E. P. Dutton, 1969.

Davidson, Leon. *Flying Saucers: An Analysis of the Air Force Project Blue Book Special Report No. 14.* White Plains, N.Y.: Blue-Book Publishers, 1976.

Eberhart, George. *The Roswell Report: A Historical Perspective.* Chicago: Center for UFO Studies, 1991.

Edwards, Frank. *Stranger Than Science.* New York: Lyle Stuart, 1959.

———. *Flying Saucers—Serious Business.* New York: Lyle Stuart, 1966.

Emenegger, Robert. *UFOs: Past, Present and Future.* New York: Ballantine Books, 1974.

Fawcett, Lawrence, and Barry Greenwood. *Clear Intent: The Government Cover-up of the UFO Experience.* Englewood Cliffs, N.J.: Prentice-Hall, 1984.

Friedman, Stanton T., and Don Berliner. *Crash at Corona: The U.S. Military Retrieval Cover-Up of a UFO.* New York: Paragon House, 1992.

Friedman, Stanton T. *Top Secret/MAJIC.* New York: Marlowe & Company, 1996.

Good, Timothy. *Above Top Secret.* New York: Morrow, 1988.

Gross, Loren. *UFOs: A History 1947.* Fremont, Calif.: Loren Gross, 1988.

Haines, Richard F. *Project Delta: A Study of Multiple UFO.* Los Altos, Calif.: L.D.A. Press, 1994.

Hall, Richard H., ed. *The UFO Evidence.* Washington, D.C.: National Investigations Committee on Aerial Phenomena, 1964.

Hendry, Allan. *The UFO Handbook.* Garden City, N.Y.: Doubleday and Company, 1979.

Hesemann, Michael and Philip Mantle. *Beyond Roswell: The Alien Autopsy Film, Area 51, and the U.S. Government Coverup of UFO's.* New York: Marlowe & Company, 1997.

Jacobs, David Michael. *The UFO Controversy in America.* Bloomington: Indiana University Press, 1975.

Klass, Philip J. *UFOs: The Public Deceived.* Amherst, N.Y.: Prometheus Books, 1989.

Korff, Kal K. *Spaceships of the Pleiades: The Billy Meier Story.* Amherst, N.Y.: Prometheus Books, 1995.

Kusche, Lawrence D. *The Bermuda Triangle Mystery—Solved.* Amherst, N.Y.: Prometheus Books, 1986.

Menzel, Donald, and Ernest H. Taves. *The UFO Enigma.* Garden City, N.Y.: Doubleday and Company, 1977.

Moore, William L., and Jamie H. Shandera. *The MJ-12 Documents: An Analytical Report.* Burbank, Calif.: Fair Witness Project, 1991.

Philips, Ted. *Physical Traces Associated with UFO Sightings: A Preliminary Catalog.* Northfield, Ill.: Center for UFO Studies, 1975.

Randi, James. *Flim-Flam!* Amherst, N.Y.: Prometheus Books, 1982.

Randle, Kevin D. *A History of UFO Crashes.* New York: Avon Books, 1995.

———. *Roswell UFO Crash Update: Exposing the Military Cover-Up of the Century.* New York: Global Communications, 1995.

Randle, Kevin D., and Donald R. Schmitt *UFO Crash at Roswell.* New York: Avon Books, 1991.

———. *The Truth about the UFO Crash at Roswell.* New York: Avon Books, 1994.

Shandera, Jamie H. "New Revelations about the Roswell Wreckage: A General Speaks Up," Burbank, Calif.: Fair Witness Project, 1990.

Story, Ronald. *The Space Gods Revealed: A Close Look at the Theories of Eric von Däniken.* New York: Harper and Row, 1976.

———. *Guardians of the Universe?* London: New English Library, 1979.

Stringfield, Leonard H. *Situation Red: The UFO Siege.* Garden City, N.Y.: Doubleday and Company, 1977.

———. *UFO Crash/Retrieval Syndrome Status Report II.* Seguin, Tex.: Mutual UFO Network, 1980.

———. *UFO Crash/Retrievals: Amassing the Evidence: Status Report III.* Cincinnati: Leonard Stringfield, 1982.

———. *UFO Crash/Retrievals: The Inner Sanctum: Status Report VI.* Cincinnati: Leonard Stringfield, 1991.

Todd, Robert G.. "Roswell: The Ruse That Laid the Golden Egg." *The Cowflop Quarterly: Reporting on UFOlogical Frauds and Fantasies.* Havertown, Penn.: 1995.

———. " 'Bolender Memo'—Reality Check." *The Cowflop Quarterly: Reporting on UFOlogical Frauds and Fantasies.* Havertown, Penn.: 1995.

———. "Randle Dumps—And Dumps On—Schmitt." *Cowflop Alert: Special Edition.* Havertown, Penn.: 1995.

———. "Major Jesse Marcel: Folk Hero or Mythomanic?" *The Cowflop Quarterly: Reporting on UFOlogical Frauds and Fantasies.* Havertown, Penn.: 1995.

———. "Roswell Record Found." *The Cowflop Quarterly: Reporting on UFOlogical Frauds and Fantasies.* Havertown, Penn.: 1996.

———. "General Twining's Majical Mystery Tour." *The Cowflop Quarterly: Reporting on UFOlogical Frauds and Fantasies.* Havertown, Penn.: 1996.

United States Air Force. *The Roswell Report: Fact vs. Fiction in the New Mexico Desert.* Washington, D.C.: Government Printing Office, 1995.

————. *History of the Eighth Air Force, Fort Worth, Texas.* Air Force Archives, Maxwell Air Force Base, Alabama.

————. *History of the 509th Bomb Group, Roswell, New Mexico.* Air Force Archives, Maxwell Air Force Base, Alabama.

U.S. House Committee on Armed Services. *Unidentified Flying Objects, Hearings.* 89th Congress, 2nd Sess., April 5, 1966. Washington, D.C.: Government Printing Office, 1966.

U.S. Committee on Science and Astronautics. *Symposium on Unidentified Flying Objects.* 90th Congress, 2nd Sess., July 29, 1968. Washington, D.C.: Government Printing Office, 1968.

Index